Medieval Academy Reprints for Teaching 39

Medieval Academy Reprints for Teaching

Edited and translated by

C.H. Talbot

THE LIFE OF CHRISTINA
OF MARKYATE:
A TWELFTH CENTURY RECLUSE

Published by University of Toronto Press
Toronto Buffalo
in association with the Medieval Academy of America

First published as an Oxford Medieval Text. General Editors:
C.N.L. Brooke, D.E. Greenway, M. Winterbottom

Dedicated to
DOM JEAN LECLERCQ, O.S.B.
my friend and collaborator
for many years

© Medieval Academy of America 1998
Printed in Canada
ISBN 0-8020-8202-5

Reprinted by arrangement with Oxford University Press
© Oxford University Press 1959

Revisions © 1997 by the author.

Printed on acid-free paper

Canadian Cataloguing in Publication Data

Main entry under title:

The life of Christina of Markyate : a twelfth century recluse

(Medieval Academy reprints for teaching ; 39)
Text in Latin and English.
"One of several lives of saintly persons which have been added at the end
of what is now the second volume of [the British Museum's] MS.
Cotton Tiberius E. 1."—Introd.
ISBN 0-8020-8202-5

1. Christina, of Markyate, Saint, ca. 1096–1160. 2. Christian women
saints – England – Biography. I. Talbot, C.H. (Charles H.).
II. British Museum. Manuscript. Cottonian Tiberius E. I.
III. Medieval Academy of America. IV. Series.

BX4700.C565I.53 1998   282'.092   C98-930397-7

GENERAL EDITORS' NOTE

THE unique manuscript of *The Life of Christina of Markyate* was fearfully damaged in the fire that devastated the Cotton library in 1731. It had been known to the antiquarians of the early seventeenth century, but never published in full. Dr C. H. Talbot's publication of the *Life* (Clarendon Press, 1959), based on his own patient transcription, was one of the most remarkable events in medieval scholarship during our time, and the book immediately established itself as a classic of historical literature. It has long been out of print, and we formed the design of joining it to Oxford Medieval Texts. This is now possible, with Dr Talbot's ready consent, and it is a special pleasure to us to welcome the book into the Series and make it available once again. Much has been written on Christina since 1959; but what is needed is a reprint, not a new edition. We have made some minor additions and corrections on pp. 194–6.

The edition of 1959 was closely followed by *The St Albans Psalter*, edited by O. Pächt, C. R. Dodwell, and F. Wormald (London, 1960), fully displaying the great psalter so closely connected with Christina (see pp. 22–7) and dating it *c*.1119–23. It has been re-dated *c*.1120–30 by R. M. Thomson, *Manuscripts from St Albans Abbey, 1066–1235* (Woodbridge, 1982), i. 25; and later still by C. Holdsworth in his wide-ranging paper 'Christina of Markyate' in *Medieval Women* (dedicated to Rosalind M. T. Hill), ed. D. Baker (Oxford, 1978), pp. 185–204. Thomson's date has been the most widely accepted, but Holdsworth's paper is a valuable commentary on the *Life* as a whole, especially on its place among the literature on hermits in this age — for which see *L'eremitismo in occidente nei secoli XI e XII* (Atti della seconda Settimana internazionale di studio Mendola, Miscellanea del Centro di Studi Medioevali, iv, Milan, 1965); H. Leyser, *Hermits and the new monasticism* (London, 1984).

One of the great virtues of this *Life* is its vivid revelation of

Christina's personal circumstances, which must be based on her own reminiscences. Even though doubts have been cast on her veracity (see R. and C. Brooke, *Popular Religion in the Middle Ages*, London, 1984, p. 111), they do not affect the main lines of the extraordinary story she told the author.

C. N. L. B.
D. E. G.
M. W.

PREFACE

THE manuscript of Christina's Life, MS. Cotton Tiberius E. 1, besides being incomplete, has been partly destroyed by fire. When Horstman used it for his edition of the *Nova Legenda Anglie*, he tried to overcome this difficulty by the use of chemicals: 'I have tried', he said, 'wherever possible to restore the text, partly by consulting the original sources, partly with the help of chemicals, which the authorities of the British Museum were kind enough to employ at my petition for the clearer bringing out of certain passages—which kindness it is my agreeable duty here publicly to acknowledge.' Fortunately for his successors Horstman was deterred from proceeding further than the first paragraph by the unrewarding condition of the rest, and contented himself with printing Roscarrock's abridgement of it with the following prefatory remark: 'which Life, in the absence of another MS. it will be impossible to decipher'. That it has been impossible to decipher every word of the text the present edition makes evident. The first lines on the top of many pages have completely disappeared, and it has not been possible, except in rare cases, to attempt even a partial reconstruction. Where a few letters have remained legible, this has given but a faint clue to what might have been written there, and for this reason these lines have been left blank in preference to making guesses that might have been wide of the mark. Where the exterior columns are defective and lacking several letters or words, the task of completing the text has not been so onerous, although many guesses, which at first sight seemed to possess a certain degree of probability, were afterwards proved wrong by the use of an ultra-violet-ray lamp. The whole text, in fact, has been controlled by employing ultra-violet-ray photographs, but even this has not been sufficient to provide absolute certainty; so that any filling in of gaps (and there are many) attempted by the editor makes no claim to finality.

All supplements of letters and words which are illegible have been placed in square brackets, but where only a few letters are missing and the restoration is certain, the reader's convenience has been taken into consideration and the brackets have been omitted. Other letters or words left out by the scribe of the manuscript, but essential to the sense of the text, have been supplied in angle brackets, though here again it has not been thought necessary to indicate that all the initial letters introducing new sections were originally omitted. I should add that early corrections in the manuscript have been silently incorporated into the text and that words obviously repeated in error by the scribe have been as silently cut out.

The sections of the text reproduce the original arrangement of the manuscript, but the numbering of these sections is my own, made for convenience of reference.

Biblical references are made according to the Vulgate, but for the translation the Authorized Version has been used: this leads to a slight discrepancy in the numbering of the psalms.

The translation necessarily suffers from gaps in the text, and there are several places where no attempt has been made to bridge them. But in less important instances, where the sense of the passage seems more or less clear, the narrative has been continued without a break and the missing portions filled in. A careful reader will notice where these parts occur and will judge them for what they are worth. The spelling and punctuation of the manuscript have been preserved.

In the course of preparing this text I have had the counsel, encouragement, and help of several people whom I should like to thank. First and foremost I should like to express my gratitude to Christopher Hohler, who, on more occasions than I care to recall, sat or stood with me in the stuffy underground chamber at the British Museum, trying to read, with the aid of an ultra-violet-ray lamp, those difficult passages where the writing had almost disappeared. His tenacity and patience never wilted. That the transcription was ever com-

pleted is due to his constant inquiries about the progress of the work. Dr. B. Schofield Keeper of Manuscripts at the British Museum then came to my rescue by arranging for ultra-violet photographs of the manuscript to be made so that I could revise and correct the first transcription. Dr. R. W. Hunt looked through it and made some useful suggestions which I incorporated, and, when everything was seemingly completed, Professor Roger Mynors generously offered to run his expert eye over the whole typescript. After some weeks he returned it to me pleasantly transformed. To him and to the other scholars mentioned above I am deeply indebted. But in spite of all their endeavours there are bound to be some shortcomings in a book like this; for these my friends are not responsible. They are all my own work.

C. H. T.

April 1959

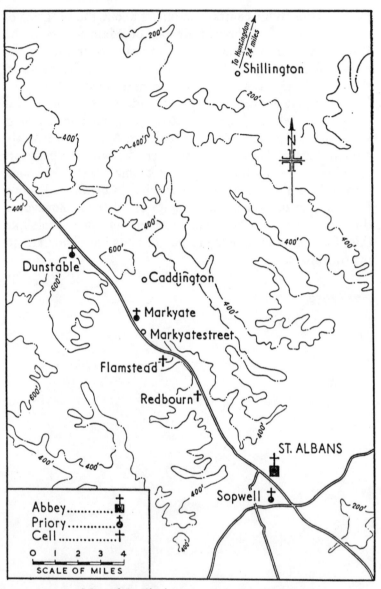

Map of the district connected with Christina

INTRODUCTION

THE Life of Christina, recluse and later prioress of Markyate, is one of several lives of saintly persons which have been added at the end of what is now the second volume of MS. Cotton Tiberius E. 1. This folio manuscript, written apparently during the second quarter of the fourteenth century, contained the *Sanctilogium Angliae* of John of Tynemouth, a collection of the Lives of English Saints arranged according to the date of the Calendar. As this is the only copy in which John of Tynemouth's original design has been carried out (for later collections have the same material arranged in alphabetical order), it has been suggested that this manuscript was prepared at St. Albans under his direct supervision.[1] Be that as it may, four other narrations of Saints' Lives have been added as an afterthought after the Life of St. Egwin (30 December) which concluded the original series; and following these, written in the same hand as the rest of the text, comes the Life of Christina.

The writing of the manuscript has been beautifully executed, and its large letters in double columns, with the titles of the separate chapters picked out in red, give the book a handsome appearance. Though it seems to have been written in one hand throughout, there are a number of corrections and additions to be found in the margin and elsewhere which suggest that at some time it has undergone a thorough revision. On folio 6 of the first volume are the remains of a contemporary inscription which runs as follows:[2] 'Hunc librum dedit Dompnus Thomas de la M[are Abbas monasterii

[1] C. Horstman, *Nova Legenda Anglie*, Oxford, 1901, i, p. xii.

[2] Fortunately, before it was damaged the inscription was copied in full by Fr. Augustine Baker, who recorded it many years later (in 1637) in MS. Jesus College, Oxford, 77, fol. 64ʳ; and by W. Nicolson, *The English Historical Library*, London, 1696–9, ii. 31, and in part by Humfrey Wanley in his copy of Smith's Cottonian catalogue, now in the Bodleian. N. Roscarrock (1549–1634?) was the first to record the provenance of the manuscript in his *Lives of the English Saints* (Brent Eleigh MS., now Cambridge University Library MS. Add. 3041), where he wrote: 'I finde in a Manuscript which was given by Thomas De la March Abbot of St. Albons to the Priorie of Rudburn . . ..'

Sti. Albani Anglorum] prothomartiris, Deo et Ecclesiae beati Amphibali [de Redburne; ut fratres ibidem in cursu ex]istentes per eius lecturam poterint celestibus instrui, [et per Sanctorum exempla virtutibus insigniri].' This shows that the manuscript came originally from St. Albans and may have been written both for and in the monastery. Abbot Thomas de la Mare was elected to St. Albans in 1349 after his term of office as prior of Tynemouth (1341–9),[1] and it was shortly after this that he sent sixteen monks to Redbourn[2] during the Plague. As he is reported to have provided them with books and other necessary things on that occasion, it may well be that this copy of the *Sanctilogium Angliae* was presented to them at that time.[3]

How the manuscript came into the hands of Sir Robert Cotton is not recorded. But when the Cottonian library passed out of his family's possession and was vested by Act of Parliament in the Queen, this manuscript together with many others suffered in the disastrous fire at Ashburnham House, where the collection had been temporarily deposited pending the erection of a new building to house it.[4] As a result the first and last leaves of the manuscript have been extensively damaged: all the corners of the rest of the pages are eaten away and the exterior columns with the first few lines on many pages are practically illegible. As the Tiberius text of the *Vita* is imperfect at the end, it might appear at first sight as if some leaves had been destroyed by the fire, particularly as Smith, in his catalogue of the Cottonian manuscripts printed in 1696, does not specifically state that any leaves were lacking at the end of the volume. It is quite

---

[1] For a portrait of Thomas de la Mare see M. D. Knowles, *The Religious Orders in England*, Cambridge, 1955, ii. 319–48.

[2] Redbourn was a cell of St. Albans, situated about four and a half miles north of the monastery. It was built after the discovery of the bones of St. Amphibalus in 1178 and served as a place of retirement for sick monks: Dugdale, *Monasticon Anglicanum*, iv. 525–7. T. Tanner, *Notitia Monastica*, ed. J. Nasmith, London, 1787, ii. 42, mentions a manuscript (Cotton Tiberius E. XI) which contained *Ordinationem tangentem socios commorantes apud Redburn factam A.D. 1366*, but this volume was lost in the fire of 1731.

[3] A further record of the abbot's gifts to Redbourn is given in MS. Cotton Nero D. VII, fol. 22ʳ⁻ᵛ. [4] *Gentleman's Magazine*, 1731, p. 451.

clear, however, that long before that date a portion of the text was already missing. Writing at the end of the sixteenth or at the beginning of the seventeenth century, Roscarrock says in his account of the Life of Christina:[1] 'In the end of this boke, I finde in part, the life of one Theodora'or Christiana, not perfitted; the effect of which I will breiflie laye downe, that others, lighting on a more exact Coppie, maie perfitt it.' And as a confirmation that the damage sustained by the manuscript in the fire of 1731 has not appreciably altered the length of the text, we have his account of the final incident recorded in it. 'And soe Concluding abruptlye with noting howe shee tolde her Abbot of som thoughtes that he had Contrarie to that which she had advised him, and ending thus, makes mee to doubt what to think, whether theyre bee anie perfitt Coppie, or whither the writer dyed before he perfitted it; or whither shee removed to anie other place, where the writer had noe intelligence of her.' This proves that the manuscript ended exactly where it does at present. Roscarrock's suggestion that the original text of the Life may have been left incomplete through the death of the author has not much to commend it. Though the excerpts taken from the Life of Christina and inserted in the *Gesta Abbatum monasterii Sancti Albani* by Thomas of Walsingham or his anonymous predecessor cover only those incidents which can be found in the Tiberius text and end exactly where the Tiberius text breaks off, this does not necessarily mean that no more was available. We cannot be certain that the excerptor's reference to a manuscript 'which is preserved at Markyate'[2] indicates his use of that source: indeed, it seems highly likely that he was basing his account on the actual version we have before us. Moreover, the existence of a copy of the Life at Markyate suggests that it was intended primarily as a work of edification for the nuns, in which the trials undergone by

---

[1] C. Horstman, ii. 532, 536. It is not possible to say when Roscarrock examined the manuscript. He was in London (though frequently in prison as a recusant) between 1580 and 1607 and could have taken his notes at any time between these two dates: see *DNB*, xvii. 220-1.

[2] *Gesta Abbatum*, ed. H. T. Riley, i. 105.

their foundress and the eventual establishment of their priory
were described. Such a work would, presumably, include all
the events leading up to and including her death. Had the
first biographer failed to complete his task, it seems hardly
likely that the followers and admirers of Christina would
have allowed the text to remain in its unfinished state, especially as there were monks at St. Albans capable of bringing
it to a conclusion. Abbot Robert (1151–66), who was on the
closest terms with Christina and who almost certainly out-
lived her, would surely see that the nuns of Markyate had
a complete biography of their foundress.

It is obvious also from the abrupt curtailment of the narrative in the middle of a sentence that the Tiberius biography
did not end at that point. The surviving twenty-three leaves
of the manuscript appear to be made up of two quires of
eight and one of seven leaves, but it is impossible at this stage
to say whether one leaf is lost or whether one leaf plus a quire
of eight is missing.

That a considerable portion of her life is not covered by
the surviving text cannot be doubted. From our knowledge
of other historical events in which Christina was directly or
indirectly involved, it is evident that the present Tiberius
version carries the story of Christina's life no further than the
year 1142. As she was still alive in 1155–6 there are at least
fourteen years of activity to account for, during which the
community of Markyate was placed on a canonical footing,
the buildings of the priory were twice burned down and
rebuilt, the church of Markyate was consecrated by Alexander, bishop of Lincoln, Geoffrey of St. Albans, her friend
and benefactor, died, and two other abbots, with whom
Christina must have had close relations, governed the monastery of St. Albans. None of these events are mentioned in the
text of her Life which has survived. Judging, therefore, by
the amount of information on Christina's later life which has
been left unrecorded, it is possible that MS. Tiberius E. 1
lacks a complete gathering, equal perhaps to a quarter of the
complete text. If this is so, then it is more reasonable to

assume that the Tiberius copy, and not the original biography, was left incomplete. But the version in Tiberius E. 1 is not merely incomplete. The hypothesis that it is also an abridgement cannot be ruled out. At one point in the narrative the writer refers to a certain Thomas, *quem supra memoravimus*. One looks in vain in the Tiberius text for any other mention of him. It would seem, therefore, that this portion of the story has been left out as being irrelevant. At another point, the writer without giving any preliminary explanation makes an abrupt transition from Christina's narrow cell at Caddington, where she could sit but could not lie at full length, to a building which housed several nuns, where there was a dormitory, a little church (*ecclesiola*), a refectory, and a kind of cloister garth in which flowers of all kinds were growing. Unless we assume that the account of the building of the priory has been omitted from the Tiberius version, it is difficult to explain this sudden change of circumstances. If, however, we take into consideration John of Tynemouth's method of dealing with the material he used for his *Sanctilogium* it will not appear at all strange that he should have omitted many details which did not expressly concern the spiritual character of his heroine.[1]

What seems more or less certain is that a dedicatory letter (and probably a prologue) have been discarded for these reasons. That there was a dedication in the original may be deduced from the later words of the author, where he addresses himself to a superior of some kind; for, in giving the reasons which prompted Christina to choose St. Albans as the place for making her profession, he says: 'Tum quia *te* super omnes sub Christo pastores in terra diligebat sicut iugi experimento *probasti*'.

The loss of this dedicatory letter (and, perhaps, prologue) is all the more to be regretted, since it would have told us

---

[1] Cf. my remarks about his use of the Saints' Lives written by Goscelin of St. Bertin, 'The Liber Confortatorius of Goscelin of Saint Bertin,' in *Analecta Monastica* (Studia Anselmiana xxxvii), Rome, 1955, p. 14.

precisely for whom the biography was composed and, what is more important still, would have revealed the identity of the writer. It would also have fixed, approximately, the date at which the Life was written. In the circumstances the text is anonymous. All that we can say is that the author was a monk of St. Albans and that he was writing in the monastery itself: these details emerge during the course of the story. He describes St. Albans, for instance, as *nostrum monasterium*; he calls Roger the hermit *noster monachus* and describes Roger's hermitage as being 'on the right side of the road as you go from *our monastery* to Dunstable'. He was well acquainted with Abbot Geoffrey's propensity for riding roughshod over the community's wishes and shows a certain familiarity with other members of the same abbey, such as Gregory (Christina's brother), Alexander, the sub-prior, and an unnamed monk who was sceptical of Christina's saintliness. That he was writing the biography in the monastery itself may be inferred from his statement that Christina decided to make her profession in the abbey where he was situated, *in hoc monasterio*.

His identity, however, remains a matter of pure guess-work. The only historical writer at St. Albans during the first half of the twelfth century about whom we have any information is Adam the cellarer whose 'ancient roll' was Matthew Paris's source for the period. But the whole emphasis of his work is on 'territorial acquisitions and litigation concerning them' and no one would think of identifying him with the author of this life.[1] Indeed, if he had written it, surely it would have been known to, and used by, Matthew.

Whoever the writer was, he was very close indeed to Christina. The whole tone of the story is autobiographical rather than historical. The usual desire to edify, to speak only of the supernatural qualities of the Saint, to borrow from or draw parallels with the lives of other saintly persons is conspicuous by its absence. There is in the narrative a frankness, a vigour of expression, and an economy of words that must reflect direct contact with Christina herself. Only where the

---

[1] R. Vaughan, *Matthew Paris*, Cambridge, 1958, p. 183.

reputations of living people are concerned is there any suppression of names or places: everything else is described with a directness that is both refreshing and convincing. Indeed, many of the incidents recorded in the biography could have originated only with Christina: the scratching of the cross on the door of St. Albans church, the shameful attempts by Ralph Flambard on her chastity, the wiles of her parents at the meeting of the Gild Merchant at Huntingdon, the encounter with the bailiff, the provisions for her escape on horseback to Flamstead, all these and many other details could have been known only to her. The writer, therefore, must have heard these things from her own lips and been in a position to question her closely on all the events that preceded her eventual settlement at Markyate. Moreover, he was writing all this down during her lifetime, for at one point he explains that so far, *usque presens*, he has been unable to discover from her how she knew about a certain event. It may be that, though he was a monk of St. Albans, he was attached to Markyate in some official capacity, such as chaplain or confessor. He apparently had enough authority to question her about her visions and her gift of foreseeing future events, for besides showing intimate knowledge of her spiritual difficulties, he knew exactly what signs gave her a premonition of some impending supernatural grace. All this is described with such naturalness as could arise only from long familiarity, a familiarity which is emphasized by his reference on one occasion to his having taken a meal with her. Though he is sparing of dates and gives but few indications of the exact year when a particular event took place, he is precise about the day or month of the occurrences he describes and always introduces them with phrases such as *post biduum, idest, .vi. kalendas aprilis, in crastino vero Pentecostes, die itaque festo Sancti Mathei, tunc erat dies dominicus,* and so on.

Whether he was personally acquainted with the many other persons who are mentioned in his pages it is difficult to say; he definitely knows their names and stations in life; he accurately describes them as *canonicus, decanus, presbyter, prior,*

yppo-prior, *laicus*, and only suppresses these details when he has been requested to do so in the public interest. But it is obvious that he knew Christina's parents and other members of her family, and from her sister Matilda he had learned some details, not only of her early, but also of her later life. He had even seen, though he does not disclose where, one of Christina's companions named Helisen, who had entered a convent to expiate her evil behaviour in trying to corrupt Christina during the year she had been held in close custody. One of his most prolific sources of information must have been Abbot Geoffrey himself, for in his account of the relationship between the abbot and the recluse, he seems to know Geoffrey's side of the story with uncanny precision, what he said and did, his perplexity over the sources of Christina's spiritual knowledge, and his reactions to her teaching.

As regards the person who encouraged the author to write the biography, gave him instructions about the form it should take, and suggested the omissions, we are not absolutely clear. All that we are told is that he was a prelate whom Christina loved and revered more than all other prelates in Christendom. There were several people to whom this might apply. Thurstan, archbishop of York, had taken considerable interest in her case, had released her from her forced marriage, and provided her with a place of retirement during her troubles with Robert Bloet, bishop of Lincoln. He had even tried to persuade her to take charge of the community of nuns which he had founded in the city of York, and it may have been Thurstan who suggested that she should go to Marcigny.[1] But as Thurstan died in 1140, it is unlikely either that the biography was written at his request or that it was dedicated to him. Another prelate for whom Christina had great reverence was Alexander, bishop of Lincoln. In

---

[1] Thurstan founded the convent of St. Clement between 1125 and 1135: Dugdale, *Monasticon*, iv. 323; W. Farrar, *Early Yorkshire Charters*, Edinburgh, 1914, i. 278. His interest in Marcigny may have been due to the fact that in 1120 he accompanied Adela, countess of Blois, to the abbey, where she took the veil: *The Historians of the Church of York*, ed. J. Raine, ii. 184.

his presence she made her monastic profession and he it was who consecrated Markyate priory church when the time came to put the community on a canonical basis. But when the biographer speaks of Alexander's capture and imprisonment by King Stephen in 1139, he recalls the event in a manner so detached as to make it quite obvious that the addressee is not involved. Might it not then be Geoffrey, abbot of St. Albans? All the indications point to the fact that Geoffrey was the mainstay of Christina's material and spiritual welfare from the time of her return to Markyate until Geoffrey's death in 1147. The biographer is at pains to emphasize the close spiritual relationship that bound these two people together, the gossip to which it gave rise, and the great advantages which both of them drew from it. Christina always called the abbot 'her beloved', whilst he on his side referred to her as his *puella*. Her affection for him was such that she was continually preoccupied with his welfare and spent more time praying for him than she did for herself, and it was mainly by his persuasion that she agreed to make her profession at St. Albans. On the other hand, if the biography were drawn up at his request, it is difficult to see how the writer could always speak of him as doing things in the past, or how he could have spoken so unrestrainedly of Geoffrey's shortcomings without some kind of apology or excuse. Taking several other points into consideration, therefore, it seems more likely that Geoffrey was not the person at whose instigation the biography was composed. The only other prelate of whom we have certain evidence as being in close relationship with Christina was Robert, the nephew of Geoffrey and (after the death of Abbot Ralph) his successor at the abbey of St. Albans. The *Gesta Abbatum* recounts that Christina sent three mitres and a pair of sandals, embroidered by her own hands, to Pope Adrian IV when Robert went to Rome in 1155.[1] This presupposes that they were on friendly terms, and it may even be suggested that these gifts were prepared for the Pope at Robert's instance. There is no direct evidence,

[1] *Gesta Abbatum*, i. 127.

however, of any further contact between these two, and the hypothesis that the biography was commissioned by him rests merely on the fact that the writer was a monk of St. Albans, was producing the work within the abbey of St. Albans, and was addressing it to a prelate who had influenced Christina in attaching herself to that monastery. There can be no absolute certainty on this score, but the probability is reasonable.[1]

If it is accepted as likely that the Life was written at the instance of Robert Gorham, it becomes possible to suggest a provisional date for its composition. As Robert governed St. Albans for fifteen years, between 1151 and 1166, and Christina was still living in 1155, the biography took shape some time during the last ten years of his rule, a date which receives some confirmation from the obits entered in the Calendar of the St. Albans Psalter, which will be discussed later.

The biographer tells us that Christina came from a family of Anglo-Saxon nobles which had relatives spread over the whole county of Huntingdonshire. This may imply that her forebears may have been thegns under the old régime, a rank corresponding to the post-Conquest barons or knights: but though the name of her father, Autti, is fairly common in the Danelaw and figures several times in the Domesday survey of other counties, it does not appear among those holding lands in Huntingdonshire.[2] He was, so we are told, an extremely rich man, a most important person at the annual meeting of the gild merchant at Huntingdon,[3] highly respected by the clergy of the town and with such influence that even the

---

[1] On fol. 151ᵛᵃ of the *Vita* there is a reference to a vision in which it was revealed to Christina that she should have a companion, *confratrem* 'strenuum in monasterio nostro indicans monachum'. For some reason the biographer was ordered to suppress his name. Could it be that this *confrater* was identical with the person who had commissioned the *Vita* or with the author?

[2] H. Ellis, *A General Introduction to Domesday Book*, London, 1833, ii. 45. The name *Auti* appears in Sussex, Hampshire, Gloucestershire, Shropshire, Derby, Lincoln, and Norfolk.

[3] This is a very early reference to the gild merchant: see C. Gross, *The Gild Merchant*, Oxford, 1927, i. 185–8.

bishop of Lincoln was prepared, after suitable bribes had been offered, to declare judgement in his favour. From such a description one might think it would be easy to discover some reference to him either in the Cartulary of the Canons of Huntingdon,[1] in the Confraternity list of Thorney abbey,[2] or in one of the many cartularies relating to other abbeys in the vicinity.[3] But the only possible identification that could be made occurs in the Ramsey cartulary, where there is mention of a certain Autti of Huntingdon who between 1114 and 1123 gave back the church of Shillington in Bedfordshire to the abbot of Ramsey in return for ten marks of silver.[4] The date of this transaction agrees with what we know of Autti's life-span. Furthermore, it is stated in the biography of Christina that when Autti and his family were returning home after one of their visits to the monastery of St. Albans they stayed the night at Shillington, a statement which seems to imply that he had at least a house there. If we could be sure that Autti's two sons, Baldwin and Burhed, named in the transaction with the abbot of Ramsey, were to be identified with Christina's brothers, Gregory and Simon, there would be no difficulty in accepting the Ramsey transaction as Autti's, but as, apart from Christina herself, there is no parallel for this double nomenclature, we must leave the question open.

None of Autti's children, with the exception of Christina, seems to have attained any eminence: Gregory became a monk of St. Albans and used to come to Markyate, with the abbot's permission, to celebrate Mass there: Simon, apparently a simple citizen of Huntingdon, signed the foundation charter of Markyate along with the others who were watching over

---

[1] MS. Cotton Faustina C. 1.

[2] B.M. MS. Add. 40000. The lists precede a tenth-century copy of the Gospels. On fol. 3ᵛ the following names occur: Rodbertus de Huntendona . . . Burred, Rogerus, Leofricus, Benedictus, Alveva, Ailwardus (in that order), corresponding to the names of some of the people connected with Christina, but it would be unwise to conclude that they are identifiable with them.

[3] e.g. the Cartulary of St. Neots, B.M. Cotton Faustina A. IV.

[4] *Cartularium monasterii de Rameseia,* ed. W. H. Hart and Ponsonby A. Lyons, London, 1884–93, i. 138: the same text in *Chronicon Abbatiae Rameseiensis,* ed. W. Dunn Macray, 1886, p. 247; cf. p. 248.

Christina's interests:[1] Margaret, who appears as the confidant of Christina throughout her biography, became a member of the community at Markyate, whilst her married sister, Matilda, lived at Huntingdon with her husband. These are the only members of the family whom we know.

The people with whom Christina was intimately connected seem to have belonged exclusively to the Anglo-Saxon element of the community. The names of Sueno, her first spiritual director, Alfwen, the recluse with whom she took shelter, Eadwin, the hermit who made provision for her escape, Loric, the boy with whom she rode to Flamstead, Wlfwinus, who brought news of her to Roger, Godescalc who accompanied her to Redbourne: all these bear witness to the fact. Even Roger, whose name suggests an origin overseas, came from the same circle, for the only words of his which are recorded in their original speech, 'myn sunendaege dohter', are Anglo-Saxon. If this is so, it would seem to suggest that the spiritual movement of which we have a conspicuous example in the biography was particularly strong among the natives of the country. It may be that the Normans, being the ruling race, were more concerned with the organized and disciplined forms of religious asceticism; but the fact remains that even apart from Christina and her circle almost all the names of those connected with the hermit movement in England, like Godric and Wulfric, are Anglo-Saxon. Indeed, running through all the accounts we have of hermits at that time, there is an undercurrent of national feeling, an indirect allusion to the differences in tongue and custom between those who led the hermit life and their spiritual superiors;[2]

[1] Dugdale, *Monasticon*, iii. 372.

[2] *Libellus de vita et miraculis S. Godrici*, ed. J. Stevenson (Surtees Soc. xx, 1847), p. 204: 'Haec omnia lingua Romana peroptime disseruit, nosque admirando stupore perfudit; erat enim quondam hujus linguae penitus ignarus, utpote simpliciter lingua materna edoctus...'; *Wulfric of Haselbury*, ed. M. Bell (Somerset Record Soc. xlvii, 1933), p. 29 (Brichtric complains of the miracle performed on a dumb man by Wulfric): 'Nam homini alienigenae cui satis erat linguam ad loquendum aperuisse, ad geminum linguae officium devotus ministrasti et mihi qui cum ad episcopum et archidiaconum venio quasi mutus silere compellor, Gallici usum sermonis non dedisti.' There is even an indirect reference to this difference in the *Gesta Abbatum*, where the writer, speaking of Abbot Paul's foreign origin (p. 60), says: 'Pronunciationes

and it is perhaps not entirely by accident that some of the Normans who appear in the Life of Christina are portrayed in a somewhat unfavourable light.

At what date Christina was born is a matter for conjecture, but the end of the eleventh century seems the most probable time. At the coming of Ralph Flambard to Huntingdon she must have been about sixteen years of age. As Ralph was accustomed to stay there with Autti's relatives whenever he was going to or returning from London, he must have had many opportunities of seeing her before the occasion on which he made his shameless advances. The persecution and enforced marriage which followed as a result of his disappointment could have been possible only if she were of marriageable age, whilst the discussions in the presence of Fredebertus, prior of the Austin Canons at Huntingdon, and the visit of the hermit, Eadwin, to Ralph d'Escures, archbishop of Canterbury, could not have taken place before 1114. We may surmise, then, that she was born between 1096 and 1098. There are no dates in the biography from which we can draw a chronological sequence of events until the mention of the death of Robert Bloet, bishop of Lincoln, which took place in 1123.[1] Before that time Christina had been under strict custody at home for a whole year, had stayed with Alfwen at Flamstead for two years, and had lived secretly with Roger in his hermitage at Markyate for four years, besides spending a long period, *multo tempore consumpto*, after Roger's death under the uneasy tutelage of Archbishop Thurstan's clerical friend. There was, then, an interval of about eight or nine years between Christina's first encounter with Flambard and her return to Markyate as Roger's successor in the

---

quorumdam nominum, vel ob reverentiam patrum nostrorum Orientalium, cujus vestigia sequi desideravit, *vel suae linguae patriae, et genialis*, corrupit.' A marginal note in Cotton MS. Nero D. 1, fol. 35ᵛ, adds: 'Unde majus, divisim, et majestas et alii. Unde Gaufridus, Garinus et Ausculta, etc.' Riley, in his note to this passage, is uncertain whether the allusion refers to the alteration in the pronunciation of Latin or English words: but it seems quite clear what is meant.

[1] William of Malmesbury, *Gesta Pontificum*, ed. N. E. S. A. Hamilton, 1870, p. 313.

hermitage: this would give us a date between 1114 and 1115 for the beginning of the story of her trials.

Between the death of Robert Bloet and the decision to send Geoffrey, abbot of St. Albans, to Rome for the confirmation of King Stephen's election in 1136, we have no exact indication of the sequence of events; but after this there are one or two details, mainly connected with Geoffrey and the king, which make it possible to see that the text of the biography carries the story no later than 1142. We may provisionally suggest, then, the following outline of her career:

c. 1096–8.   Birth of Christina on the feast of St. Leonard at Huntingdon.

c. 1111–12.   She visited St. Albans with her family and made her vow of virginity, which was confirmed on her return by Sueno, canon of Huntingdon.

c. 1114.   Ralph Flambard called on Alveva on his way to London and made his advances to Christina. On being repulsed, he encouraged Burhred to ask for her hand in marriage.

c. 1114–15.   Christina was kept in close custody for one year, whilst discussion on her proposed marriage took place, and eventually was forced to consent. She was brought before Fredebert, prior of Huntingdon, and the case was remitted to Robert Bloet, bishop of Lincoln, who at first decided in her favour, but later was bribed to give judgement against her.

c. 1115–16.   Eadwin the hermit consulted the archbishop of Canterbury, Ralph d'Escures, and made provision for Christina's escape. She took refuge with Alfwen at Flamstead.

c. 1115–18.   Christina remained at Flamstead for two years. Roger the hermit sent for her.

c. 1118–22.   She stayed with Roger in the hermitage at Markyate for four years. In the meantime she was absolved from her betrothal by Burhred, and after her meeting with Thurstan, archbishop of York, at Redbourn, her marriage was annulled and Burhred declared free to marry someone else.

c. 1122–3.   Roger died and was buried at St. Albans. Christina found shelter elsewhere until Archbishop Thurstan arranged for her to stay with a friend of his.

c. 1123.	Robert Bloet, bishop of Lincoln, died, and Christina returned to Markyate to take up her abode there.
c. 1124.	First intimation of her contact with Geoffrey, abbot of St. Albans.
c. 1130.	Thurstan invited her to become superior of his newly-founded community of nuns at St. Clement's York. She decided to stay at Markyate.
c. 1131.	Christina made her monastic profession at St. Albans before Alexander, bishop of Lincoln.
1136.	Geoffrey, abbot of St. Albans, was chosen to go to Rome for the confirmation of King Stephen's election.
1139.	Innocent II called a Council to which Geoffrey was destined to go as a delegate, but the decision was revoked. The bishops of Salisbury and Lincoln were taken prisoner, and at the subsequent meeting of the king and the legate at Winchester Geoffrey was again chosen to travel to the Roman Curia to champion the rights of the Church. Through the prayers of Christina he was released from this dangerous mission.
c. 1140–1.	Geoffrey was summoned to the king's court and told by Christina of the favourable outcome of his journey.
1145.	Agreement reached between Geoffrey, abbot of St. Albans, and the canons of St. Paul's about the land on which Markyate priory was founded. The church was consecrated by Alexander, bishop of Lincoln.
1147.	Geoffrey, abbot of St. Albans, died.
1155.	Henry II made a grant to Christina. She sent gifts to Pope Adrian IV through Robert, abbot of St. Albans.
c. 1155–66.	Death of Christina.

Whether Christina would have chosen the life of a recluse if left to her own devices is not at all certain. All that the biographer tells us is that on her visit as a young girl to the monastery of St. Albans she was so struck with the religious demeanour of the monks, that she made a vow of virginity. It is possible that this action merely reflected her desire to become a Benedictine nun, for on the famous occasion when she spent the night telling Burhred the story of Saint Cecilia and Valerian she ended her exhortations by proposing that

both of them should later enter a monastery. Indeed, we see that the life of a recluse was more or less forced on her by circumstances. Even after Burhred had released her from her obligations and offered to provide a dowry so that she could enter a convent, it is doubtful whether the adverse judgement of the bishop of Lincoln would have allowed any community to accept her. It was only by taking refuge with another recluse, where her presence could be kept secret and where the bishop would have no power to intervene, that she was able to gain some degree of freedom to follow out her ideals. Once embarked on this step, however, she had no alternative but to continue in it.

This course of action was facilitated by the existence in the vicinity of a remarkable number of hermits. We hear of Roger with five other hermits at Caddington (of whom two, Azo and Leofric, are named), several recluses at Huntingdon itself, Guido at a place six miles outside Huntingdon, Alfwen at Flamstead, Sigar at Northaw, Eadwin probably at Higney,[1] and many other hermitages whose names and inhabitants, though known to Eadwin and Burhred, are not specifically listed. From so restricted a district this is extraordinary testimony to the appeal of the solitary life. That it had always exerted an attraction on people with ascetic ideals is evident from the frequent references to it in hagiographical literature.[2] But on account of its manifold dangers it had been considered, even from the days of St. Benedict,[3] as suitable only for those who had been well tried in the crucible of monastic life.[4] The voice of warning had been raised on many occasions, but in spite of the general attitude of disapproval shown by

---

[1] *Cartularium monasterii de Rameseia*, i. 162. This charter for Saltrey is dated 1146–53. Whether this date is too late to refer to Roger's cousin is a matter for conjecture.

[2] L. Gougaud, *Ermites et reclus*, Ligugé, 1926: id., 'Essai de bibliographie érémitique', *Revue Bénédictine*, 1933, p. 281.

[3] *S. Benedicti Regula*, ed. C. Butler, Freiburg-im-Breisgau, 1927, c. 1.

[4] Council of Vannes (Mansi, *Concilia*, vii. 954) and Council of Agde (viii. 331) use the same words; Council of Toledo (x. 769); Peter Damian, *Epist.* 12, *PL* 144. 393; Stephen of Tournai, *PL* 211. 447: 'Expertus es in conventu rigorem ieiuniorum, vigiliarum fastidium, frenum silentii, stabilitatem loci, nonnunquam et duritiem lecti, et ariditatem cibi, diuturnum (*sic*) simul et nocturnum pensum obsequii divini.'

ecclesiastical authorities[1] the popularity of the solitary life continued unabated, and during the eleventh and twelfth centuries it seemed to grow in strength. Sufficient witness to this phenomenon in England are the hermits in the Life of St. Wulstan,[2] the letter from Ralph of Durham to William of Wycombe,[3] the biographies of Godric of Finchale and Wulfric of Haselbury, and the pages of Giraldus Cambrensis.[4] Moreover, the rules that were written for them at that time, such as Goscelin's *Liber Confortatorius* and Ailred's *De Institutione Inclusarum*, are an indication that it was not such a haphazard affair as might appear at first sight.

The usual procedure was for the hermit or recluse to undergo a period of probation under strict monastic discipline and to retire to a hermitage only when sufficient proof of holiness and stability had been given to the superiors. If the hermit were a monk he needed the permission of his abbot: if a layman or a woman, the approval of the bishop:[5] only then could he be officially recognized as possessing ecclesiastical status. This does not mean that private vows, such as were taken by Christina, were of no consequence. They were binding in conscience, but did not give her a recognized

---

[1] Ivo of Chartres, *Epist.* 256. *PL* 162, 260–2: 'Vita vero solitaria ideo inferior est, quia voluntaria et importunis cogitationibus plena, quae tanquam muscae minutissimae de limo surgentes volant in oculos cordis et interrumpunt sabbatum mentis'; Dom G. Morin, 'Rainaud l'Ermite et Ives de Chartres; un épisode de la crise du cénobitisme au XI–XIIᵉ siècle', *Revue bénédictine*, xl, 1928, pp. 99–115; Abaelard, *Epist.* 8, *PL* 178. 265; Peter the Venerable, *Epist.* i. 20, *PL* 189. 92; Bernard of Portes, *Epist.* 3, *PL* 153. 897; J. L. Jusserand, 'Les Contes à rire et la vie des recluses au XIIᵉ siècle', *Romania*, xxiv, 1895, p. 122; Archer Taylor, 'The Three Sins of the Hermit', *Modern Philology*, xx, 1922, p. 61; J. A. Herbert, *Catalogue of Romances in the Dept. of MSS. in the British Museum*, London, 1910, iii, pp. 20, 53, 66, 468, 563.

[2] *The Vita Wulfstani of William of Malmesbury*, ed. R. R. Darlington, Camden third series, xl. 65–67.

[3] Durham University Library, MS. Cosin V. 5. 8, fol. 2.

[4] Giraldus Cambrensis, *Opera*, i. 186, iv. 18, vi. 204, ed. J. S. Brewer, J. F. Dimock.

[5] Council of Frankfort (Mansi, *Concilia*, xiii. 908): 'Ut reclusi nisi ex episcopi et abbatis approbatione non fiant'; ibid. xxiii. 425; Wilkins, *Concilia*, i. 628, lists the inquiries to be made by the archdeacons throughout the diocese of Lincoln (no. 48): 'An aliqua anacorita facta sit sine assensu episcopi'. F. D. S. Darwin, *The English Mediaeval Recluse*, London, 1944, p. 53, points out that the bishop's licence for official recognition as a recluse does not appear to have been required till about 1236, when it is mentioned in the Constitutions attributed to St. Edmund Rich, *Constitutiones*, cap. 35. 2.

place in the ecclesiastical system. This problem had already
been discussed by canonists from the time of Burchard of
Worms onwards,[1] and in this connexion all the authors[2] based
their conclusions on a passage taken from the works of Pope
Innocent, to the effect that private vows, even when the veil
was not taken later in a monastery or convent, were as binding
in conscience as those professed publicly before a bishop.[3]
The decision of the bishop of Lincoln at the first meeting
with Christina was, therefore, perfectly correct according to
canon law, and we see the same judgement pronounced by
both Ralph d'Escures and Thurstan of York. It was only
when Robert Bloet had been bribed by Autti and his associates that the bishop changed his mind and decreed that
the espousals and not the private vows should be considered
valid. That the espousals ordinarily contracted had all the
force of a marriage bond was not in doubt, and when these
had been confirmed by a subsequent marriage as in Christina's
case, the position was indeed difficult. But for her both these
actions were completely nullified, not only by the private
vow which had preceded them, but also by the element of
compulsion which her parents had exercised.[4] Her flight to
the hermitage in the face of the bishop of Lincoln's judgement
and without his express permission was sufficient reason for
the subsequent episcopal 'persecution', but on Christina's side
were the precedents to be found in the lives of various early
saints.[5] Though the authenticity of some of these stories may
be open to suspicion, the mind of the Church in this matter

[1] Burchardus, *Decretorum*, lib. viii, c. 12, *PL* 140. 794.

[2] Ivo of Chartres, *Decreti*, pars vii, c. 18, *PL* 161. 549; Gratian, *Decreti*, pars ii,
causa xxvii, qu. 1, cap. 9, *PL* 187. 1376–7; Peter Lombard, *Comment. in Psalmos*,
lxxv, v. 11, *PL* 191. 709.

[3] 'Hae vero quae, necdum sacro velamine tectae, tamen in proposito virginali
semper se permanere simulaverunt, licet velatae non fuerint, si forte nupserint, his
agenda aliquanto tempore poenitentia est, quia sponsio earum a Domino tenebatur.
Si enim inter homines solet bonae fidei contractus nulla ratione dissolvi, quanto
magis ista pollicitatio, quam cum Deo pepigit, solvi sine vindicta non debet?'

[4] W. Holtzmann and E. W. Kemp, *Papal Decretals relating to the Diocese of
Lincoln*, The Lincoln Record Soc. xlvii, 1954, pp. xxvi–xxvii, 20.

[5] B. De Gaiffier, 'Intactam sponsam relinquens. A propos de la vie de S. Alexis',
Analecta Bollandiana, lxv, 1947, pp. 157–95. He gives about twenty parallel
instances.

appeared to be expressed in them, and the fact that the solution chosen by the saints was not expressly condemned in ecclesiastical circles seemed only to endorse the decision taken by them (and Christina) in such circumstances.

We have surprisingly few details about the kind of life which Christina spent during her two years' probation with Alfwen. All we are told is that on her arrival she divested herself of the garments which she had worn at home and clothed herself with a rough habit, so strangely contrasted to the silks and furs of her worldly life. Of her occupations we are told nothing. The copying of books, tilling of the garden, making of garments, weaving mats, or other forms of manual labour usually undertaken by hermits are not even mentioned,[1] and we are left to surmise that most of, if not all the hours of her day, were occupied in reading and meditating on the psalter. That she had much to bear during her stay at Flamstead is implicit in Roger's later decision to summon her to his cell, but the mention of a *dissidium* and the further statement that she was under necessity to leave Alfwen makes one wonder whether there had been a difference of opinion between the two women. It is certainly strange that, after the protection and shelter which Alfwen had afforded her during this difficult period, her name should not be mentioned again in the biography nor be found even among the obits of those who, in the St. Albans Psalter, are recorded for their close relationship to her. On the other hand the

---

[1] Cf. Stephen of Tournai, *Epist.* 159, *PL* 211. 448: 'Ne prolixitate autem legendi, aut oculos obtundas caligine aut vertigine caput graves; post modicam lectionem deambula per cellulam tuam, aut in hortulum egrediens, virentibus herbulis, quae tamen paucae sunt et rarae, visum refice languentem; aut apud alvearia conspice, quae tibi et solatio sint et exemplo.' Besides making combs, needle-cases, pots, mats, baskets, and other things, Peter the Venerable suggests the writing of books, *Epist.* I, 20, *PL* 189. 97–98: 'Plantari non possunt arbusculae, rigari nequeunt sata, neque aliquid ruralis operis exerceri, reclusione perpetua prohibente; sed (quod est utilius), pro aratro convertatur manus ad pennam, pro exarandis agris divinis litteris paginae exarentur, seratur in chartula verbi Dei seminarium: quod maturatis segetibus, hoc est, libris perfectis, multiplicatis frugibus, esurientes lectores repleat, et sic panis coelestis lethalem animae famem depellat.' In the *Gesta Abbatum Fontenellensium*, ed. S. Loewenfeld, Hannover, 1886, two hermits are mentioned as having enriched the monastic library with their work—Milo (p. 21) and Harduin (pp. 47–48). Cf. Wulfric of Haselbury (ed. Bell, p. 45).

pressure to leave Flamstead may have come from the bishop of Lincoln.

When Christina put herself under the guidance and authority of Roger she removed herself from further episcopal interference. Roger, being a monk of St. Albans and having the permission of his own abbot to lead the solitary life, did not fall under the jurisdiction of the bishop, and Christina, as his subject and companion, would most probably enjoy the same exemption. That the bishop could not brook this flouting of his authority is made clear by the marginal passage in William of Malmesbury where a story is told of the reproaches made to Roger by Robert Bloet and the brusque and uncompromising answer given by the hermit.[1] But there were other complications besides that of scandal, and the hardships which Christina had to endure during her four years of close confinement in the small cell adjoining Roger's oratory were not lessened by the secrecy which necessarily shrouded her presence there.

About the early life of Roger the hermit we know little. He first appears in the biography of Christina as a monk of St. Albans, living under obedience to the abbot, but pursuing his solitary life in the hermitage that stood 'on the right side of the road as you go from St. Albans to Dunstable'.[2] We are not told how long he had been a monk, under which abbot he had made his profession, how he had gained permission to undertake a pilgrimage to Jerusalem, or how he had come to settle on a piece of land at Caddington[3] that belonged, not to his own abbey, but to the canons of St. Paul's.

It is evident from the biography that the writer had the greatest admiration for both the personality and the holiness of Roger. He praises his rigorous discipline, his spirit of

[1] William of Malmesbury, *Gesta Pontificum*, ed. N. E. S. A. Hamilton, lib. iv, p. 314.

[2] In the *Gesta Abbatum*, i. 97, where this passage is reproduced, the place is said to be that 'now called Markyate' which is about eight miles from St. Albans along the Watling Street.

[3] Caddington, a church belonging to St Paul's cathedral, is two miles to the north of Markyate.

prophecy and contemplation, and his profound compassion for the poor and downtrodden. He calls him a *deacon*, though in the *Gesta Abbatum* there is mention only of his being ordained subdeacon by Gilbert, bishop of Limerick, in the church of St. Stephen at St. Albans.[1] We do not know what qualifications were demanded before a monk could be ordained priest in the twelfth century: but it is evident that the earlier tradition of St. Benedict whereby the priests in a monastery would be in the minority was still in force.[2] That it did not imply any lack of influence or regard in the community may be judged from the description of Alveredus, who appeared to Abbot Geoffrey in his sleep, and who, though but a sub-deacon, was described as *vir magni testimonii*. Such a one was Roger. Unlike his contemporary hermit Sigar of Northaw, who walked each night to St. Albans to attend the divine services,[3] Roger appears to have remained continually in his solitude and we must therefore surmise that the local priest at Caddington ministered to his spiritual needs. The recitation of the psalms, probably coinciding with the time of the services in the monastery, must have been his main spiritual exercise.[4] The fact that Roger had five other hermits under his charge besides Christina is evidence enough of his authority. Alfwen, the recluse of Flamstead (two miles down the road towards St. Albans), was under his spiritual direction; Eadwin, his cousin and also a hermit, relied on his counsel; Godescalc of Caddington and his wife were under his spiritual direction; whilst Archbishop Thurstan of York, *familiaris et fidus amicus*, obviously regarded him with great veneration. It is a pity that the biographer did not think it necessary to record more than one or two scattered details about his life, for beyond this no literary memorial to him

---

[1] *Gesta Abbatum*, i. 148, though later, the *Annales Monasterii Sancti Albani*, Amundesham, i. 433, speak of 'Rogeri Heremitae et Levitae'. In MS. Cotton Nero D. VII, fol. 66ʳ, there are several deacons named Roger listed among the obits.

[2] *S. Benedicti Regula*, c. 62.

[3] *Gesta Abbatum*, i. 105.

[4] Cf. *Libellus de vita et miraculis S. Godrici*, p. 110: 'Omnes horas canonicas quas Ecclesia celebrare consuevit, vir iste, quamvis pene laicus et illiteratus fuerit, congruis temporibus, prout horarum diversa immutatio expetiit, imitari non destitit.'

remains. The tomb which was erected for him in St. Albans after his death (and which remains in part to this day) has a short inscription of vague comment on the holiness of his life,[1] whilst the Golden Book of St. Albans merely records his obit along with that of many other deacons of the monastery. These fragments, together with the statement that Henry III made a pilgrimage to his shrine in 1257 and made gifts of rich embroidered hangings (*baudekinos*),[2] are the only morsels of information about him that we possess.

It has been said that the St. Albans psalter, now preserved in St. Godehardskirche at Hildesheim,[3] was most probably written by the hermit Roger.[4] It is true that all the prayers in the psalter are written in the masculine as if the text was meant to be read by a man; all the illustrations to the psalms (with two exceptions) depict monks, and the passage at the end of the manuscript about the use of pictures for those who cannot read is taken from a letter of St. Gregory addressed to a hermit. Furthermore, there occurs the following note among the obits which have been inserted in the calendar which precedes the text: 'ii. Idus Septembris Rogeri heremite monachi Scti Albani. Apud quemcumque fuerit hoc

---

[1] *Annales Sancti Albani*, i. 433; R. M. Clay, *The Hermits and Anchorites of England*, London, 1914, p. 113, gives a photograph of the tomb and records the inscription:

> Vir domini verus iacet hic Heremita Rogerus
> Et sub eo clarus meritis Heremita Sigarus.

[2] *Gesta Abbatum*, i. 106.

[3] The manuscript came from Lamspring in the seventeenth or eighteenth century as the inscription shows: 'Liber Monasterii Lambspringensis, Congregationis Anglicanae Ordinis Sancti Benedicti'. This abbey, founded in A.D. 873 and dedicated to SS. Adrian and Denis, was secularized by the Lutherans and given to the English Benedictines in 1643, by Ferdinand, archbishop of Cologne, with the consent of the Congregation of Bursfeld; L. H. Cottineau, *Répertoire topo-bibliographique des abbayes et prieurés*, i. 1545. That the manuscript was in England at the time of the Reformation is proved by the erasure in the calendar of the word *papa*. How it reached Germany is not known.

[4] So A. Goldschmidt, *Der Albanipsalter in Hildesheim*, Berlin, 1895, p. 32. He identifies it (p. 34) with the one described in the *Gesta Abbatum*, i. 94, as having been written at the instance of Abbot Geoffrey: 'unum psalterium pretiosum totum similiter auro illuminatum'. But this psalter, known as the Golden Psalter of St. Albans, is quite a different manuscript: F. Wormald, *English Benedictine Kalendars after 1100*, Henry Bradshaw Soc. lxxvii, 1938, i. 32.

psalterium fiat eius memoria maxime hac die.' The writing
of this obit is in a different, and certainly earlier hand, than
that of the rest of the insertions in the calendar. Though
these details indicate that the manuscript must have been
connected in some way with Roger, there are one or two
difficulties against accepting the supposition that it was
written specially for his use. In the first place, were this so we
should expect the calendar of the psalter to conform to that
of St. Albans abbey where Roger was a monk. This is far
from being the case. Several omissions of importance seem
to suggest that whoever was using it was not following the
liturgical prescriptions of the abbey. Not only are several
feasts missing which are a feature of the normal St. Albans
calendar (for instance, the dedication of the church), but
even the name of St. Alban has been spelt *Albinus*, a mistake
which no one familiar with the place where his relics were
preserved could have made.[1] Furthermore, there are several
features in the rest of the manuscript which could not have
found a place there during Roger's lifetime, such for instance as the occurrence of the name of St. Margaret in the
litany: this addition to the litany, which probably reflects a use
of St. Albans, was made during the lifetime of Abbot Robert
Gorham, perhaps about 1155. The fact, however, that the
psalter is so handsomely produced cannot constitute an argu-
ment against its having been in the possession of a hermit
such as Roger, for though the outward circumstances of his
life might suggest that he was averse to valuable possessions
and anything that savoured of luxury, the parallel cases of
Godric of Finchale and Wulfric of Haselbury seem to show
that asceticism did not exclude an appreciation of illumin-
ated devotional books.[2]

[1] It is hardly likely that there was a confusion with St. Albinus, bishop, whose
relics, preserved at Thorney abbey, are mentioned in B.M. MS. Add. 40000,
f. 11ᵛ under the following entry: 'Hec sunt nomina sanctorum Thornensi cenobio
requiescentium . . . S. Albini episcopi'.

[2] *Libellus de vita et miraculis S. Godrici*, p. 109: 'et libello de sinu sibi protracto,
imaginem Salvatoris, cum Beatae Mariae imaginis (*lege* virginis) similitudine, et
Sancti Johannis pictura honeste in folio depicta, protulit'. Cf. *Wulfric of Haselbury*,
p. 45.

The most powerful objection against deciding that the psalter was written for Roger comes from the claim of Christina. The obits in the calendar refer almost exclusively to her family and friends. Among them we find the names of her father and mother, her two brothers, Gregory and Simon, her sister Margaret, and probably her aunt Alveva, Roger the hermit, Azo the hermit (probably Roger's companion), Geoffrey, abbot of St. Albans, Alveredus, subdeacon of St. Albans, Matilda, nun of Markyate. These and the names of various other monks and nuns,[1] connected with her and her foundation, point in the same direction. Moreover, the calendar has been altered by introducing a number of entries which reflect an interest in female saints. These saints are Juliana, Milburga, Faith, Etheldrith, Frideswide, Hilda, and Felicity. If we examine the lives of these saints we discover that at least four of them have something in common with Christina, in that they rejected their suitors and fled from the joys of marriage to devote themselves to the religious life. In the case of St. Hilda, the first abbess of Whitby, there was the additional reason for her inclusion in that she was considered to be a patroness of hermits and recluses, whilst Juliana was an example of a holy woman who separated from her husband in order that he might become a priest. Besides these additions which indicate that a woman is responsible for their inclusion, there are three others which give a clue

---

[1] A. Goldschmidt, p. 31, has attempted to identify some of these: *Robertus monachus* with Robert, dean of St. Albans (*Gesta Abbatum*, i. 82); *Richard* and *Godwin* with the witnesses present at the dedication of the church of St. Stephen (i. 148); *Michael son of Aileva* with Michael the cantor (i. 82, 147). With the same degree of probability one might go on to identify *Ailwinus canonicus* with Ailwin, head of the Augustinian canons at Holyrood, who signed a charter of David I of Scotland at Huntingdon about 1124 (*Registrum Antiquissimum of the Cathedral Church of Lincoln*, ed. C. W. Foster, iii. 150). He became abbot of the Augustinian house at Holyrood founded by David I in 1128 (D. R. Parsons, *Scottish Historical Review*, xiv. 370–2), resigned his office in 1150, and died 1155 (*Chronicon coenobii Sanctae Crucis Edinburgensis*, Bannatyne Club xxi, 1828, pp. 30, 32). Unfortunately there are no obits in the Holyrood calendar (F. Wormald, 'A Fragment of a thirteenth-century Calendar from Holyrood Abbey', *Proc. of the Soc. of Antiquaries of Scotland*, lxix, 1934–5, pp. 471–9), so the problem must be left unsolved. The only certain identifications are Ailwardus heremita, whose obit appears in MS. Cotton Nero D. VII, fol. 72ᵛ, and Avicia and Adelaisa, who became foundation members of Sopwell priory.

to the locality she was interested in. These entries are St. Felix, the *Tumulatio* of St. Benedict, and St. Yves. All these show a definite East Anglian loyalty and are probably connected with the abbey of Ramsey. The other feasts in the calendar which were copied into the text after the original list had been completed have no significance, since most of them fall on the kalends of each month and their omission in the first place was due to palaeographical rather than to liturgical reasons. The accumulation of these details, however, tends to show that the manuscript has its main connexions not with Roger the hermit, but with Christina, the prioress. Furthermore, in the body of the psalter itself there are two drawings which are most revealing: one of them, which occurs between the end of the Athanasian creed and the beginning of the litany, depicts six nuns with an abbot in their midst holding up before the Blessed Trinity two books, on which are inscribed the opening invocations of the litany.[1] These invocations are addressed separately to the Father, Son, and Holy Spirit, with the fourth and final appeal, *Sancta Trinitas unus Deus*, summing them up. This is an obvious reference to the name of the priory of Markyate, Sanctae Trinitatis de Bosco, and must, presumably, have some connexion with the dedication of the church there. The other drawing, inserted into the margin on a new piece of vellum at some date posterior to the painting of the other initials, shows a nun introducing four monks into the presence of Christ with the following prayer expressed in hexameter leonine verse:

Parce tuis queso monachis clemencia Jesu.

This is almost certainly intended to depict Christina interceding with Christ for the monks of St. Albans, with whom, as the biographer is careful to point out, she had the closest relations. Indeed, it may even represent the monks whom she is said to havei nfluenced into joining the community: '. . . quia in nostra congregatione nonnulli erant quorum

[1] Surprisingly enough Goldschmidt gives no explanation at all of this illustration, though he describes it, p. 136, no. 204.

animas omnibus aliorum locorum cariores habebat, de quibus aliquot ipsa fecerat in ea monachos' (*Vita*, f. 158ᵛᵃ).

What makes it almost certain that the psalter belonged to Christina is the appearance in it of the Life of St. Alexis,[1] a text which is quite irrelevant to a purely liturgical book. This is an obvious addition to the volume and, considering that it is written in French, an incongruous intruder on the Latin psalms: but when one realizes that its story mirrors exactly the experiences of Christina, that it is a kind of *pièce justificative* of her action in leaving her husband and retiring to the hermitage, its presence there, far from being puzzling, becomes intelligible.

The conclusion, then, seems to be that the psalter, if not originally destined for Christina, eventually found its way into her hands and was altered perhaps and completed during the course of its preparation to conform to her interests.

At what date the psalter was written is not clear, but it is worth noting that the invocations in the litany accompanied by the illustration of the Blessed Trinity seem to imply a date somewhat later than the consecration of the church of Markyate in 1145, whilst the duplication of the name of St. Alban, reflecting the liturgical practice of the monastery, together with the inclusion of the name of St. Margaret (made at the instance of Abbot Robert after his escape from a disaster at sea),[2] would place the writing of this particular part of the psalter some time after 1155. It has been suggested that the writing of the psalter was carried out by Michael the Cantor, whose name occurs as a witness in the *Gesta Abbatum*, mainly because the entry in the obits, *Aileva mater Michaelis*, seems to point this way. But the identification is by no means certain. There is no evidence to connect Michael the Cantor with Christina of Markyate, and it is perhaps significant that

[1] Goldschmidt, p. 35, infers from this and the reference to the dedication of a chapel at St. Albans to St. Alexis during the abbacy of Abbot Richard (1097–1119), *Gesta Abbatum*, i. 148, that the psalter was written between 1115 and 1119. He does not explain the omission from the psalter, from MS. Egerton 3721, and from the St. Albans calendar of the feast of St. Alexis; cf. W. v. Wartburg, 'Alexis in Liturgie, Malerei und Dichtung', *Zeitschrift f. romanische Philologie*, lxxii, Tübingen, 1956, pp. 165–94.   [2] *Gesta Abbatum*, i. 126.

his name does not occur among those who witnessed the charter of foundation or, indeed, in any document concerned with Christina. All that one can say is that the writer of the running titles over the psalms in the St. Albans psalter is not responsible for the Alexis story, but only for the obits in the calendar: his hand appears also in the breviary that belonged to St. Albans and in several other manuscripts now preserved in Oxford and Cambridge.[1]

After Roger's death Christina's trials began once more, mainly owing to the pressure brought to bear on her by the bishop of Lincoln, and she was compelled not only to abandon her hermitage at Markyate, but also to seek shelter in various other places to avoid his attentions. Under what circumstances her plight became known to Thurstan, archbishop of York, we are not told, but as he had formerly absolved her from her marriage and applied for an apostolic indult to allow her former husband, Burhred, to marry again, it may be that she applied to him once more for assistance. In the event his provision of a 'protector' was not entirely happy; and after Christina had spent a long time repulsing the importunities of this unnamed cleric, in a house which was evidently not far from a monastery, she returned to her former dwelling. From that moment the tide of her fortunes seemed to turn.

In the meantime her reputation as a person of great holiness had spread far and wide and she was visited by prelates, who came not only from distant parts of England but even from overseas, entreating her to become abbess of communities in which they were interested. The invitations to make her abode at Marcigny[2] and Fontevrault[3] may have been the result of

---

[1] Goldschmidt, pp. 34–37: B.M. MS. Royal 2 A. x: Pembroke College, Cambridge, MS. 180.

[2] Marcigny-les-Nonnains, founded in 1080 by St. Hugh of Cluny and his brother Godefroy. Raingard, the mother of Peter the Venerable, was a nun there, and about Easter 1120 Thurstan accompanied Adela, countess of Blois, to the convent, where she took the veil: *Gallia Christiana*, Paris, 1728, iv. 486; M. Marrier, *Bibliotheca Cluniacensis*, Macon, 1915, pp. 456, 734–51, 755.

[3] Fontevrault was founded about 1100 by Robert D'Arbrissel for the women who had previously lived as hermits under his direction: *Gallia Christiana*, ii. 1311.

her expressed desire to leave England and find some peace
where she was less well known. She was persuaded by her
friends, however, to remain at Markyate and to make her
monastic profession at St. Albans. In this course of action no
one played a greater part than Abbot Geoffrey. For a long
time she hesitated to carry out her decision, deterred by a too
tender conscience and a remembrance of the dangers she had
barely escaped; and several months, perhaps a year, elapsed
before she finally pronounced her solemn vows in the presence
of Alexander, bishop of Lincoln. Though, as a result of this,
she would come within the jurisdiction of the abbot of St.
Albans, it is probable, judging by the date of the erection of
the community into a fully constituted priory, that she and
her companions continued to live as a congregation of hermits.
But with the increase in the number of her associates this state
of affairs could not endure for long, and it was inevitable
that, like many other similar groups of recluses, they should
seek a more permanent and organized form of religious life.

Here we may see, perhaps, the decisive influence of Abbot
Geoffrey. Christina had known the abbey from her early
childhood: she had made her first vow of virginity there when
she came on a visit with her parents: she was acquainted with
several members of the community (Alveredus among them)
and had even persuaded some of them to become monks
there. But she had never met the abbot and only knew of him
by reputation. Geoffrey was in some ways the antithesis of
Christina. He was a man of affairs, a former schoolmaster of
Dunstable, who had offered himself as a monk to St. Albans
in compensation for the loss of some valuable copes which he
had borrowed from the abbey for a play and which had been
accidentally burnt whilst they were in his keeping.[1] From the
hints dropped by the biographer in the Life one gets the
impression that he was a worldly man, rather proud of his
success as an administrator and inclined to pay little heed to
the opinions and advice of others. It is not surprising, then,
that he should have brushed aside with disdain (*Norman-*

[1] *Gesta Abbatum*, i. 73.

norum more, says the chronicler) what he considered the pious vapourings of an hysterical woman. But this first personal encounter with Christina, unpromising as it seemed, marked the turning-point in his career, and the gradual change which came over his character as a result of his closer intimacy with her had in it all the elements of a spiritual conversion. Preoccupation with material interests gave place to a desire for prayer and solitude, personal ostentation was superseded by compassion for the poor and lowly. He expended his energies less on the aggrandizement of his own monastery than on the hermits and recluses who dwelt in the neighbourhood. Not only did he take on himself the economic burden of providing for the needs of the nuns of Markyate, but he also established the recluses from Eywood in the priory of Sopwell[1] and converted the hermitage of Moddry into a regular cell of Benedictine monks dependent on St. Albans.[2] In doing this he appears to have been willing to run counter to the wishes of his own community, though no suspicion of this emerges from the biographer's description of Geoffrey's relations with Christina. As time progressed he became more and more dependent on Christina for advice and direction, and it is evident from the stories about his abortive journeys to the Roman Curia during the early years of King Stephen's reign that he did nothing without first consulting her. It is small wonder that tongues began to wag and that rumours spread from mouth to mouth about the constant visits of the abbot to Markyate.

We are not told either in the Life or in the *Gesta Abbatum* at what precise date Geoffrey decided to build the priory of Markyate. This is rather surprising in view of the fact that the foundation of Sopwell is assigned to a definite year in the *Gesta*. All we know for certain is that in 1145 the canons of St. Paul's granted the land on which the buildings were to be erected and that some time later in the same year the church was consecrated by Alexander, bishop of Lincoln.[3] What is

---

[1] *Gesta Abbatum*, i. 80; Dugdale, *Monasticon*, iii. 362–6.
[2] *Gesta Abbatum* i. 78; Dugdale, iii. 274–7.
[3] Dugdale, iii. 372; M. Gibbs, *Early Charters of the Cathedral Church of St. Paul, London* (Camden third series, lviii, 1939), nos. 154 and 156.

interesting about the grant made by the canons of St. Paul's is the list of witnesses. These are not, as one might imagine, taken exclusively from the community of St. Albans, but fall into three groups: Benedictines, Austin Canons, and laymen. Among the Benedictines we find, besides Geoffrey (and five monks who may come from St. Albans, though it is not certain), Germanus, prior of Belvoir (a cell of St. Albans), Gervase, a monk from the Cluniac priory of Bermondsey, and Hugh, abbot of Colchester. Christina's relationship with the priory of Bermondsey is already known through the incident in the biography where Simon, the sacrist, has a vision confirming her integrity; but what the abbot of Colchester has to do with Markyate is difficult to discover. The appearance of so many Austin Canons at the founding of the priory is surprising and seems to indicate that the relations she had with the Order whilst she was still a girl at Huntingdon had continued even after her flight to the hermitage. One of them, indeed (Robert, prior of Merton), had originally been a canon of Huntingdon and may have known Christina and her family before he left to found the house at Merton; but of the rest—Norman, prior of Holy Trinity, Aldgate, Thomas, prior of St. Bartholomew, Smithfield, and John, prior of St. Julian and St. Botolph, Colchester—nothing specific is known to connect them with either Christina or her hermitage. It may be that they were chosen as representing the most important Augustinian houses in the south and, if so, the order in which they appear in the charter is significant.[1] Of the laymen who signed the charter only one, Simon, Christina's brother, is known. The canons, on their side, are represented by Ralf, the dean of St. Paul's, William, archdeacon of London, Richard Belmeis, archdeacon of Middlesex, Alwaldus, archdeacon of Colchester, and several others, among whom we may single out Odo, prebendary of Caddington Minor.

One of the more pleasant aspects of the Life of Christina

---

[1] J. C. Dickinson, *The Origins of the Austin Canons and their Introduction into England*, pp. 99–108, 117–19.

is its comparative freedom from the miraculous elements which invariably creep into hagiographical literature. The desire to show the reader that Christina possessed all the marks of sanctity is no doubt present, but this purpose is not flagrant, and as a result one is not plagued with a series of incredible occurrences calculated to tax the imagination. Though the writer begins in the approved hagiographical style by recounting the supernatural signs which accompanied her birth and thus prepares the way for her inevitable life of virtue, the story soon comes down to earth and proceeds to narrate, with admirable conciseness and detail, the events, far from miraculous, which led Christina to embark on the religious life. Unlike many of his predecessors working in this field the writer does not borrow events and scenes from the lives of other saints in order to make his story more picturesque, but contents himself with the bare facts which he describes as simply and objectively as he can. Indeed, the narrative is refreshingly unconventional, and it is only towards the end that any emphasis is laid on the unusual events in Christina's life.

The supernatural element in the story is, for the most part, confined to the visions of the recluse, and these visions are concerned not so much with the external affairs of the world as with her own religious vocation. Their effect was to confirm her in her way of life and to give her confidence and fortitude to bear the trials which were thrust upon her. Whether these visions had any mystical content or were merely her own intuition sharpened by anxiety we have no means of knowing; but it is significant that at one point the writer, who seems conversant with the works of Pseudo-Dionysius, is at pains to point out that these experiences were not imaginary. For the most part they concerned herself and Abbot Geoffrey.

Her gift of knowing beforehand what was going to happen was one commonly attributed to hermits and recluses. Roger, her religious director, is said to have possessed the power of prophecy, and other hermits like Godric and Wulfric are

known to have predicted events with amazing precision.[1] But in the case of Christina the instances of her clairvoyance had no public import: she does not appear to have been consulted as a seer by those outside her own circle, and her presentiments and thought-reading were connected only with her most intimate friends and subjects. Whether this implies that her faculty of anticipating the thoughts and actions of those about her had a supernatural explanation is a matter for conjecture, but it is interesting to note that she was always careful to have witnesses of these events when they occurred. Only one physical miracle is recorded as having been performed by Christina—the cure of the girl from Canterbury who was afflicted with the falling sickness. We are given no description of the seizures which the girl suffered beyond the fact that they occurred every Tuesday between nine in the morning and midday; but the regularity with which they came upon her gives rise to the suspicion that their source was psychological rather than physical. Christina's intervention, therefore, which she herself tried to depreciate, may not have had the supernatural implications which her companions were inclined to give to it, though, taking into account the medieval attitude towards this affliction, they had every reason to believe that no other explanation was possible.[2]

Christina's own illnesses, which seem to have resulted from her four years' confinement in the cell attached to Roger's oratory, are described with great accuracy. The story of her paralysis and the portrayal of its effects on her eyes and limbs is extraordinarily precise, and sufficiently detailed to provide a fair picture of a patient afflicted with hemiplegia. Her sudden recovery from this condition, though considered by her attendants to be due to the miraculous intervention of Our Lady, is an occurrence which is by no means rare, and it may have been as natural as the onset of the malady. Her many other ailments which, the writer is quick to point out,

[1] *Libellus de vita et miraculis S. Godrici*, pp. 302–4; *Wulfric of Haselbury*, pp. lix–lxiv.
[2] On the popular attitude to the falling sickness see O. Temkin, *The Falling Sickness*, Baltimore, 1954, pp. 94–116.

left her completely after she had overcome the initial troubles in the hermitage, may have been nervous complaints, brought on by a continual state of fear and anxiety; and her recovery from them may have been due to peace of mind and freedom from the constraints under which she had lived so long. The biographer does not indeed lay too much stress on the supernatural aspect of this sudden restoration to health: he merely points out that after her visions she was filled with such consolation and strength that every manifestation of her sufferings disappeared. The fact that Christina lived to a good age despite the heavy and constant drain made upon her energies is an indication, perhaps, that the ailments from which she suffered may have been psychological rather than physical in origin and that their relief may have been due to natural rather than supernatural causes. But at all events, they were worth recording to give us a complete picture of a woman, highly strung but not hysterical, overcoming her physical disabilities and finding her equilibrium in a life of prayer and contemplation.

Christina was, as far as one can see, a well-balanced and integrated person. We find no mention in her life of excessive fasts, mortifications, wearing of hair-cloth or a lorica (the iron-mail shirt worn by male hermits), nor indeed of any extraordinary modes of penance. There is very little of this kind of medieval extravaganza. But it may be that some readers may find her temptations, which are the normal stock-in-trade of the lives of the saints, rather exaggerated. It is difficult to believe in the monstrous appearances of the devil which were so frightening that, according to the biographer, they would have driven any normal person out of his mind. This we should now perhaps ascribe to a disturbed imagination. But the extraordinary tale of the headless body which lay at the entrance to the church and which gave such a fright to all her nuns is not easy to explain on a purely natural basis: nor is the presence of the pilgrim at the procession. These must be accepted in the same spirit of simplicity as that in which they are described.

[DE S. THEODORA, VIRGINE, QUAE ET CHRISTINA DICITUR.]

FUIT virgo mire sanctitatis et gracie orta nobiliter in civitate huntendonie. Pater eius Aucti. mater vocabatur Beatrix. Ipsa vero nomen sortita Theodoram in baptismate. novissime pro Theodora nomen sibi Christinam accepit ex necessitate. Virgo sane non dum nata. iam electa Deo ac ostensa est hominibus. Quam dum mater sua gestaret in utero. contigit eandem matrem de domo sua prospectare monasterium beate dei genitricis quod in civitate situm erat.[1] Et ecce columbam unam nive candidiorem egressam de monasterio vidit ad se recto itinere. modesto volatu venire. et in dexteram manicam tunice qua erat induta. iunctis alis sese totam immergere. Erat autem tunc dies sabati. qua die precipue celebratur a fidelibus memoria Genitricis Dei. Erat eciam inter assumpcionis et nativitatis dies ipsius. Porro columba cum pregnante muliere sicut ipsa michi retulit. septem continuos dies in mansuetudine egit. ut et attrectari manibus eius inevitabiliter plauderet. et libencius nunc in gremio nunc in sinu ipsius requiescere gauderet.

2. Monstratum est igitur tali presagio. quicquid illud erat quod intus latebat replendum fore spiritu sancto qui super dominum ihesum in specie columbe apparuit. et per Ysaiam prophetam septiformi gracia se descripsit.[2] Nec non beate marie semper virginis et erudiendum exemplo et communiendum presidio ut esset sanctum corpore et spiritu. ab hiis que sunt mundi vacans. et in contemplacione supernorum (f. 145rb) requiescens perhibuit . . . et colum[ba] . . . [mat]ris et perpetue virginis quibus aut mundum ingressa . . . per diem sabati prodiit. et gra[tia repl]eri sese mansuetissimam* comm[od]avit. Hec illa considerans frequenter pronu[nci]abat quod talem partum haberet. qui multum deo placeret. Portavit itaque conceptum suum cum gaudio.

---

* mansuetutissimam *MS*.

[1] Though there was a parish church of St. Mary, the reference is probably to the Augustinian priory of St. Mary's, Huntingdon. The precise date of foundation is not known, but it is usually placed between 1086 and 1092; J. C. Dickinson, *The Origins of the Austin Canons and their Introduction into England*, London, 1950, pp. 103–4.   [2] Isa. 11. 2.

OF S. THEODORA, A VIRGIN, WHO
IS ALSO CALLED CHRISTINA

IN the town of Huntingdon there was born into a family
of noble rank a maiden of uncommon holiness and beauty.
Her father's name was Autti, her mother's Beatrix. The
name which she herself had been given in baptism was
Theodora, but later on, through force of circumstance, she
changed it to Christina. Even before the maiden's birth she
was chosen as a servant of God and shown as such to men.
For whilst her mother was bearing her in the womb, she
looked out one day from her house towards the monastery
of Our Lady which was situated in the town.[1] And suddenly
she saw a dove, whiter than snow, leave the monastery and
come straight towards her in a gentle flight; and, with its
wings folded, it took shelter in the sleeve of the tunic she
was wearing. This occurred on a Saturday, a day specially
set aside by the faithful for the devotion to the Mother of
God. It was between the feasts of the Assumption and the
Nativity of Our Lady. Furthermore, as she told me herself,
the dove stayed quietly with her for seven whole days, allow-
ing itself to be stroked with her hands, showing no sign of
uneasiness, and nestling comfortably and with evident pleasure first in her lap and then in her bosom.

Such a sign was evidently meant to convey that the child
she was bearing would be filled with the Holy Spirit who
hovered over Jesus in the form of a dove and who was
described by the prophet Isaiah as being endowed with grace
sevenfold.[2] It showed also that she would be taught by the
example and strengthened by the protection of Blessed Mary,
ever a virgin, and be holy both in mind and body; detaching
herself from the things of the world and finding peace in
the contemplation of the things that are above. . . . As she
considered these things, she frequently gave it as her opinion
that she would have such a child as would be very pleasing
to God. And so she bore her pregnancy with gladness until

donec veniret dies expectati partus. Quo illucescente. vadit
mulier ad ecclesiam. audivit matutinas et reliquas horas cum
celebracione misse. Et intente per singula⟨s⟩ commendans se
Deo ac eius integerrime matri sanctoque Leonardo cuius
tunc celebraver[unt] natalicium. expleto officio repedavit
domum. Et inter primam et terciam eodem die. hoc est. viii.
Idus Novembris peperit filiam. propter spem sobolis equani-
miter sustinens horam tribulacionis. Crevit infans et ab-
lactata est. et cum incremento corporis proficiebat virtutum
incrementis. Inde fuit quod cum adhuc per etatem discernere
nequiret inter rectum et iniquum suam tenellam carnem
virgis cedebat quociens aliquod illicitum se fecisse putabat.
Nec tamen adhuc scire potuit propter quid diligeret iusticiam.
et odisset iniquitatem.[1] Interea quoniam audierat de Christo
quod bonus est. quod pulcher. quod ubique presens. in
noctibus et lectulo suo loquebatur ad ipsum quasi ad hominem quem videret. et hoc alta voce et clara. ut audiretur et
intelligeretur ab hiis qui in eadem domo iacebant. estimans
cum Deo loquentem non posse audiri ab homine. At illis
deridentibus eam morem mutavit.

3. Fuit tunc temporis quidam canonicus Huntendonie
Sueno dictus. provectus etate. vita clarus et doctrina potens.
Hic casu vidit eam adhuc parvulam et mox tanti (f. 145va)
[amoris eius captus] uehementer apud . . . concepit tamen
men[te] . . . rei quam magnum erat olim . . . futura. et ideo
querebat sem[per occas]ionem et plerumque reperiebat quomodo videret illam uel eciam alloqueretur. Multum proficiebat uterque ex alterna sermocinatione. Porro virguncula
statuit integritatem suam Deo servare. vir Dei omnimodo
intendebat animum illius in statuto roborare. Modo difficultatem exprimebat. modo gloriam extollebat virginitatis.
difficultatem servande. gloriam servate. Quadam vice. cum

[1] Cf. Ps. 44. 8.

the day of the expected birth should come. When that day dawned, she went to church, heard matins and lauds, and attended Mass. And commending herself at each one devoutly to God, to His Virgin mother, and to St. Leonard, whose feast day it then was, she returned home after the service was concluded. And between six o'clock and nine o'clock of the same day, that is on November 6th, she gave birth to a daughter, bearing with fortitude the pains of labour for her hope in her offspring. The child grew and was weaned, and as it grew in strength so it made progress in virtue. Hence it came about that while she was still too young to see the difference between right and wrong, she beat her own tender body with rods whenever she thought she had done something that was not allowed. But even so the child was still unable to understand why she should love righteousness and hate wickedness.[1] In the meantime, as she had heard that Christ was good, beautiful, and everywhere present, she used to talk to Him on her bed at night just as if she were speaking to a man she could see; and this she did with a loud clear voice, so that all who were resting in the same house could hear and understand her. She thought that if she were speaking to God, she could not be heard by man. But when they made fun of her, she changed this mode of acting.

At that time there was a certain canon at Huntingdon named Sueno, a man advanced in age, conspicuous for his good life, and influential in his teaching. This man saw her by chance when she was a small child. . . . For this reason he was always seeking opportunities (and often found them) of seeing and speaking to her. From this mutual conversation both gleaned great profit. Furthermore, as the maiden had decided to preserve her virginity for God, the man of God strove by all the means in his power to confirm her in her decision. Sometimes he described the difficulties, at other times he extolled the glory of virginity, the difficulty of preserving it, and the glory of having preserved it intact. On one occasion when he was speaking about these matters,

de hiis ageret. dixit illi quidam: Adhuc tanta libidine arderet. quod nisi maiore virtute Dei cohiberetur impudenter cuilibet deformi fracteque leprose se supponeret. Hoc illa cum magno tedio audivit. et cum indignacione subintulit. dicens: Si vis loqui de bono. loquere et audiam: si de contrario protinus abscedam. Que responsio tantum confirmavit eum in virtute sanctitatis ab eo quod fuit antea. quantum ferrum a plumbo differt in fortitudine. Et quemadmodum cementum solidat lapides in muro. sic asperitas huius verbi solidavit illum in amore divino. Set et illa nichilominus per doctrinam et exhortacionem Suenonis profecit tantum. quod umbram estimaret queque bonorum temporalium.

4. Interea divina disponente providencia contigit Autti ac Beatricem sumpta secum sua karissima filia Christina nostrum adire monasterium ac beati martiris Albani cuius inibi sacra venerantur ossa; sibi sueque proli flagitare patrocinium. Perscrutans ergo puella sedulo visu locum. et considerans reverendam maturitatem inhabitancium monachorum. pronunciavit felices et consorcii eorum optavit fieri particeps. Denique exeuntibus paren(f. 145vb)tibus suis de templo. postquam expleverint propter que venerunt. illa signum crucis uno unguium suorum scripsit in porta scilicet quod in illo specialiter monasterio suum recondidisset affectum. Et notandum quod erat tunc natalicium sancti Leonardi; sicut quando prius edita fuit in lucem huius seculi. Deinde venerunt ad villam que dicitur Scetlyndunum[1] et pernoctaverunt ibi. Cetero comitatu variis prout libuit intendente vanitatibus. sola virgo Christi iugiter in sanctis exercebatur meditacionibus. Denique prescripsit secum in animo quasi iam fuisset quod futurum erat se mortuam exponi. exanimi cadavere locum exalati spiritus non licere prenosci. Pro certo tamen habebat in bonis illum fore si bene fecisset. sin autem male deputari tormentis. Proinde omnem pompam seculi

---

[1] Shillington is a village on the Bedfordshire/Hertfordshire border, 25 miles from Huntingdon and 17 from St. Albans nearly on a direct line.

someone said to her that he was still so stimulated by lust
that unless he were prevented by the greater power of God
he would without any shame lie with any ugly and mis-shapen
leper. To this she listened with deep disgust and angrily
interrupted him, saying: If you wish to speak on edifying
matters, speak and I will listen; but if not, I will go away
immediately. This remark so strengthened him in the pursuit
of holiness that his former life compared to his later was as
lead compared to iron. And as cement makes firm the stones
in a wall, so did this biting remark establish him immovably
in the love of God. She also made such progress through the
teaching and encouragement of Sueno that she accounted
all the things of this world as but a fleeting shadow.

In the meantime, by an act of divine providence, Autti
and Beatrix brought their dear daughter Christina with them
to our monastery of the blessed martyr St. Alban, where his
sacred bones are revered, to beg his protection for themselves and for their child. When the girl therefore had looked
carefully at the place and observed the religious bearing of
the monks who dwelt there, she declared how fortunate the
inmates were, and expressed a wish to share in their fellow-
ship. At length, as her parents were leaving the monastery,
having fulfilled all the things they had come to do, she made
a sign of the cross with one of her fingernails on the door as
a token that she had placed her affection there. And it should
be remarked that it was then the feast day of St. Leonard,
the very day on which she had been brought into this world.
Then they came to the vill which is called Shillington[1] and
spent the night there. The rest of the party gave themselves
up to various amusements according to their whim: the
maiden of Christ spent her time alone in holy meditation. In
that hour she imagined herself lying on her deathbed (as if
the future were already present) and she reflected that after
life had departed from the body no one could foretell the
abode of the freed spirit. One thing, however, was certain—
that if she lived well it would enjoy bliss, but if wickedly
it would be given over to torments. Thenceforward she lost all

fastidivit et ad Deum toto corde conversa dixit: Domine ante
te omne desiderium meum et gemitus meus a te non est
absconditus.¹ Quid enim michi est in celo et a te quid volui
super terram? Defecit caro mea et cor meum; Deus cordis
mei et pars mea Deus in eternum. Quia ecce qui elongant se
a te peribunt: perdidisti omnes qui fornicantur abs te. Michi
autem adherere Deo bonum est. ponere in Domino Deo
spem meam.² In crastina pergit ad ecclesiam ubi celebrante
missam sacerdote. post evangelium accessit Christina ad altare et optulit unum denarium. dicens in corde suo: Domine
Deus clemens et omnipotens. suscipe tu per manum sacer-
dotis tui meam oblationem. Tibi namque in resignatione mei
ipsius denarium istum offero. Dignare queso candorem et
integritatem virginitatis conferre michi quo reformes in me
ymaginem filii tui.³ qui tecum vivit et regnat in unitate spiritus
sancti Deus per omnia secula seculorum. Amen.

5. (f. 146ʳᵃ) Postquam autem venit Huntendoniam Suenoni suo quid vovisset aperuit* et ille qui tanquam lucerna
Dei in locis illis habebatur. votum virginis coram Deo confirmavit. porro Christina mansit in domo patris sui in pace.
gaudens se de die in diem in virtutibus sacris et amore supernorum succrescere. Ceterum hoc invidia diaboli ferre diu
non potuit. unde ad conturbandam illam exardescens. hoc
inicium sumpsit. Rannulphus episcopus Dunelmi⁴ ante episco-
patum dum esset tocius Anglie iudex. secundus post regem;
Christine materteram Alvevam nomine habuerat. de qua
filios procrearat. Quam postea cuidam civium Huntendonie
dedit in uxorem. et illius causa reliquam eius honorabat
propinquitatem. Apud ipsam semper hospitabatur. quando
de Nordanhumbria Londoniam ibat vel inde revertebatur.
Quodam tempore cum esset illic. et de more venisset ad eum
amicus suus Aucti cum liberis suis: factum est ut episcopus
elegantem puellam intencius consideraret. continuo misit in

---

* aperuit: apparuit *MS.*

¹ Ps. 37. 10.　　　² Ps. 72. 25–28.　　　³ Rom. 8. 29.
⁴ Ralph Flambard, originally in the service of Maurice, bishop of London, was
consecrated bishop of Durham 5 June 1099. He died in 1128.

interest in worldly ostentation and turned to God with all her heart, and said: 'Lord, all my desire is before Thee, and my groaning is not hid from Thee.[1] Whom have I in heaven but Thee? and there is none upon earth that I desire besides Thee. My flesh and my heart faileth, but God is the strength of my heart and my portion for ever. For lo, they that are far from thee shall perish: Thou hast destroyed all them that go a-whoring from Thee. But it is good for me to draw near to God: I have put my trust in the Lord God, that I may declare all Thy works.'[2] The following day she went to the church where the priest was saying Mass. After the gospel Christina approached the altar and offered a penny, saying in her heart, 'O Lord God, merciful and all powerful, receive my oblation through the hands of Thy priest. For to Thee as a surrender of myself I offer this penny. Grant me, I beseech Thee, purity and inviolable virginity whereby Thou mayest renew in me the image of Thy Son:[3] who lives and reigns with Thee in the unity of the Holy Spirit God for ever and ever, Amen.'

After she had returned to Huntingdon she revealed to Sueno what she had vowed and he, who was considered in those parts as a light of God, confirmed the virgin's vow before God. Christina, however, remained peacefully in her father's house, rejoicing that she could grow from day to day in holy virtue and in the love of supernatural things. But the envy of the devil could not long endure this; and burning with desire to upset her, took the initiative in this way. Whilst Ralph the bishop of Durham[4] was justiciar of the whole of England, holding the second place after the king, but before he became a bishop, he had taken to himself Christina's maternal aunt, named Alveva, and had children by her. Afterwards he gave her in marriage to one of the citizens of Huntingdon and for her sake held the rest of her kin in high esteem. On his way from Northumbria to London and on his return from there he always lodged with her. On one occasion when he was there Autti, his friend, had come as usual with his children to see him. The bishop gazed intently at his beautiful daughter, and immediately

cor eius[1] incentor libidinis Satanas ut eam male concupisceret.
Quamobrem. officiose querens quonam ingenio pot[ir]etur
illa. tandem nichil mali suspi[can]tem introduci fecit in
cameram [su]am cortinis decenter ornatam. in quo ipse
nocte dormiebat. illis solis [rema]nentibus cum innocente
qui e[rant] de familia episcopi. patre suo et matre ceterisque
cum quibus venerat in aula seorsum indulgentibus ebrietati.
Iam obtenebrescente nocte innuit occulte suis episcopus et
egressi sunt. dominumque suum et Christinam. lupum videlicet et agnum in una domo simul dereliquerunt. Pro pudor.
impudicus episcopus virginem per alteram tunice manicam
irreverenter arripuit et ore (f. 146[rb]) sancto quo misteria
[divina solebat] conficere. de re nephanda [sollicitavit]. Quid
ergo faceret m[isera puell]a inter tales angustias appr[e-
hensa]? Clamaretne parentes? Iam [dor]mitum abierant.
Consentire nullo modo voluit. aperte contradicere ausa non
fuit. Quia si aperte contradiceret. proculdubio vim sus-
tineret.*

6. Audi ergo quam prudenter egit. Respexit ad hostium.
et vidit clausum quidem sed non obseratum. Dixitque. Di-
mitte me. ut eam hostium obserare. Quia licet minime Deum
metuimus. saltem homines opere tali ne superveniant vereri
debemus. Exegit ab ea iusiurandum quod eum non falleret.
quin ostium sicut dixit obfirmaret. Et iuravit illi. Itaque
dimissa. protinus† [prosi]liit, et forinsecus ostio firmiter ob-
serato. domum festina cucurrit. Quod fuit inicium suarum
que secute sunt immanium tribulacionum. Tunc ille miser
videns quia illusus esset ab adolescentula. contabuit dolore
[ut nisi] contemptum ulcisceretur. nichili [pend]eret quantumcumque videbatur habere [po]tencie. Set nullo alio
modo se ultum iri credidit quam ut vel per se vel [per] alium
auferret Christine florem pudicicie. propter quam tutandam
episcopum quoque spernere non dubitavit.

* vim+pateretur, *eras. MS.*   † protinus+dimissa, *eras. MS.*

[1] Cf. John 13. 2.

Satan put it into his heart[1] to desire her. Busily, therefore, seeking some trick of getting her into his power, he had the unsuspecting girl brought into his chamber where he himself slept, which was hung with beautiful tapestries, the only others present with the innocent child being members of his retinue. Her father and mother and the others with whom she had come were in the hall apart giving themselves up to drunkenness. When it was getting dark the bishop gave a secret sign to his servants and they left the room, leaving their master and Christina, that is to say, the wolf and the lamb, together in the same room. For shame! The shameless bishop took hold of Christina by one of the sleeves of her tunic and with that mouth which he used to consecrate the sacred species, he solicited her to commit a wicked deed. What was the poor girl to do in such straits? Should she call her parents? They had already gone to bed. To consent was out of the question: but openly resist she dared not because if she openly resisted him, she would certainly be overcome by force.

Hear, then, how prudently she acted. She glanced towards the door and saw that, though it was closed, it was not bolted. And she said to him: 'Allow me to bolt the door: for even if we have no fear of God, at least we should take precautions that no man should catch us in this act.' He demanded an oath from her that she would not deceive him, but that she would, as she said, bolt the door. And she swore to him. And so, being released, she darted out of the room and bolting the door firmly from the outside, hurried quickly home. This was the beginning of all the frightful troubles that followed afterwards. Then that wretch, seeing that he had been made a fool of by a young girl, was eaten up with resentment and counted all his power as nothing until he could avenge the insult he had suffered. But the only way in which he could conceivably gain his revenge was by depriving Christina of her virginity, either by himself or by someone else, for the preservation of which she did not hesitate to repulse even a bishop.

7. Interim tamen dissimulabat quid [mo]liretur. et Londoniam proficiscitur. [Cum re]diit. venit Huntendunum.
sericas vestes et queque preciosa ornamenta secum attulit.
virgini obtulit; que omnia tanquam lutum respexit atque
despexit. Ille vere captivus prius luxurie post invidie. cum
vidisset quia per se nichil proficeret. locutus est cum nobili
quodam iuvene Burthredo nomine. [inci]tans eum ut Christinam sibi postularet (f. 146ᵛᵃ) [in uxorem. promittens quod]
ipse modis omnibus [secundaret] eius postulacionem. Igitur
[agente iuv]ene secundum consultum episcopi. tan[ta in-
stan]cia aggressus est episcopus exequi quod promiserat
quod non prius destitit. quam assensu⟨m⟩ parentum ipso
tradente. vellet nollet Christina Burthredus illam sibi despon-
sandam accepit. Quo facto; presul quasi gloriose compos
victorie letus abiit Dunelmum. virgo remansit tristis in domo
parentum suorum. Post hec convenit predictus adolescens
patrem illius et matrem. quatinus sibi desponsarent quam
pepigerant ei coniugem. Quibus loquentibus. cum filia de
sponsaliis. avertit aurem. Causam querentibus. malo respondit casta manere. nam et votum feci. Audientes. deriserunt
temeritatem eius. Illa nec vultum mutavit. unde magis eam
redarguerunt stulticie. et abdicata illa exortati sunt ut ad feli-
cia sponsalia festinaret. Noluit. Optulerunt munera. promise-
runt magna. recusavit. Blanditi sunt. minas addiderunt. non
cessit. Novissime quandam ipsius collateralem et individuam
comitem Helisentem vocabulo seduxerunt. que virginis aures
sedulo demulceret lenociniis. ut vel assiduitas confabulacionis
huiusmodi suscitaret in audientis animo appetitum fastigii
matronalis. Hanc Helisentem postea velatam vidimus. credo
propter illud expiandum scelus. Infatigabiliter quippe laboravit in studio depravandi sodalem. spem triumphandi sumens
a proverbio. gutta cavat lapidem non vi sed sepe cadendo.¹

---

¹ This is a medieval version of Ovid, *Epistulae ex Ponto,* IV. x. 5. Cf. Job 14. 19.

In the meantime he concealed his intentions and set out for London. On his return he came to Huntingdon, bringing with him silken garments and precious ornaments of all kinds. These he offered to the maiden; but she looked on them as dirt and despised them. But he, first a slave to lust and afterwards to malice, seeing that he made no headway on his own account, spoke to a young nobleman named Burthred, egging him on to ask for Christina's hand in marriage, promising that he would further his request by every means in his power. When the young man acted on the bishop's advice, the bishop backed his promise with such malicious persistence that he did not stop until, against Christina's will, he had gained the parents' consent for her to be betrothed to Burthred. When this was accomplished, the prelate, glorying in his conquest, went off to Durham, leaving the maiden sad at heart in her parents' home. After this the aforesaid young man called on her father and mother to arrange his betrothal with the girl who they had promised should be his wife. When they spoke to her about preparations for the wedding, she would not listen. And when they asked the reason, she replied: 'I wish to remain single, for I have made a vow of virginity.' On hearing this, they made fun of her rashness. But she remained unmoved by it: therefore they tried to convince her of her foolishness and, despite her rejections, encouraged her to hurry on the marriage preparations. She refused. They brought her gifts and made great promises: she brushed them aside. They cajoled her; they threatened her; but she would not yield. At last they persuaded one of her close friends and inseparable companions, named Helisen, to soothe her ears by a continuous stream of flattery, so that it would arouse in her, by its very persistence, a desire to become the mistress of a house. We saw this same Helisen afterwards when she took the veil for the purpose, I believe, of expiating this criminal behaviour. She left no stone unturned in her efforts to undermine her friend's resistance, deriving hope of ultimate triumph from the proverb: *Constant dripping wears away a stone.*[1] But she

Verumptamen nullo modo potuit ab ea saltem verbotenus
extorqueri consensus. cum annus integer fuisset in huiusmodi machinamentis expensus. Postea vero quadam die con-
gregati ad ecclesiam. aggressi sunt simul omnes ex improviso
puellam (f. 146ᵛᵇ) Quid multa? Nescio quomodo. scio quod
nutu dei tot impinguentibus lingua concessit. et eadem hora
Burthredus illam in coniugem sibi desponsavit.

8. Desponsata virgo reducitur rursus in domum parentum dum sponsus suus quanquam alibi haberet edificia. nova
faceret et ampliora prope suum socerum. Ipsa tamen etsi
desponsata perseverabat eodem animo quo prius. libere pro-
testans collum suum nulla racione contaminandum fore
carnali⟨bu⟩s viri amplexibus. Parentes vero sui quo pertinaciam illius considerabant. eo nichil intemptatum pretermit-
tebant. modo blandiciis. modo obiurgacionibus. interdum
muneribus amplisque promissis. necnon minis atque terrori-
bus insistentes. ut eius possent emollire constantiam. Cumque
simul omnes domestici sui ceteraque cognatio desudarent
unanimiter in hoc. Aucti tamen pater suus omnes in hoc
studio superabat; et ipse superatus ab eiusdem virginis genitrice. sicut in sequentibus clarebit. Qui postquam multis
eam modis nequicquam temptaverant; tandem hac callidi-
tate sunt usi. Deputantes ei duram ac diligentem custodiam.
omnem hominem religiosum et timentem Deum arcebant
ab eius colloquio. iocosos nitore carnis elatos omni levitate
seculi facetos. quorum mala collo[quia] corrumpunt mores
bonos.[1] admitteb[ant] ultro. Hiis addiderunt ut prohiber[ent]
eam ab ingressu monasterii beate [Dei] genitricis semper
virginis eo quod [videba]tur illis. quociens id intrabat soli-
[dita]tis aliquid suis pristinis viribus [contrib]uere. Que res
valde gravis erat illi. unde eciam prohibentibus sic respondit
cum magna commotione animi: Etsi vos aditum monasterii
mee dilectissime domine michi intercluditis nunquam certe
dulcem ipsius memoriam a pec[tore] (f. 147ʳᵃ) meo divelletis.

---

[1] 1 Cor. 15. 33.

was quite unable to extort one word signifying her consent even though she had spent a whole year trying out these stratagems. Some time later, however, when they were all gathered together in the church, they made a concerted and sudden attack on her. To be brief, how it happened I cannot tell. All I know is that by God's will, with so many exerting pressure on her from all sides, she yielded (at least in word), and on that very day Burthred was betrothed to her.

After the espousal the maiden returned once more to her parents' home whilst her husband, though he had houses elsewhere, built her a new and larger dwelling-place near his father-in-law. But although she was married, her former intentions were not changed, and she freely expressed her determination not to submit to the physical embraces of any man. The more her parents became aware of her persistence in this frame of mind, the more they tried to break down her resistance, first by flattery, then by reproaches, sometimes by presents and grand promises, and even by threats and punishment. And though all her friends and relatives united forces together in this purpose, her father Autti surpassed them all in his efforts, whilst he himself was outclassed by the girl's mother, as will become evident later on. After they had tried out many methods without result, they finally hit on this subterfuge. Putting her under strict and rigorous guard, they prevented any religious god-fearing man from having any conversation with her: on the other hand they freely invited to the house people given to jesting, boasting, worldly amusement, and those whose evil communications corrupt good manners.[1] Furthermore, they stopped her going to the monastery of Our Lady because it became apparent that whenever she paid a visit there she came back confirmed and strengthened in her resolution. This was very hard for her to bear, and to those who forbade her she said with great feeling: 'Even though you may deny me access to the monastery of my beloved Lady, you cannot wrench its memory from my breast.' They forbade her access to the chapel which was most dear to her and would not allow her to go

S[ed illi totaliter arcentes] cubilia que libentissime [vis]eret.
non permittebant illum adire locum. deducebant autem secum
invitam ad convivia. ubi ciborum exquisita varietas diversorum infundebatur alternatione poculorum. ubi cythare
lireque melodiis illecebrosa respondebant modulamina can-
tantium. ut ista conculcate mentis robur enervarent. et ita
demum ad seculi luxum deducerent. Sed illorum ubique
delusa calliditas. maiorem demonstrabat in victrice pruden-
ciam.

9. Denique vide quid egit. quomodo se continuit in gilda
que vocatur mercantium. maximo videlicet negociatoribus
atque celeberrimo festo.[1] Quadam die congregata illic nume-
rosa multitudine nobilium; presidebant illis Aucti et Beatrix
nobilissimi omnium. Tunc placuit ut coram tam honorabili
congregatione sua maior natu atque dignior filia. idest Christina. gereret officium pincerne. Quapropter iubent illam
surgere. et posito pallio quo* erat circumdata. strictam laqueo-
lis vestes ad latera. manicas ad brachia; venerande nobilitati
pocula decenter ministrare.† Si⟨c⟩ quidem sperabant hinc in-
tuentium laudibus. illinc nimietate paulatim sumpta potus.
subigendum animum illius ad consensum. corpus ad opus
corrupcionis. Illa preceptum adimplens; contra utrumque
iaculum satis conveniens opposuit scutum. Contra favores
laudis humane Genitricem Dei defixam memoriae. Ad
quod non parum iuvit aula presentis conventus. quam
propter enormitatem sui necesse fuit patere pluribus ostiis.
quorum unum ante quod erat Christine frequentius trans-
eundum. respiciebat ad sancte genitricis Dei monasterium.
(f. 147ʳᵇ) . . . dicendo ave Maria ‡ . . . templi quoque aḍu . . .
contra incentivum ebrietatis scu[tum oppo]suit ardorem sitis.
Quid mirum si aruit. quia per totum diem ministra[ndo]
iure bibentibus ipsa nichil gustavit. Vespere sero siti pariter
et estu deficiens. bibit pauxillum aque. sicque sedavit pariter
utrumque.

---

* quo: qua *MS.*　　　† ministraret *MS.*　　　‡ Two lines completely missing.

[1] See Introduction, p. 10.

to that place. But they took her with them, against her will, to public banquets, where divers choice meats were followed by drinks of different kinds, where the alluring melodies of the singers were accompanied by the sounds of the zither and the harp, so that by listening to them her strength of mind might be sapped away and in this way she might finally be brought to take pleasure in the world. But their wiles were outwitted at all points and served but to emphasize her invincible prudence.

See finally how she acted, how she behaved herself at what is called the Gild merchant, which is one of the merchants' greatest and best-known festivals.[1] One day, when a great throng of nobles were gathered together there, Autti and Beatrix held the place of honour, as being the most important amongst them. It was their pleasure that Christina, their eldest and most worthy daughter, should act as cup-bearer to such an honourable gathering. Wherefore they commanded her to get up and lay aside the mantle which she was wearing, so that, with her garments fastened to her sides with bands and her sleeves rolled up her arms, she should courteously offer drinks to the nobility. They hoped that the compliments paid to her by the onlookers and the accumulation of little sips of wine would break her resolution and prepare her body for the deed of corruption. Carrying out their wishes, she prepared a suitable defence against both attacks. Against the favours of human flattery she fixed in her memory the thought of the Mother of God, and for this purpose she was not a little helped by the hall where the gathering took place, for because of its size it had several entrances. One of these before which Christina had frequently to pass looked out on the monastery of the blessed Mother of God . . . reciting the *Hail Mary* . . ..* Against the urge to drunkenness, she opposed her burning thirst. What wonder is there that she felt dry, since though she had been pouring out wine all day for others to drink their fill, she had tasted nothing? But in the evening, when it was late and she was fainting with the heat and thirst, she drank a little water and thus satisfied both desires at the same time.

10. Parentes vero sui sic in hoc illusi aliud moliti sunt.
et noct[u] clam in cubiculum illius sponsum suum intro-
duxerunt. quatinus si forte dormientem virginem reperiret:
repente oppresse illuderet. At vel providencia cui se com-
miserat inventa vigilans atque vestita. iuvenem quasi ger-
manum letabunda suscepit. et apud lectum suum cum ipso
residens. multum ad caste vivendum exhortans. exempla
quoque sanctorum ei proposuit. Historiam ordine retexuit
illi beate Cecilie et sponsi sui Valeriani. qualiter illibate
pu[dici]cie coronas eciam morituri meru[erunt] accipere de
manu angeli. Nec solum [hoc] sed et illi et per illos alii
postmodum [ad] viam martirii pervenerunt. sicque a Domino
duppliciter coronati: in celo et [in ter]ra honorati sunt. Et
nos inquid [quan]tum possumus sequamur illorum exempla. ut consortes efficiamur in eorum [per]henni gloria.
Quia si compatimur: et con[reg]nabimus.[1] Non pudeat te
repudia[ri. sci]licet ne tui concives improperent tibi [quasi]
a me repudiato viliter ingrediar [in do]mum tuam. et co-
habitemus in ea ali[quan]to tempore. specietenus quidem
con[iuges] ⟨.⟩in conspectu Domini continentes. Verum[pta-
men] prius interdemus alterutrum dextras quod interim
neuter contingat alterum impudice. neuter alterum aspiciat
nisi simplici et angelico oculo. promittentes Deo quod post
revolucionem trium aut quatuor annorum (f. 147[va]) habitum
suscipiemus [religionis] et nos ex toto mancipabimus . . .
monasterio quod sibi providentia elegerit. Huiusmodi ser-
mocinacionibus pertracta plurima parte noctis. [tandem] a
virgine recessit iuvenis. Per eum edocti qui introduxerant
illum quid factum fuerat. ignavum ac nullius usus iuvenem
conclamant. Et multis exprobracionibus animum eius denuo
accendentes: alia nocte impingunt in thalamum magnopere
prestructum. ne infinitis ambagibus et candidis sermonibus
fallentis effeminetur. Sed omnino seu prece seu vi voto suo

---

[1] A conflation of Rom. 8. 17, 2 Tim. 2. 12.

But as her parents had been outwitted in this, they tried something else. And at night they let her husband secretly into her bedroom in order that, if he found the maiden asleep, he might suddenly take her by surprise and overcome her. But even through that providence to which she had commended herself, she was found dressed and awake, and she welcomed the young man as if he had been her brother. And sitting on her bed with him, she strongly encouraged him to live a chaste life, putting forward the saints as examples. She recounted to him in detail the story of St. Cecilia and her husband Valerian, telling him how, at their death they were accounted worthy to receive crowns of unsullied chastity from the hands of an angel. Not only this: but both they and many others after them had followed the path of martyrdom and thus, being crowned twice by the Lord, were honoured both in heaven and on earth. 'Let us, therefore,' she exhorted him, 'follow their example, so that we may become their companions in eternal glory. Because if we suffer with them, we shall also reign with them.[1] Do not take it amiss that I have declined your embraces. In order that your friends may not reproach you with being rejected by me, I will go home with you: and let us live together there for some time, ostensibly as husband and wife, but in reality living chastely in the sight of the Lord. But first let us join hands in a compact that neither meanwhile will touch the other unchastely, neither will look upon the other except with a pure and angelic gaze, making a promise that in three or four years' time we will receive the religious habit and offer ourselves ... to some monastery which providence shall appoint.' When the greater part of the night had passed with talk such as this, the young man eventually left the maiden. When those who had got him into the room heard what had happened, they joined together in calling him a spineless and useless fellow. And with many reproaches they goaded him on again, and thrust him into her bedroom another night, having warned him not to be misled by her deceitful tricks and naïve words nor to lose his manliness.

pociatur. Quod si neutro prevaleat per se: sciat ipsos protinus
sibi suffragio adesse. modo meminerit esse virum.

11. Hoc animadvertens Christina, concita de stratu suo
exiliit [et] utraque manu tenens clavum qui defixus [in]
pariete fuit inter ipsum parietem et cortinam tremefacta
pependit. Accessit interim Burthredus ad lectum. nec inveniens [quo]d speravit; mox innuit expectantibus [eum]
ad ostium. Qui protinus irrumpentes. accensis luminaribus
huc illuc discurrentes querunt. eoque studiosi[us] quo certi
fuerunt illam tunc intus [esse] quando intravit nec uspiam
e[gredi] potuisse nisi illis inspicientibus. [Quid] queso. quid
animi tunc illi fuisse putes? quomodo trepidabat inter tot
fremitus querentium animam suam.[1] Nonne [evan]ida est in
corde suo trementi descr[ips]it sese iam in medium trahendam. iis circumstantibus. intuentibus minantibus ludibrio
corruptori suo tradendam. Denique unus ex eis casu pedem
pendentis manu palpando tenuit. Sed mediante cortina ex-
cecato sensu ignorans quid esset; continuo dimisit. Tunc
ancilla Christi resumpto spiritu oravit ad Dominum dicens:
Avertantur retrorsum qui volunt michi mala.[2] et illis statim
abeuntibus (f. 147[vb]) [cum] rubore salva facta est sic ex illa
hora.[3]

12. Nichilominus in crastino rediit ad illam idem Burthredus simili furore agitatus. Qui dum per unum ostium
intravit. ipsa per alium sibi fugam consiluit. habensque ante
se quidem sepem quandam, que per altitudinem et super-
eminentibus preacutis sudibus transcensum prohibere videbatur; a tergo vero iuvenem instantem qui eam iam iamque
comprehendere videbatur. sepem incredibili facilitate tran-
siliit; et ex altera parte stantem nec transire valentem insecu-
torem suum tuta respiciens ait: Vere nunc in isto demonem
evasi. quem nocte preterita vidi; viderat namque per som-
pnum quasi demonem horribilem aspectu atris dentibus se

[1] Ps. 34. 4.   [2] Ps. 69. 4.   [3] Cf. Matt. 9. 22.

Either by force or entreaty he was to gain his end. And if neither of these sufficed, he was to know that they were at hand to help him: all he had to mind was to act the man.

When Christina sensed this, she hastily sprang out of bed and clinging with both hands to a nail which was fixed in the wall, she hung trembling between the wall and the hangings. Burthred meanwhile approached the bed and, not finding what he expected, he immediately gave a sign to those waiting outside the door. They crowded into the room forthwith and with lights in their hands ran from place to place looking for her, the more intent on their quest as they knew she was in the room when he entered it and could not have escaped without their seeing her. What, I ask you, were her feelings at that moment? How she kept trembling as they noisily sought after her.[1] Was she not faint with fear? She saw herself already dragged out in their midst, all surrounding her, looking upon her, threatening her, given up to the sport of her destroyer. At last one of them touched and held her foot as she hung there, but since the curtain in between deadened his sense of touch, he let it go, not knowing what it was. Then the maiden of Christ, taking courage, prayed to God, saying: 'Let them be turned backward, that desire my hurt:'[2] and straightway they departed in confusion, and from that moment she was safe.[3]

Nevertheless, Burthred entered her room a third time in a similar state of agitated fury. But as he came in one door, she fled through another. In front of her was a kind of fence which, because of its height and the sharp spikes on top of it, was calculated to prevent anyone from climbing over it: behind her almost on her heels was the young man, who at any moment would catch hold of her. With amazing ease she jumped over the fence and, looking back from her place of safety, saw her pursuer on the other side, standing there unable to follow. Then she said: 'Truly in escaping him, I have escaped from the devil I saw last night.' For, in her sleep, she had seen as it were a devil of horrible appearance with blackened teeth who was unavailingly trying to seize

voluisse comprehendere. sed nequivisse; eo quod illa fugiendo sepem excelsam saltu transvolasset. Porro parentes eius dum istis insidiis ac multis intendunt; frequenter dies nupciarum genero suo constituunt. Siquidem speraverunt illam aliqua decipiendam occasione. que enim femina putaretur tot laqueos posse eludere? Et tamen respiciente votum sponse sue Christo. nullatenus potuit nupciarum provenire celebracio. Nimirum imminente die quem illi statuissent. et preparatis que ad nupcias opus essent: contingebat nunc improviso igne preparata devorari. nunc ipsam sponsam febre corripi. Et illi quidem febricitantem quandoque iactabant in aquam frigidam. quandoque nimis torrebant; ut fugarent febrem.

13. Interea fama de Christine nupciis; pervenit ad aures supradicti canonici domini Suenonis. Et quoniam dura diligensque custodia Christine deputata nullo modo permittebat Suenonem ad illam venire. nec ab illa mandatum accipere⟨.⟩ tunc cre(f. 148ra)[dens] eam penituisse virginalis propositi [infremuit] et redarguit illam muliebris inconstancie dicens: Vere nulli amplius . . . cam, quando quidem illa [decepit] me cui maxime credebam. Relatum est igitur hoc Christine. et quod unicus amicus suus versus sit in adversarium. et penitencia ductus condemnavit se fuisse illi vel amicum vel consiliarium. Quo audito illa tunc demum immenso concussa dolore diriguit. et ita immobilis aliquandiu sedit: ut posset putari non esse homo sed pocius insculpta marmori hominis imago. Post hec trahens alta suspiria in profusionem lacrimarum erupit. et singultu querimonias interrumpente: se miser⟨r⟩imam. sese orphanam sepius [con]clamavit. Quippe a parentibus et a[micis] omnibus spreta et afflicta: solum Suenonem habebat consolatorem. Cuius amica familiaritas atque compassio tantum illi ministrabat fortitudinis: ut pro minimo deputaret quantumcumque pateretur ab omnibus illis. Et ecce iam puella perseverante vir defecit. unica* sua in medio inimicorum contra spem derelicta: ille retrorsum

* Perhaps for *amica*; but cf. Ps. 34. 17.

her, because in her flight she had sprung at one leap over a high fence. Whilst her parents were setting these and other traps for her they fixed the day for the marriage with their son-in-law several times. For they hoped that some occasion would arise when they could take advantage of her. For what woman could hope to escape so many snares? And yet, with Christ guarding the vow which his spouse had made, the celebration of the wedding could nohow be brought about. Indeed, when the day which they had fixed approached and all the necessary preparations for the marriage had been arranged, it happened first that all the things prepared were burned by an unexpected fire, and then that the bride was taken with fever. In order to drive away the fever, sometimes they thrust her into cold water, at other times they blistered her excessively.

In the meantime the news of Christina's marriage reached the ears of master Sueno, the canon mentioned earlier. But since Christina was consigned to a close and rigid custody, which did not allow him to visit her, nor to receive any message sent by her, thinking that she had changed her mind about the vow of virginity, he accused her of feminine inconstancy, saying: 'Truly, to no other ... since she in whom I put all my trust deceived me.' This was eventually told to Christina, namely that her only friend was now turned against her, and that, filled with regret, he reproached himself for ever having been her friend and counsellor. When she heard it, she was struck with profound grief and sat so rigid and still for some time that you would have thought she was not a living person but an image carved in stone. Then, heaving deep sighs, she broke out into floods of tears and, with sobs punctuating her laments, she bewailed her lot over and over again as the most wretched and abandoned of all. Indeed, despised and afflicted as she was by her friends and relatives, Sueno was her only comfort. His friendly intimacy and sympathy had been to her such a source of strength that what she had suffered from others was accounted of little consequence. But now, whilst the maiden stood firm, the man had wilted: she was left

abiit. Sed numquid Christus deseruit sperantem in se? Non.
immo benigne respexit humilitatem ancille sue.[1] Illa mox ad
eum conversa dixit. Domine. multiplicati sunt qui tribulant
me. [multi] insurgunt adversum me.[2] Sustinui [qui] simul
contristaretur. et non fuit. [et]* qui consolaretur: et non
inveni.[3] Et ego ad te Domine animam meam [lev]avi[4] qui
fidelibus tuis per temetipsum [dixi]sti. Beati eritis cum vos
oderint homines. et cum separaverint vos et exprobraverint
et eiecerint nomen vestrum tanquam malum propter filium
hominis. Gaudete in illa die: et exultate. Ecce enim merces
vestra: copiosa est in celo.[5] Quoniam igitur quod ego puta-
bam michi causam (f. 148[rb]) iusticie [fore] in die [iudicii
factum est] in seculo. [te a]mando. te consequendo. propter
te [ob]probia persecuciones hominum su[stinen]do: et in te
solo omnia michi spera[ndo]. Quanto namque despectior quis
homi[ni]bus fuerit. tanto tibi preciosior erit. Hec dicens:
spiritu sancto roborata. perrexit in tota fiducia. Nec dubium
quin hoc in articulo meruerit illo nomine sui [crean]tis in-
signiri. quo postea vocabatur [nempe] Christina. cui nomen
a baptismate fuerat [Theodora]. Nimirum sicut Christus
prius a Iudeis reprobatus.[6] post ab ipso apostolorum prin-
cipe Petro qui eum ardencius ceteris amaverat negatus.[7]
factus est obediens Patri us[que] ad mortem:[8] sic et hec
virgo prius a parentibus afflicta. post ab unico amico suo
Suenone derelicta: Christum sequens co[nten]debat ipsius
solius infa[ti]gabiliter im[pl]ere voluntatem.

14. Hiis ita se habentibus et [in op]primendo famulam
Christi [quantum] potuerunt magis ac magis insanientibus
innotuit Suenoni [ve]ritas rei. Qui considerans cons[tanci]am
beate virginis. sue pariter reco[rdatus] est infidelitatis. Tunc
miser [homo] ingemuit. pectus suum pugnis [tun]dens.

---

* [et non] fuit qui *MS.*

[1] Luke 1. 48.   [2] Ps. 3. 2.   [3] Ps. 68. 21.   [4] Ps. 24. 1.
[5] Luke 6. 22–23.   [6] Cf. Mark 8. 31.   [7] Matt. 26. 70, 72.   [8] Phil. 2. 8.

alone, contrary to her expectations, to face all her enemies; he
had turned his back on her. But did Christ desert the one who
placed her trust in Him? Not so. Rather, He looked with pity
on the lowliness of His handmaid.[1] She, turning to Him after
a little while, said: 'Lord, how are they increased that trouble
me. Many are they that rise up against me.[2] I have looked
for some to take pity, but there was none, and for comforters,
but I found none.[3] Unto Thee O Lord do I lift up my soul,[4]
to Thee who hast said to Thy followers: Blessed are ye when
men shall hate you: and when they shall separate you from
their company and shall reproach you, and cast out your
name as evil for the Son of Man's sake. Rejoice ye in that
day and leap for joy: for behold your reward is great in
heaven.[5] I believed that He would be the source of righteousness to me but in the day of trial, I have been forsaken, truly
loving Thee, following Thee, bearing reproaches for Thee,
enduring the persecutions of men and in Thee placing all my
trust. For the more a person is despised by men, the more
precious he is in Thy sight.' Saying this, she was strengthened by the Holy Spirit and went on with utter confidence. And there is no doubt that at this juncture she,
whose name was Theodora from baptism, deserved to be
signed with the name of her creator by which she was afterwards called, namely Christina. Indeed, just as Christ was
rejected by the Jews,[6] afterwards denied by the prince of the
apostles, Peter,[7] who loved Him more than the rest, and was
made obedient to His Father even unto death,[8] so this maiden
was afflicted first by her parents, then abandoned by her
only friend, Sueno. Following Christ, she strove tirelessly to
fulfil His will.

In these circumstances, whilst her parents were oppress-
ing the servant of Christ and growing more and more furious
with her, the truth of the matter was made known to Sueno.
Turning over in his mind the constancy of the blessed maiden
and recalling at the same time his own lack of loyalty, the
wretched man broke out into laments; and, striking his breast
with his fists, became the harsh unmerciful avenger of his

durus et immitis in se sui erroris ultor extitit. Et anxie
querens cum lesa amica loqui. nec omnino lo[cum] inveniens
propter vigilanciam custodum. tandem audivit eam venisse
cum parentibus suis ad sepe nominatam ecclesiam beate
Genitricis Dei Marie causa sepeliendi corpus cuiusdam nobilis [cogna]ti. Et puto quod arte Suenonis [hoc] fuerat procu-
ratum. Ubi nactus opportunitatem: misit ad eam latenter
semel. secundo. ac tercio. suppliciter orans propter amorem
Christi ne colloquium miseri senis aspernaretur que illum
diffidencie sue merito iustius aversaretur. Unde (f. 148ᵛᵃ)
. . . improbe . . . [elevan]sque manum eius et apponens
faciei. ita flevit largiter ut flumina lacrimarum ipsam manum
perlavarent. et testem invocans Deum se nunquam alterius
commissi tantum quantum huius penituisse impetravit errori
suo veniam et sibi reformavit pristinam amice familiaritatem.
Hinc uterque lecior effectus: remansit senex in monasterio⟨.⟩
virgo repedavit domum cum parentibus.

15. Quam rursus alia vice pater Aucti illuc reduxit. statu-
ensque coram reverendo Fredeberto priore[1] ac reliquis canonicis eiusdem loci: affatus est illos dicens voce lacrimabili.
Scio domini mei scio. et testimonium huic filie mee perhibeo
quod ego et mater sua com[pule]ramus invitam ad coniugium et contra voluntatem suam suscepit hoc sacramentum.
Verumtamen qualitercumque ad hoc [ded]ucta sit. si nostra
auctoritate contemta illud respuerit facti sumus obprobrium
vicinis nostris. abominacio et illusio hiis qui in circuitu nostro sunt.[2] Quocirca vos obsecro rogate [eam] ut misereatur
nostri et in Domino nubens[3] [aver]tat a nobis notam immi-
nentis ob[pro]brii. Ut quid degeneret? Ut quid parentes dis-
honoret? Mendicitas illius universe nobilitati erit notabile
dedecus. Fiat modo quod nos volumus. omnia eius erunt.
Hec cum dixisset Aucti: separavit eum Fredebertus a con-
sorcio et cum canonicis suis cepit affari virgini hoc modo.
Miramur Theodora valde tuam pertinaciam. immo ut verius

---

[1] Not otherwise known: the earliest recorded prior of St. Mary's, Huntingdon, is
Robert, 1147. *V.C.H. Hunts.* i. 395. Cott. MS. Aug. II. 112.

[2] Ps. 78. 4.   [3] Cf. 1 Cor. 7. 39.

own mistake, and seeking anxiously to have converse with his friend whom he had hurt and being unable to find an occasion because of the watchfulness of her guard, he heard at length that she had come with her parents to the church of the blessed Mother of God for the purpose of burying some noble kinsman who had recently died. And I believe that this was arranged by Sueno. When he found an opportunity, he sent secretly to her two or three times asking her for the love of Christ not to spurn the company of a wretched old man though she might more justly turn from him because of his lack of trust. [   ] and raising his hand and putting it to his face, he wept so copiously that a flood of tears ran over his hand: and calling God as his witness that he repented of this deed more than of any other, he obtained pardon for his error and renewed his former friendship with her. Both of them being happier at this turn of events he remained in his monastery, but the maiden went back home with her parents.

Her father brought her back there another time, and placing her before Fredebert,[1] the reverend prior, and the rest of the canons of the house, addressed them with these doleful words: 'I know, my fathers, I know, and I admit to my daughter, that I and her mother have forced her against her will into this marriage and that against her better judgement she has received this sacrament. Yet, no matter how she was led into it, if she resists our authority and rejects it, we shall be the laughing-stock of our neighbours, a mockery and derision to those who are round about.[2] Wherefore, I beseech you, plead with her to have pity on us: let her marry in the Lord[3] and take away our reproach. Why must she depart from tradition? Why should she bring this dishonour on her father? Her life of poverty will bring the whole of the nobility into disrepute. Let her do now what we wish and she can have all that we possess.' When Autti had said this, Fredebertus asked him to leave the assembly and with his canons about him began to address the maiden with these words: 'We are surprised, Theodora, at your obstinacy, or rather we

dicamus tuam insaniam. Nos scimus te fuisse desponsatam
ecclesiastico more. Nos scimus sacramentum coniugii divina
sancitum institucione non posse solvi. quia quos Deus
coniunxit homo non separet. Propter hoc relinquet homo
patrem suum et matrem et adherebit uxori (f. 148vb) sue et
erunt duo in carne una.[1] Et apostolus. uxori inquid vir
debitum reddat. similiter autem et uxor viro. Mulier sui
corporis potestatem non habet. sed vir. Similiter autem et
vir sui corporis potestatem non habet sed mulier. Iis autem
qui matrimonio iuncti sunt. precipio non ego. sed Dominus.
uxorem a viro non discedere. Et vir uxorem non dimittat.[2]
Et scimus preceptum filiis obedire parentibus: et honorem
deferre. Hec precepta. id ⟨est⟩ de observando coniugio et
obediendo parentibus magna quidem sunt: et in Veteri et
Novo Testamento magnopere commendata. Verumptamen
matrimonii virtus adeo precellit [iuss]ionem parentum. quod
nequaquam audires eos si iussissent tibi solvere matrimonium. Nunc autem cum [illud] tibi iubeant quod eciam
obedi[encie] prelatum auctoritate divina novimus quando
illos non audis: profecto rea [dup]pliciter existis. Nec putes
quod sole [salvantur] virgines quando pereuntibus multis
virginibus multas matresfamilias salvari non ignoramus.
Que cum ita sint: nichil restat nisi ut nostrum consilium
sanamque doctrinam suscipias. et honestis amplexibus viri
cui legitime desponsata fuisti collum tuum submittas.

16. Hiis perhoratis; Christina respond[it]. Nescio scri-
pturas quas nominasti. ex sensu vero desuper [intellec]to
domine prior respondebo tibi. [Pater] meus et mater mea
sicut audistis perhibent michi testimonium. quod contra
voluntatem meam. suo com[pulsu] [cele]bratum est super
me hoc quod [dicis esse sa]cramentum. Non tamen uxor
[ante] extiti. nec unquam fore cogitavi. Quantocius
scitote quod elegerim ab infancia castitatem et voverim
Christo me permansuram virginem. et feci coram testibus

[1] Cf. Mark 10. 7–9.   [2] 1 Cor. 7. 3–4, 10–11.

should say, your madness. We know that you have been betrothed according to ecclesiastical custom. We know that the
sacrament of marriage, which has been sanctioned by divine
law, cannot be dissolved, because what God has joined together, no man should put asunder. For this a man will leave
his father and mother and cleave to his wife. And they shall
be two in one flesh.[1] And the Apostle says: let the husband
render unto the wife due benevolence and likewise also the
wife unto the husband. The woman has no power over her
own body, but the husband: and likewise also the husband
has not power over his own body, but the wife. Unto the
married I command, yet not I, but the Lord, let not the wife
depart from her husband and let not the husband put away
his wife.[2] And we know the commandment given to children:
obey your parents and show them respect. These two commandments, about obedience to parents and faithfulness in
marriage, are great, much commended in the Old and New
Testaments. Yet the bond of marriage is so much more
important than the authority of parents that if they commanded you to break off the marriage you should not listen
to them. Now, however, that they order you to do something
which we know on divine authority to be more important
than obedience itself, and you do not listen to them, you
are doubly at fault. Nor should you think that only virgins
are saved: for whilst many virgins perish, many mothers of
families are saved, as we well know. And since this is so,
nothing remains but that you accept our advice and teaching
and submit yourself to the lawful embraces of the man to
whom you have been legally joined in marriage.'

To these exhortations Christina replied: 'I am ignorant of
the scriptures which you have quoted, father prior. But from
their sense I will give my answers thereto. My father and
mother, as you have heard, bear me witness that against my
will this sacrament, as you call it, was forced on me. I have
never been a wife and have never thought of becoming one.
Know that from my infancy I have chosen chastity and have
vowed to Christ that I would remain a virgin: this I did

qui etsi deessent: adesset tamen consciencie (f. 149ra) mee
testis michi Deus. . . . Quare diu hoc quantum licuit operibus
ostendi. Quod si parentes mei iusserunt me subire quod nunquam volui matrimonium: et a voto quod ab infancia me
fecisse sciunt fraudare Christum. hoc quantum ⟨et⟩ quam iniquum sit. vos iudicate qui videmini reliquos homines in
sciencia scripturarum precellere. Non ergo contra preceptum
Domini parentibus inobediens ero. si me ad reddendum
Christo votum meum expediero. Quod ecce ipso invitante
nunc facio. cuius dicitis istam esse vocem in evangelio: Omnis
qui reliquerit domum vel fratres. aut sorores. aut patrem aut
matrem. aut uxorem aut filios aut agros. propter nomen
meum centuplum accipiet. et vitam eternam possidebit.[1] Nec
tamen puto solas virgines salvari. Sed dico quia multe virgines ⟨pereunt⟩ sicut vos dicitis et verum est: utique multo
magis pereunt coniugate. Et si multe matres familias salvantur. quod vos dicitis similiter et verum est. utique multo
facilius salvantur virgines.

17. Obstupescens Fredebertus super prudencia et responsis Christine: interrogavit eam dicens. Quomodo pro-
babis michi quod hec facis propter amorem Christi? quia
forsitan spretis Burhredi nupciis: diciores affectas. Vere inquid diciores. quis namque Christo dicior? Cui ille: non
iocor inquid. sed serio tecum ago. Et si vis ut credamus tibi.
satisfac nobis iureiurando. quia non nuberes nec regis filio.
etsi desponsata illi fuisses quemadmodum desponsata fuisti
Burhredo. Ad hanc vocem Christi virgo suspiciens in celum.
hillari vultu respondit. Non modo iureiurando sed eciam
calidum (f. 149rb) candensque ferrum hiis nudis portando
manibus parata sum probare. Votum etenim quod ut sepe
dixi vovi eterni regis unico filio sua preveniente gracia ipsi
omnimodo reddere me oportet et reddam. eadem gracia co-
operante. Et confido in Domino quoniam adhuc tempus erit.
quando me non aliud quam Christum habuisse in causam
clarebit.

[1] Matt. 19. 29.

before witnesses, but even if they were not present God would be witness to my conscience continuously. This I showed by my actions as far as I was allowed. And if my parents have ordered me to enter into a marriage which I never wanted and to break the vow to Christ which they know I made in my childhood, I leave you, who are supposed to excel other men in the knowledge of the scriptures, to judge how wicked a thing this is. If I do all in my power to fulfil the vow I made to Christ, I shall not be disobedient to my parents. What I do, I do on the invitation of Him whose voice, as you say, is heard in the Gospel: Every one who leaves house or brothers or sisters or father or mother or wife or children or possessions for My name's sake shall receive a hundredfold and possess eternal life.[1] Nor do I think that virgins only will be saved. But I say as you do, and it is true, that if many virgins perish, so rather do married women. And if many mothers of families are saved, which you likewise say, and it is true, certainly virgins are saved more easily.'

Fredebertus, astonished at the common sense and answers of Christina, asked her, saying: 'How do you prove to me that you are doing this for the love of Christ? Perhaps you are rejecting marriage with Burthred in order to enter a more wealthy one?' 'A more wealthy one, certainly,' she replied. 'For who is richer than Christ?' Then said he: 'I am not joking. I am treating with you seriously. And if you wish us to believe you, take an oath in our presence that, were you betrothed to him as you have been to Burthred, you would not marry even the king's son.' At these words the maiden casting her eyes up to heaven and with a joyful countenance replied: 'I will not merely take an oath, but I am prepared to prove it, by carrying red-hot iron in these my bare hands. For, as I have frequently declared, I must fulfil the vow which through the inspiration of His grace I made to the only Son of the Eternal King, and with the help of this same grace I mean to fulfil it. And I trust to God that the time is not far off when it will become clear that I have no other in view but Christ.'

18. Tunc Fredebertus vocavit Aucti et dixit ei: Satis quidem animum filie tue conati sumus ad voluntatem tuam inclinare. sed nichil omnino per nos valemus proficere. Scimus autem episcopum nostrum Rodbertum in proximo venturum ad Buchendoniam.[1] villam videlicet suam huic civitati vicinam. Hoc igitur exigit racio quatinus ad ipsum retexatur huiusmodi causa: monstretur ei postquam venerit. et tandem accipiat finem saltem ex episcopali sentencia. Ut quid enim viscera tua laceras et in vanum laboras? Suspicimus quippe mentem huius virginis alta quadam et inaccessibili virtute stabilitam. Ad quem [Aucti]. Consilio tuo inquid assentior. et episcopum hac de causa per te requiri precor. Annuit ille. et sic Aucti reductam filiam [red]didit assuete custodie.

19. Interea audivit episcopum venisse Buchendoniam. Quem Fredebertus mox requisiuit missus ab Aucti. et cum eo non[nul]li qui erant in civitate nobilissimi. arbitrati propter sacramentum coniugii iam celebratum: quod statim iuberet desponsatam mulierem omnino [intra]re sub mariti dominium. Unde [que] pertinere sciunt ad susceptum negocium incunctanter revolvunt ei per ordinem. [que] scilicet vel Christina gesserit. vel que [circa] illam ab aliis gesta sint ab infancia sua usque in hodiernum diem. Novissime (f. 149[va]) rogant quare . . . sponsam constringerent ad nupcias suas vel episcopali auctoritate quam nulla alia vel adversitas vel prosperitas ad hoc potuit adducere. Episcopus vero singulis subtiliter notatis. protestor vobis. inquid. et Deum ac Dei genitricem iuro. quia non est episcopus sub celo qui ad nupcias illam constringere possit. si iuxta votum suum Deo non alteri viro servare se voluerit. domino libere famulandi. Hoc illi contra spem audientes; confusi redeunt; et episcopale responsum Aucti reddunt. Quo audito ille omnem spem perdidit. et valde dolens magisque dolendus Christine dixit: Ecce hodie pax. quin eciam domina mea facta es quam episcopus super omnes nos laudibus extulit et liberiorem

---

[1] Buckden is a residence of the bishops of Lincoln on the Great North Road, 4 miles south-west of Huntingdon.

Fredebertus then called in Autti and said to him: 'We have tried our best to bend your daughter to your will, but we have made no headway. We know, however, that our bishop Robert will be coming soon to his vill at Buckden,[1] which is near this town. Reason demands that the whole question should be laid before him. Let the case be put into his hands after he comes and let her take the verdict of the bishop, if of no other. What is the point of tearing your vitals and suffering to no purpose? We respect the high resolution of this maiden as founded on impregnable virtue.' To which Autti replied: 'I accept your advice. Please seek the bishop on this affair.' He agreed, and so Autti brought back his daughter and placed her under the usual restraint.

In the meantime he heard that the bishop had come to Buckden. Fredebertus immediately sought him out, being sent by Autti: and with him went the most noble citizens of the town, who thought that, as the marriage had already been performed, the bishop would immediately order the betrothed woman to submit to the authority of her husband. Hence they laid before him in detail and without delay all the facts which they knew pertained to the business in hand, namely what Christina had done, what others had done to her, beginning with her childhood and bringing it up to the present day. At last they brought forward the proposal . . . that since neither adversity nor prosperity could bring her to it she should be forced to accept her marriage at least by episcopal authority. After weighing all the evidence minutely, the bishop said: 'I declare to you, and I swear before God and His blessed Mother that there is no bishop under heaven who could force her into marriage, if according to her vow she wishes to keep herself for God to serve Him freely and for no man besides.' Hearing this unexpected answer, they returned in confusion and reported the bishop's reply to Autti. When he heard it, he lost all hope: and full of self-pity, but more to be pitied, he said to Christina: 'Well, we have peace today, you are even made mistress over me: the bishop has praised you to the skies and declared that you are

pronunciavit. Ingredere itaque et egredere sicut ego et vive tibi ut libet: verumtamen solacium vel auxilium a me ne quicquam expectabis. Hoc dicens; merore suo die [in] diem consumebatur. Quod videns Ro[bertus]* decanus[1] et quidam alii; misero condolebant homini. Et convenientes ut dolorem eius lenirent. susurrant ei in aure qualiter potest [fili]am suam nuptum cogere. dicentes: [Vis] scire quare episcopus egit alia die contra [illud] profecto quod insipienter requisitus [erat]? At si obtulisses illi pecuniam. peregisses utique causam tuam. An ignoras cupiditatem ipsius pariter et in-[continentiam]? Quodlibet horum satis erat. Quan[to] magis, ubi simul sunt? Avaricia per[suade]bit iudicia pervertere. incontinentia castimoniam aliis invidere. Cuius igitur am[i citia] munera speraverit; eiusdem consilio totus erit. Et ideo fac ut tibi fa[veat] nec erit qui ultra voluntati tue contradicat. Quod ut possis facilius impetrare; nobis qui presto sumus intercessoribus utere. Ex hoc Aucti spem recuperavit; et omnem curam illis imposuit. O miranda impudencia hominum (f. 149[vb]) qui potest[atem Dei contempnentes] insurgere potuerunt in idipsum. Et due quidem maxime extiterunt huius rei causae quas hic libet et non ab re forsitan interserere. Quia dum quis eas cognoverit, parentes adversus sanguinem suum tales esse posse non dubitabit.

20. Igitur una causarum fuit quod haec parentela pro natura habuit non desistere ceptis seu bona fuissent seu mala donec consummavit ipsa; si non obstitisset impossibilitas efficiendi. At in bono persistere virtus. in malo facit improbitas. Altera fuit causa hec. In Christina iam tunc eluxit tanta morum honestas. tale decus. tanta gratia. [ut] omnibus qui nossent eam merito super reliquas feminas esset

---

* The MS. has XV, a misreading for Ro.

[1] A Robert, priest of Huntingdon, witnessed the agreement between Autti and the abbot of Ramsey about the church of Shillington between 1114 and 1123; *Cart. de Rameseia*, i. 138 and 139. He also appears on pp. 135–6.

freer than ever. So come and go as I do, and live your own life as you please. But don't expect any comfort or help from me.' When he had said this, his sadness grew upon him from day to day. Seeing this, Robert the dean[1] and certain others took pity on the wretched man. And, putting their heads together to see how they could assuage his grief, they whispered in his ear a way of compelling his daughter to marry, saying: 'Do you know why the bishop gave that decision the other day contrary to what was so foolishly asked of him? If you had given him money, you would certainly have won your case. Are you not aware of his greed and his vicious nature? Either of these would be sufficient; how much more when both are together! His greed will teach him to pervert justice and his vice to hate other people's virtue. When he hopes to get money from anyone's friendship, he will take that man's side. So see to it that he is on your side, and there will be no one to oppose you in the future. In order to gain your end more easily, make use of our services as your advocates.' From this, Autti recovered hope and put all his cares into their hands. How astonishing is man's shamelessness, to despise the power of God and to rebel against it! But there were two reasons for this, which it may be worth while to give here. For when they are understood, there can be no hesitation in believing that parents can behave in this way against their own flesh and blood.

One reason, therefore, was this family's characteristic of pursuing to the bitter end anything it had begun, whether it was good or bad, except where success was impossible. Whilst to persevere in good is counted a virtue, to persevere in evil is the work of wickedness. Another reason was that Christina was conspicuous for such moral integrity, such comeliness and beauty, that all who knew her accounted her more lovable than all other women. Furthermore, she was so intelligent, so prudent in affairs, so efficient in carrying out her plans, that if she had given her mind to worldly pursuits she could have enriched and ennobled not only herself

amabilior. Insuper inerat ei tantum acumen in sensu. talis
providencia in gerendis. ea efficacia in deliberatis. ut si seculi
rebus tota vellet incumbere crederetur non se tantum suam-
que familiam. sed reliquum genus suum posse diviciis et
honoribus ampliare. Huc accessit quod sibi speraverunt ex
illa nepotes proles matri non dissimiles. Et hos fructus intendentes vitam ei celibem inviderunt. Quippe si propter
Christum casta permaneret. metuebant quod et ipsam et
quod per ipsam haberi possent, una perderent. Qui pensare
non noverant nisi bona presentis seculi; istis carentem. sola
invisibilia querentem iudicantes profecto perditum iri. Sed
hec vidimus aliter evenisse. Nam et ipsa derelinquens secu-
lum sese penitus dedidit sponsam Christo domino. non frau-
dando a desiderio suo.[1] et illi postmodum a seculo derelicti
ad [ean]dem quam* a se torquendo fugaverant. confugiebant
et penes illam consilium salutis animabus suis atque corpori-
bus recuperabant. Sic parentum opinionem Christina cassavit
que sibi prius (f. 150ʳᵃ) [sperabant fore] illis† . . .

21. . . . igitur ut ad ordinem historie redeamus. Aucti
sedulo privatimque tractante cum familiaribus suis de re-
quirendo episcopo. Christina considerabat eorum clandestina
conventicula. et nescio quid suspicata: sicut est feminea con-
suetudo metuebat omnia. Interim excogitanti secum siquid
adversum se molirentur quonam modo contrairet: venit in
mentem ut illum aditum quo coniciebat illos maxime tendere
preveniens obstrueret. Duas itaque personas magne auctoritatis id est Suenonem canonicum et capellanum patris sui
misit: et sponsum suum per illos de absolucione sua re-
quisivit. Inter alia commemoravit ei testimonium episcopi.
ne contra se nequicquam ille contenderet: quam auctoritas
tanta absolvisset. Quibus iuuantibus mandata sibi credita
persuasionibus suis: respondit Burhredus provocatus exemplo pontificis. Si ut vos dicitis qui locum Christi tenetis: pro
contemptu mei non querit hoc sponsa mea ut alterum virum
accipiat. sed ut votum suum Christo reddat: ecce coram
Deo et vobis illam absolvo et de mea substancia liberaliter

* quam: quem MS.   † A complete line missing.
[1] Ps. 77. 30.

and her family but also all her relatives. To this was added
the fact that her parents hoped she would have children who
would be like her in character. So keen were they on these
advantages that they begrudged her a life of virginity. For
if she remained chaste for the love of Christ, they feared
that they would lose her and all that they could hope to gain
through her. They could not bring their minds to consider
anything but the joys of the present world, thinking that anyone lacking them and seeking only invisible things would
end in ruin. But we saw things turn out quite differently.
For she abandoned the world and devoted herself completely
as a spouse to Christ the Lord, fulfilling her resolution:[1]
whilst they afterwards were abandoned by the world and
had to take refuge with her whom they had driven out, finding with her both salvation for their souls and safety for
their bodies. In this way Christina brought the hopes of her
parents to naught . . ..

But let us return to the course of our story. Whilst Autti
was secretly taking counsel with his friends about approach-
ing the bishop, Christina was wondering what their stealthy
meetings meant, and being suspicious, became fearful of
everything, as the habit of women is. In the meantime, as
she wondered how she could counter any plots they might
make against her, it came into her head to forestall them
by blocking that avenue which she thought they would
take. She sent two persons of great authority, namely Sueno
the canon and her father's chaplain, to her husband to ask
him to release her. Among other things she reminded him of
the bishop's pronouncement and begged him not to strive in
vain against her, since she had been dispensed by so important
an authority. When these two added their own persuasive
words to the message of Christina, Burthred, encouraged
by the bishop's precedent, replied: 'If, as you say (and you
are Christ's lieutenants), my wife is acting in this way, not
out of disrespect for me through a desire to marry someone else, but in order to fulfil her vow to Christ, then I
am prepared to release her before God and you, and I will

do: quo si monasterium intrare voluerit. ab inhabitantibus sine difficultate colligi possit. Aiunt ad eum illi. Sapienter et catholice loqueris. Ne de virginis sponsione dubites: en accipe nos integritatis ipsius incontaminande fideiussores. Et substancia quidem tua interim tibi maneat integra. sponsam vero tuam si absolvis. absentem ac si presens esset. trade nunc absolutam in manibus nostris. Et fecit sic. Ut autem in noticiam parentum Christine ⟨venerit⟩: incredibili furore succensi. tam intercessores absolucionis illius quam auctorem in(f. 150ʳᵇ)dignis affecerunt contumeliis. iurantes nec posse nec debere stare: quod absque suo arbitrio illi fecissent. Et Burhredum quidem ad penitenciam non sine labore compulerant. Quem post hec hiis exprobracionibus et blandimentis multo exagitatum. cum decano ceterisque quos supra memoravimus destinaverunt ad episcopum. Et ei pauca loquendo sed multam largiendo pecuniam inclinaverunt facile cor illius ad voluntatem suam. Porro Christina non cognovit hoc.

22. Post hec precipiente episcopo: convenerunt ante se Burhredus et virgo. Quam dum calumniaretur Burhredus: ait episcopus. Consule tibi Christina. Que corruptum ignorans et eiusdem priori iudicio freta: respondit. Cuius consilium salubrius michi quam Dei et tuum sanctissime pater? Recte respondisti. Et tradidit eam calumniatori. Tunc reducta est iterum in domum patris sui. Sedens autem secus Burhredus cum insultaret. iactaretque quod ⟨ante⟩ duos episcopos Dunelmi scilicet et Lincolnie scilicet. eam conquisierit nec ultra iam ante tercium cum illa venturus sit: oravit illa dicens. Utinam hoc ultimum tam sit verum quam constat illud prius esse falsum. Quomodo namque iactas tu quia conquisisti me. que propicio Deo nunquam ero tua sicut nunquam fui. nec si contingat membratim me secando dividi. Dic michi Burhrede sic propicietur tibi Deus. si veniret

make provision for her out of my own pocket: so that if she wishes to enter a monastery she can be admitted by the community without hindrance.' They said to him: 'These are wise and religious sentiments. And to remove any doubt about your wife's agreement, take our word for it her virginity shall remain unsullied. For the moment, keep your property to yourself; but if you release your wife from her engagement, do so now to us as if she were not absent but present.' And he did so. When this came to the ears of Autti and Beatrix, they were inflamed with unbelievable fury and heaped insults both on the petitioners for her release and on the prime mover in the affair, swearing that such an agreement could not and should not be valid, because it had been done without their consent. And they forced Burthred to change his mind, but not without a great deal of trouble. After this, they sent him, harassed as he was by scolding and flattery, with the dean and the others, whom we have mentioned above, to the bishop. And by saying little but by giving him large bribes they shaped his mind to their will. Besides, Christina did not know of this.

Sometime later, on the bishop's orders, Burthred and Christina appeared before him. Whilst Burthred was pleading his case against her, the bishop said: 'Take counsel, Christina.' And she, not being aware that he had been bribed, and putting her reliance on his earlier judgement, replied: 'Whose counsel can be better for me than God's and yours, most holy father?' 'That's the right answer,' said the bishop, and handed her over to the plaintiff. Then she was taken to her father's house once more. And as Burthred sat beside her, scoffing at her and boasting that he had bettered her before two bishops, of Durham and Lincoln, and had no intention of bringing her again before a third, she prayed and said: 'I wish to God this last judgement were as true as the first one was false. For how can you boast that you have succeeded, since, with the help of God, I have never been yours and never shall be, even if I should be cut to pieces. Tell me, Burthred, as you hope God may have mercy on you: if

aliquis qui me vellet a te tollere et sibi matrimonio copulare.
quid ageres? Ait. Hoc ego quoad viverem nullatenus tolle-
rarem. Immo meis ipse manibus interficerem illum. si te
aliter habere nequirem. Quo dicto: subintulit illa. Et tu ergo
cave sponsam Christi velle tibi tollere. ne in ira sua interficiet
te. Et cum hoc dixisset: surrexit ut abiret. Ille (f. 150va) vero
apprehendit pallium surgentis ut retineret eam. quod ubi
secessit. caute solvens illud a collo suo. et exemplo Ioseph[1]
relinquens in manu eius; secessit* in secretiorem cameram
expedite.

23. Tunc pater suus vehementer iratus omnibus eam in-
dumentis preter camisiam expoliavit et claves suas quas ei
commendaverat rapiens: ipsam de nocte sic expellere de
domo sua disposuit. Porro Aucti ditissimus argenti et auri.
queque preciosissima habere poterat: fidei Christine custo-
dienda securus credebat. Is tunc ira turbatus. tenens claves
in manibus. puelle corporalibus quidem exute vestimentis.
sed beacius indute virtutum ornamentis: ait. Exi cito. Si
enim Christum vis habere: Christum nuda sequere. Eadem-
que nocte sic illam effugasset: si quidam notus sibi qui de
iure hospitis tunc aderat: pro illa non intercessisset. Et illa
quidem et nuda et de nocte preoptabat expelli. quatinus sibi
daretur libertas Christo serviendi. Unde facto mane. ipsa
exivit arcente nemine. At pater ut agnovit misit festinanter
post eam: et reduxit invitam. Ex illo die mater eius Beatrix
Dei permissu. diabolico instinctu totas furoris habenas in
propriam filiam relaxavit. nullum penitus omittens genus
malicie: quo putaret integritatem illius posse nocere. Et ante
quidem ei valde inhumana extiterat. sed ex tunc inauditis
illam nunc occultis nunc apertis insidiis iniuriisque persecuta
est. Denique iurabat quod non consideraret quis filiam suam
corrumperet. ⟨si⟩ tantum aliquo casu corrumpi potuisset.

---

* sesensit *MS*.

[1] Gen. 39. 12.

another should come and take me away from you and marry
me, what would you do?' He replied: 'I would never allow
it, as long as I lived. Indeed I would slay him with my own
hands, if there was no other way of keeping you.' As he said
this, she retorted: 'Beware then of taking to yourself the
spouse of Christ, lest in His anger He will slay you.' And
when she had said this, she rose to go away. But as she got
up he seized hold of her mantle to keep her back: as she
moved away, she loosened it at the neck, and, leaving it, like
another Joseph,[1] in his hands, she quickly escaped into her
private room.

   Then her father was violently incensed and stripped her
of all her clothes, with the exception of her shift, and, taking
from her the keys which he had placed in her keeping, decided
to drive her naked from the house that night. Now Autti was
very rich and always entrusted to Christina his silver and gold
and whatever treasures he possessed. So, maddened with
anger and holding the keys in his hands, he said to the
maiden, stripped as she was of her bodily garments, but
more blessedly clothed with the gems of virtue: 'Get out, as
fast as you can. If you want to have Christ, follow Him stripped
of everything.' And he would have driven her out on that
same night had there not been a guest staying with them at
that time who interceded for her. And she on her part
preferred to be sent away, both naked and at night, for the
sake of getting her freedom to serve Christ. Hence, when
morning came, she left the house without anyone preventing
her. But as soon as Autti found out, he sent after her with
all haste and brought her back against her will. From that
day forward her mother, Beatrix, with God's permission but
at the instigation of the devil, loosed all her fury on her own
daughter, neglecting no sort of wicked artifice which might,
in her opinion, destroy her integrity. Even before this she
had been most harsh to her, but from then onwards she persecuted her with unheard-of cruelty, sometimes openly, at
other times secretly. In the end she swore that she would not
care who deflowered her daughter, provided that some way

Proinde plurimum substancie dissipavit in annosas vetulas. que veneficiis et incantacionibus suis insanire facerent illam amore turpitudinis. Sed earum sapientissima (f. 150vb) pocula . . .]tudin . . . serat in hoc. Voluit tandem iudea prestigiis contra solitum potentibus Christinam ledere. Intravit igitur in domum Aucti. vidit virginem pretereuntem: dixit Beatrici ipsius genitrici. In vanum laboravimus. video duo fata quasi duas candidas personas que cum illa iugiter gradiuntur et ab omnibus impugnacionibus hinc inde defendunt. Iccirco melius est vobis cessare iam: quam ultra laborare nequicquam. Ceterum Beatrix obstinato animo persistebat in malicia. et que non potuit filie victrix fieri: sategit vel probrosis illius penis saciari. Erat quando repente de convivio illam eduxit. et in secreciori loco crinibus arreptam quamdiu lassata est verberavit. Scissamque rursus introduxit coram convivantibus ad ludibrium. relictis in dorso eius verberum vestigiis que nunquam potuerunt ipsa superstite deleri.

24. Inter has angustias volens Christus suam fidelem sponsam confortare. per suam virginem matrem confortavit eam sic. Nocte quadam cum dormiret: videbatur sibi quod in quoddam pulcherimum templum cum aliis mulieribus introducta fuisset. Et ecce stabat ad altare quidam indutus vestimentis sacerdotalibus quasi ad solemnia missarum celebranda paratus. Qui respiciens: innuit Christine quatinus ad se veniret. Et accedenti cum tremore: porrigebat ramum frondium speciosarum et florum inestimabilium. dicens. Accipe cara. et offer ille* domine. Pariterque monstrabat ei quandam similem imperatrici non longe ab altari sedentem in tribunali. Cui genu flexo. acceptum ramum offerebat. Suscipiens autem illa domina de manu Christine ramum: de ipso sumens redonabat offerenti ramusculum. et dice(f. 151ra)bat. Custodi michi hoc diligenter. adiciensque interrogat eam: Quomodo tecum est? Aiebat: male domina:

---

* ille *MS.*; *perhaps for* illi.

of deflowering her could be found. Henceforward she wasted a great deal of money on old crones who tried with their love potions and charms to drive her out of her mind with impure desires. But their most elaborate potions had no effect. One Jewess wanted to harm Christina with tricks which were more powerful than the rest. She therefore entered Autti's house. As she saw the maiden walking by, she said to her mother Beatrix: 'Our trouble has been all for nothing: I can see two phantoms, two persons, as it were, dressed in white, who accompany her at all times and protect her from assaults at all points. It is better for you to give up now rather than to waste time in vain.' But Beatrix, in her obstinacy, would put no term to her malice, and as she could not break her daughter's will, tried to gain satisfaction from the shameful sufferings she inflicted on her. There was one time when on impulse she took her out from a banquet and, out of sight of the guests, pulled her hair out and beat her until she was weary of it. Then she brought her back, lacerated as she was, into the presence of the revellers as an object of derision, leaving on her back ,uch weals from the blows as could never be removed as long as she lived.

Amidst all these trials Christ, wishing to comfort His spouse, gave her consolation through His holy Mother. It happened in this way. One night whilst she was sleeping, it seemed to her that she was brought with some other women into a most beautiful church. At the altar stood a man clothed in priestly vestments, as if ready to celebrate Mass. Looking over his shoulder, he beckoned to Christina to come to him. And when she approached with trembling, he held out to her a branch of most beautiful leaves and flowers saying: 'Receive this, my dear, and offer it to the lady.' At the same time he pointed out to her a lady like an empress sitting on a dais not far from the altar. Curtsying to her, she held out the branch which she had received. And the lady, taking the branch from Christina's hand, gave back to her a twig and said, 'Take care of it for me'; and then added as a question: 'How is it with you?' She said: 'Ill, my lady: they all hold me

omnes subsannant me:[1] et coangustant undique.[2] Non est
similis mei in sorte dolencium. Unde nec die nec nocte a
fletu et singultu meo temperare possum. Ne timeas inquid.
vade modo quoniam ego de manibus eorum eripiam te:[3] et
educam clara luce diei. Recedebat igitur ut sibi videbatur
leta. portans florentem ramusculum in dextera. Et ecce qua
illi descendendum erat. Burhredus iacebat prostratus super
pavimentum. versus faciem ad terram. et atra circumamictus
cappa. Qui cum videret transeuntem: extendebat manus in
illam ut apprehenderet atque teneret. Illa vero colligens et
stringens ad se vestimenta sua que habebat candidissima et
subtus ampla: pertransibat intacta. Quam sic evadentem
torvis persecutus oculis horribiliter ingemescebat et pro-
prium caput pavimento repetitis ictibus hostiliter infligebat.

25. Interea virgo prope prospiciebat et videbat quasi
solarium unum altum et quietum. ad quod ascendere volenti:
per interpositos gradus arduus et gravis patebat ascensus.
Huc eciam Christine habenti magnam ascendendi voluntatem. sed hesitanti propter ascensus difficultatem: subito
regina quam paulo ante viderat ministrabatur adiutorium et
sic ascendebat in solarium. Cumque resideret ibidem delectata loco. Ecce predicta regina veniebat. Et instar quiescere
volentis. caput suum reclinabat in gremio sedentis: sed
aversa facie. Cuius adversionis Christinam non mediocriter
tedebat et non ausa loqui: tantum in corde suo dicebat. O si
licuisset michi vultum tuum contemplari. (f. 151ʳᵇ) Et continuo convertit vultum suum imperatrix illa dixitque blanda
affabilitate. Et licet et contemplare contemplativa postmodum
ad sacietatem: quando introduxero te in thalamum meum.
te et Judith una tecum. Post hec visa evi⟨gi⟩lavit et cervical
suum multis lacrimis maduisse reperit. ut sicut verum flere
fuit quod sompniasse putabat. ita de reliquorum eventu non
ambigeret. que per idem somnium viderat. Itaque videris
eam totam repente mutatam. Magnitudinem leticie quam
conceperat ex spe liberacionis sue. vultus propalabat hilaritas.

[1] Jer. 20. 7.   [2] Luc. 19. 43.   [3] Cf. Ps. 30. 16.

up to ridicule[1] and straiten me from all sides.[2] Among those
that suffer there is none like me. Hence I cannot stop crying
and sobbing from morning till night.' 'Fear not', she said.
'Go now, since I will deliver you from their hands[3] and bring
you to the brightness of day.' So she withdrew, full of joy
as it seemed to her, carrying in her right hand the little
branch of blossoms. And where she had to go down, there
lay Burthred prostrate on the ground swathed in a black cape
with his face turned downwards. And as soon as he saw her
passing by he stretched out his hand to seize her and hold
her fast. But she, gathering her garments about her and
clasping them close to her side, for they were white and
flowing, passed him untouched. And as she escaped from
him, he followed her with staring eyes, groaning horribly,
and struck his head with repeated blows on the pavement to
show his rage.

Meanwhile, the maiden looked closely in front of her, and
saw an upper chamber, lofty and quiet, which could be
reached only by a series of steps, steep and difficult for anyone wishing to climb. Christina had a great desire to climb
up, but as she hesitated on account of its difficulty, the queen
whom she had seen just a short time before helped her, and
so she mounted to the upper chamber. And as she sat there
enjoying the beauty of the place, behold, the aforesaid queen
came and laid her head in her lap as if she wished to rest,
with her face turned away. This turning away of her face
was a source of disquiet to Christina, and not daring to
speak, she said inwardly: 'O, if only I were allowed to gaze
upon your face.' Straightway the empress turned her face
towards her and said to her with winning kindness: 'You
may look now; and afterwards when I shall bring both you
and Judith also into my chamber, you can gaze to your full
content.' After this vision she awoke and found her pillow
wet with tears, so that she was convinced that as the tears
she dreamed she had shed were real, so were the rest of the
things which she had dreamed. From that moment you could
see she was completely changed, and the immense joy which

26. Interea quesita repertaque oportunitate loquendi cum Suenone secretorum suorum conscio. non valens cum illo novum gaudium non communicare: narravit visionem ex ordine. Sueno vero: retulit eam Fredeberto priori suo. Tunc Fredebertus vocans Aucti dixit illi. Audi consilium meum. et ne relucteris contra divinum iudicium. Noli Christinam amplius angere. sed tanquam sponsam Christi venerare. Quia si verum est quod audivi: in vanum laborant. quicumque nocere sive renuere violenter illam temptant. Et aperuit illi causam. Audiens Aucti magis turbatus est. et omnis domus sua cum illo conceptumque furorem quo semel imbuti sunt: nulla racione prout super docuimus deponere valuerunt. Hoc intuita virgo virginum: adiecit iterum apparere Christine. quod factum [est hoc] ordine. Videbat se ancilla Christi quiete stare et reginam celi ex insperato stantem ante se ⟨.⟩ Cuius decorem vultus cum miraretur et cum magno intenderet affectu: dicebat illa sibi. Quid me tantopere miraris? Ego sum maxima feminarum. Vis scire quanta? Hic michi stanti facile est manu contingere culmen celi. Et scito quod elegi te de domo (f. 151ᵛᵃ) p[atris tui et] confratrem tuum. Et nomina[vit ali]quem vita post mutatum et . . . strenuum in monasterio nostro indicans monachum. Ego vero nomen suum hic tacui eo quod sic preceptum fuit michi.

27. Porro Sueno dum nullam medicinam recipiebat obstinacio predictorum hominum die ac nocte pro afflicte virginis erepcione interpellabat Christum. Qui tandem exaudivit vocem fletus eius.[1] Nam quadam die dum ad altare missam celebraret: facta est vox ad eum dicens. Ne timeas Sueno ecce liberabo illam pro qua rogasti me. Et oculis tuis videbis [et] ore

[1] Ps. 6. 9.

filled her at the thought of her freedom was displayed for all
to see in the cheerfulness of her countenance.

Meantime she sought and found an opportunity of talking
with Sueno, the sharer of her secrets, being unable to with-
hold from him this new source of gladness. She told him the
vision in detail. Sueno then recounted it to his prior Fredebert. So Fredebert summoning Autti said to him: Take my
advice and do not resist the judgement of God. Do not cause
Christina any more pain, but respect her as the spouse of
Christ: because, if what I have heard is true, those who
attempt to harm her in any way or to oppose her are wasting
their time. And he gave him the reason. When Autti heard
this, he was more disturbed than ever, as were all those
around him: but once having been aroused to anger, they
were not prepared on any account, as I explained above, to
desist. Having seen this, the Virgin of Virgins appeared once
more to Christina: and it happened in this way. The handmaid of Christ saw herself standing quietly, and quite unexpectedly the queen of heaven stood before her. And as she
was admiring the beauty of her countenance and looking
upon her with great affection, she said to Christina: 'Why
are you gazing upon me so intently? I am the greatest of
women. Do you wish to know how great? As I stand here it
is quite easy for me to touch the highest point of heaven.
And be assured that I have chosen you from your father's
house, and not only you but your companion also.' And she
named a certain man who, after his conversion, became a
most observant monk in our monastery. His name I shall
not reveal here, because I was told not to do so.

As the obstinacy of the aforesaid people could not be
remedied, Sueno prayed to Christ day and night for the
afflicted maiden's deliverance. And at last his prayers and
tears were heard.[1] For one day whilst he was standing at the
altar to say Mass, a voice was heard saying to him: 'Fear not,
Sueno: the woman for whom you have prayed I will make
free. And with your own eyes you shall see her and with your
lips you shall speak to her when she is free, and your heart

tuo alloqueris liberatam et gaudebit cor tuum. Hiis dictis siluit. Nec parcitur interim electe Christo virgini. immo cotidie
contra suam erepcionem ceperunt acriora prioribus irrogari
sibi. Et ecce instabat tempus ut expleretur divina promissio
in quo libet intueri quanta fuerit in virgine prudencia sive
fortitudo.

28. Mansit in regione vir quidam Eadwynus[1] nomine soli-
tariam vitam religiose ducens. Huius colloquium desideravit
Christina. capiendi consilii gracia. Custodibus itaque suis
mercede data. hec namque sola via erat. accepta licencia
mittitur timide ad hominem. Venit ille latenter. Ac sumpta
opportunitate: soli colloquuntur pro loco et tempore breviter.
Petit illa consilium fuge. Spondet ille sedulitatem suam.
Finito colloquio discedit et res callide dissimulatur. Tunc ille
plurima loca mente percurrens semper ad cognatum suum
nomine Rogerum animo recurrebat. Qui videlicet Rogerus
tunc etate senior. sensu maturior. diaconus ordine: monachus
(f. 151vb) professione: meritis sanctitatis par habitus est
antiquis patribus. Noster quidem monachus erat. sed vivebat
in heremo servans et in hoc obediencia⟨m⟩ abbati suo. Porro
locus heremi quem inhabitabat: gradientibus de nostro monasterio Dunstapulam apparet a dextris secus viam.[2] Hunc
locum acceperat noster Rogerus divino munere. perductus
illuc eo angelico ministerio. Nam cum rediret de Ierusalem:
exceperunt eum Wyndosoram tres angeli niveis vestibus et
stolis induti singuli singulas cruces in manibus ferentes. et
desuper totidem cereos ardentes. Inde visibiliter ambulantes
cum illo usque ad prefati heremi locum comitem deducunt.
et ibidem statuunt. ubi postea multa mala perpessus: multa
vicissim consolacione meruit relevari divinitus. Hac animatus

---

[1] Probably Eadwine of Higney mentioned in the Chartulary of Ramsey, ed.
W. H. Hart and Ponsonby Lyons, London, 1884–93, i. 162; R. M. Clay, p. 21.

[2] Dunstable is 13 miles north of St. Albans, and Markyate, the site of Roger's
hermitage, is rather over half way. There was a dense wood along this stretch of
Watling Street, which was flanked on the south-west by barren downs. For many
centuries settlers in the district were few and it was perhaps for this reason that Roger
made his hermitage there. G. H. Fowler, *Tractatus de Dunstaple et de Houcton*,
Publications of the Bedfordshire Historical Record Soc., xix, 1937, p. 4.

shall rejoice.' After this the voice was silent. In the meantime, however, the maiden was not spared any suffering, nay every day increasingly stringent steps were taken to prevent her from gaining her liberty. But the time was not far off when the divine promise would be fulfilled, and in this one can see how great was her prudence and fortitude.

In the district there lived a certain man named Eadwin,[1] who was leading a religious life in solitude. Christina wished to have converse with him for the purpose of taking his advice. As the only way of achieving this was by giving bribes to her keepers, she gave them money and, having received permission, sent a message to the man with some apprehension. He came to her by stealth. And, seizing an opportunity, they spoke with one another briefly as the time and place permitted. She asked his advice about her escape. He promised his help. After the conversation was over, he departed and the matter was cleverly hushed up. Then as he turned over several suitable places in his mind, his thoughts always turned to a relative of his, named Roger. This Roger was at that time an old man, mature in wisdom, a deacon in holy orders, a monk by profession, and by virtue of his holy life considered as equal to the fathers of old. He was a monk of ours, but lived in a hermitage, though even here he kept obedience to his abbot. The position of the hermitage where he dwelt was on the right hand near the road as you go from our monastery towards Dunstable.[2] Roger had been given this place through divine generosity, and was brought there by the ministry of angels. For, when he was returning from Jerusalem, he was met at Windsor by three angels clothed in white garments and stoles, each one bearing in his hand a cross over which there were the same number of burning tapers. Accompanying him visibly from thence, they brought him to the site of the hermitage and established him there: here he afterwards endured many sufferings, but on the other hand was sustained by divine consolation, which so encouraged him that suffering had no fears for him, because he dwelt faithfully in the commandments of the Lord.

illa derisit. quia fideliter in mandatis domini vixit.* Cui unquam callidus hostis vel acriores temptaciones immisit. vel
plures tetendit insidias? Ille vero virtute crucis Christi arma-
tus et has vincebat. et cavebat illas. Quis unquam in carnem
suam crudelior extitit? Nulli quippe animum voluptati dedit.[1]
Illud insistebat omni conatu perficere. quo possit magis ac
magis Deo placere. Erat eciam ei super afflictis compassio ut
eorum miserias non ferret tam egre: si proprie sibi fuissent
illate. Hec de nostro sene breviter prenotavimus: eo quod ad
rem pertinere rati sumus. Tacemus cetera. tum quia ineffabilia
tum quia non hic necessario dicenda. De spiritu prophecie
loquor et de contemplativis illius. in quibus habebatur ineffa-
biliter egregius.

29. Hunc ergo senem consobrinus (f. 152ra) suus Eadwynus cuius supra meminimus incunctanter adiit. ut ille virginem
Christi susciperet in sua cura: quod ipse propter parentes
eius ausus non fuit. Siquidem ea duxerat originem ex antiquis
anglis nobilibus atque potentibus. quorum stirpe multipliciter
propagata: omnis illa regio circa Huntendoniam longe lateque
repleta est. Vir Dei ut audivit quod esset de Huntendonia:
diligenter interrogavit de illa. mores illius et fortunas omnes
cupiens agnoscere. Erat enim ex multo tempore expectans
videre quiddam quod de Huntendonia sibi venturum esse
noverat: verumtamen quid illud esset ignorabat. Ille diserte
replicabat. iste singulis totus intendebat. At ubi retulit illam
fuisse desponsatam. continuo Rogerus torvis illum respiciens
oculis, tandem fremebundus ait: An tu venisti quo doceres
me matrimonia solvere? Fuge hinc quantocius, letus si contingat intactum abire qui vapulares iustius. Et eiecit illum
extra cellam. Eadwynus interea nesciens quid ageret quando-
quidem tantus vir tale desponsatorum discidium abhorreret.
desperare cepit et forsitan cepti penituit. Iamque reversus
esset unde venerat infecto negocio. si non subveniret sibi

* vixit: vicit *MS.*

---

[1] St. Gregory, *Dialogues,* ii, prol.; *PL 66. 126.*

No one suffered more violent temptations of the devil or had more snares laid for him. But armed with the power of the cross of Christ, he overcame the first and avoided the second. Who could have been more cruel to his own flesh? He allowed himself no pleasure.[1] His whole endeavour was to progress more and more in the service of God. His compassion on the afflicted and their wretchedness was such that he could not have borne their miseries so hardly if they had been inflicted on himself. We have written these few words about our old man by way of preface, because we think that they are pertinent to our story. The rest we pass over in silence, both because it is difficult to describe and because it is not necessary to tell here. I refer to his spirit of prophecy and his contemplative spirit in which he was considered to excel.

This old man, therefore, was visited immediately by his cousin Eadwin, whom we have mentioned earlier, who asked him to take the maiden of Christ under his care, as he himself dared not do so because of her parents. For indeed she came of a family of ancient and influential English nobles, and the whole of that district about Huntingdon for miles around was full of her relatives. When the man of God heard that she was from Huntingdon, he carefully inquired about her, desiring to learn about her character and her way of life. For a long time he had been expecting to see something which he knew would come to him from Huntingdon: but what it would be, he knew not. Eadwin unfolded the whole story clearly: the old man listened intently. But when he told him that she had been married, Roger, straightway turning his glaring eyes upon him, said angrily: 'Have you come here to show me how to dissolve marriages? Get out of here quickly and think yourself lucky if you get away safe and sound: you deserve a whipping.' And he drove him from his cell. Since the holy man refused to consider this separation of marriage partners, Eadwin, not knowing what to do next, began to lose hope and perhaps regretted having undertaken such a commission. And he would have returned whence he came without doing anything, had he not thought of going

de archiepiscopo Cantuarie in hac difficultate consulendo.
Ra[dulph]us erat tunc illic archiepiscopus[1] in utraque sciencia
divine scilicet legis et seculi sicut decebat personam apprime
eruditus et gracia pietatis omnibus amabilis.

30. Igitur Eadwynus Cantuariam proficiscitur. ut quod
ille venerabilis pater decreverit: hoc modis omnibus exequa-
tur. Pervenit eo. petit colloquium presulis. admittitur intro.
Sequestratis aliis qui aderant: remanet here(f. 152rb)mita
cum presule solus: et narrat ei vitam Christine seriatim. ut
scilicet integritatem suam Christo voverit ab infancia [et]
quid ob hoc fuerit a parentibus patratum. Nec tacet de sacra-
mento coniugii quin plene commemoret qua arte perducta
sit ad hoc et qua vi. Novissime voluntatem quam habet ipsa
fugiendi aperit. et de hoc utrum liceat consilium querit.
Sciscitatur antistes de virginis innocencia: heremita docet
quod mente et corpore sit incorrupta. Tunc ille verus Dei
servus super angustiis afflicte virginis ingemuit. ceterum de
perseverancia eiusdem fortissime militis Deo gracias egit. et
dixit Eadwyno. Crede michi frater. si illa malidicta mulier
veniret ad me ad confessionem. cuius astu virgo de qua
loquimur seducta est ad coniugium: non iniungerem aliam
illi penitenciam quam si perpetrasset homicidium. At illam
benedictam virginem sic desponsatam securus absolverem.
immo absolvo et benedico vice Christi summi pontificis. qui
michi potestatem istam dedit. Unde nunc illam exhortor in
proposito virginitatis permanere. Deum obsecro quatinus
angelicam voluntatem quam ei ipse dedit dignetur perficere.
Tibi vero fili mi Eadwyne non est morandum hic. sed festina
cito. et succurre preciose Dei columbe quacumque poteris
ope vel consilio et Dominus vobiscum sit.

31. Secessit itaque letus ille et in redeundo locutus cum

---

[1] Ralph d'Escures, archbishop of Canterbury, 17 May 1114 to 20 Oct. 1122.

to the archbishop of Canterbury for advice in this difficulty. At that time the archbishop[1] there was Ralph, a man deeply versed in both the divine and civil law, as a man in his position should be, and acceptable to all for his piety.

So Edwin set out for Canterbury, resolved to carry out whatever the venerable father should decide. He arrived there, asked for an interview with the archbishop, and was received into his presence. When the others who were there had withdrawn, the hermit remained alone with the archbishop and recounted to him step by step the life of Christina, how she had vowed her virginity to Christ in her childhood, and what her parents had done on account of it. Nor did he pass over in silence her marriage, but explained with what guile she had been led into it and under what compulsion. At last he revealed her intention of trying to escape and asked advice whether this was permissible or not. The bishop questioned him about the maiden's innocence; the hermit replied that she was inviolate in both mind and body. Then as a true servant of God he grieved over the trials and afflictions of the maiden, but gave thanks to God for her perseverance as a staunch soldier of Christ: and he said to Edwin: 'Believe me, brother: if that accursed woman by whose wiles the maiden, of whom we are speaking, was seduced into marrying, were to come to me in confession, I would impose on her the same penance as if she had committed manslaughter. But the blessed maiden who thus entered into marriage I would absolve without a scruple: indeed, I absolve her now, and as the deputy of Christ, the high priest, who gave me that power, I bless her. Hence I now exhort her to persevere in her vow of virginity and I pray God that He will bring to fulfilment that angelic desire which He Himself inspired in her. But you, my son Edwin, must not tarry here: but hasten away and sustain the precious dove of God with as much help and advice as you can, and may the Lord be with you both.'

So he joyfully departed and having spoken with hermits at various places on his return journey, made his way to

anachoretis diversorum locorum: perrexit Huntendoniam:
Quo cum venisset invenit Aucti et uxorem eius et filios in
monasterio sancte Dei Genitricis. Affuit inter eos et Christina
cui oculi omnium erant custodia. Unde factum est. quod
visum procuratorem suum non potuit alloqui (f. 152va) quippe
quod viderit illum ausa fuit insinuare nulli. cum haberet tale
desiderium cognoscendi quid pro [illa] gestum in itinere fuerat. sicut ipsa me audiente postea referebat: quod si daretur
opcio sibi vel loquendi cum homine. vel habendi tante quan-
t⟨it⟩atis aurum quante videbatur illud in quo sedebat monasterium. aurum quidem incunctanter abiceret: ut cum illo
tunc loqui posset. Veniens autem domum tristis comes parentum. postera die convenit sororem suam Matihildem ut ad
se veniret Eadwynus quod nullo pacto obtinuit. Verumtamen
data mercede cum puero viri pauca loquendi licenciam accepit. Puer ille ierat cum Eadwyno. et noverat que dominus suus
gesserit. A quo audiens virgo plura sibi loca receptui latibulo-
que satis apta patere. Flamstedam[1] elegit eo quod erat vicina
Rogero hermite. cuius famuli plerumque visitabant anachore-
tam ibi sedentem nomine Alfwen. Rogero valde dilectam
propter sanctitatem suam. Et dixit ad eam puer inter colloquendum. Utinam tenuissem te extra civitatem. Ad quod
verbum etsi Christina verecundaretur et obstupesceret. tum
quia indignum ut Aucti filia reperiretur in campo. cum tali
puero. tum quia difficillimum propter vigilanciam custodum.
acceptavit tamen erga se promptissimum illius animum. et
precepit ei dicens. Vade dic domino tuo quatinus prepararet
duos equos. unum michi. alterum tibi: in illum diem. et deter-
minavit ei feriam: Apparente aurora expectabis me cum equis
in prato illo: ultra hoc. Digitoque locum ostendit. Eo descen-
dam ad te. Neu fallaris ut occurras alteri pro me: equo parato
hoc signo discernes me. Dextram manum michi (f. 152vb)
supreme fronti opponam. indice tantum sursum erecto. Hoc

---

[1] Flamstead is a village in Hertfordshire, 2 miles on the St. Albans side of Markyate, where Roger's hermitage stood.

Huntingdon. When he came thither he found Autti with his wife and children in the monastery of Our Blessed Lady. Christina also was there with them, watched over carefully by them all. Hence it came about that though she saw her helper, she could not speak to him. Indeed, she dared give no one a hint that she had seen him, although she had such a longing to know what had been decided on her behalf on the journey that, as she afterwards averred in my hearing, if she had been given the choice of speaking with the hermit or of having a lump of gold as big as the monastery she was sitting in, she would have set aside the gold without hesitation in order to speak with him at that moment. Coming home sadly with her parents, she resorted to her sister Matilda on the following day to get Edwin to come to her, but was peremptorily refused. Nevertheless after giving a present she got permission to say a few words to the man's servant. This servant had accompanied Edwin on the journey and knew what his master had done. The maiden, hearing from him that there were several places open to her as refuges and hiding-places, chose Flamstead[1] because it was near Roger, whose servants often visited a recluse near by named Alfwen, a woman very much loved by Roger because of her holiness. And whilst he was talking to her, the servant said: 'I wish I could have you with me outside the town.' At these words Christina blushed and was embarrassed, not merely because it was beneath her dignity as a daughter of Autti to be found in the open countryside with such a youth, but also because it would be most difficult to elude the vigilance of her keepers: but she accepted his evident goodwill towards her and commanded him saying: 'Go and tell your master to prepare two horses, one for me and one for you, at a precise time', and she fixed the day of the week. 'When dawn is breaking wait for me with the horses in that field over there': and she pointed to the spot with her finger. 'I will come to you there. Do not make a mistake and accost someone else instead of me: and when the horse is ready you will recognize me by this sign. I will place my right hand to my forehead with only the

cum videris. protinus equos infrenabis. Quod si moram fecero: prestolanti oportunitatem ascribe. Nam pater meus et mater mea ibunt illa die more suo locutum cum domno Guidone. Erat autem Guido locum inhabitans solitudinis distantem ab urbe sex ferme miliariis. Ponens in corde mandata rediit et retulit domino suo. Placent illi. Preparat equos et cetera que opus erat.

32. Venit votiva dies. et abeuntibus parentibus ad solitudinem: Christina progreditur ad flumen. curiose prospiciens an videat in prato sodalem. Quo nusquam apparente: deputans ignavie. perrexit ad ecclesiam sancte Marie semper virginis. ut a Sueno[ne] licenciam accipiat eundi. At non inveniens illum. reliqua propter que venerat haut segniter explevit. scilicet Deo supplicat quo socius suus expedite veniat. quo prosperetur iter quod molitur. Deinde vadit ad domum matertere sue. cuius animum ita largicionibus illexerat. ut non solum neptem non proderet. sed ad fugiendum expediret. Inde erat quod sub illius quasi custodia. ambulabat quo volebat illo die ab aliis incustodita. Apud illam conquesta de socii tardacione: recepit pro munere consolacionis animum condolentis. Et iugiter habens oculos ultra amnem frustra. iamiamque parentum formidans reditum. iterum perrexit ad prefatum beatissime Marie templum. Cui venit obviam in itinere prepositus civitatis non[nullis] comitantibus civibus. Et tenens eam per pallium: adiuravit ut sibi diceret (f. 153ra) an fugere voluisset. Surrisit et ait. volo. Et ille quando inquid? Respondit. hodie. Sicque dimissa: ingreditur in templum. Et procidens in faciem suam: cum magna contritione cordis oravit sic. Domine Deus meus. unica spes mea. scrutator cordis et renum.[1] cui soli placere desidero. placetne tibi quo frauder ab hoc desiderio?[2] Si non hodie liberes me. relinquar*

---

* relinquam *MS.*

[1] Cf. Apoc. 2. 23.   [2] Cf. Ps. 77. 30.

forefinger raised. When you see this, rein in the horses immediately. And if I do not come at once, take it that I am waiting for the right moment. For on that day my father and mother will go as usual to speak with Guido.' Now Guido was dwelling in a secluded spot about six miles distant from the town. Keeping all these things in mind, the servant returned and told them to his master. He was pleased. He prepared the horses and everything else that was necessary.

The longed-for day arrived: after her parents had gone to the country, Christina went out towards the river, carefully scanning the meadow to see if her accomplice was there. As he was nowhere to be seen, she put it down to his laziness and set off for the church of Our Lady the Virgin to receive Sueno's permission to depart. But not finding him, she did all the other things for which she had come, that is, she prayed to God that her companion would come quickly and that the journey on which she was embarking would be successful. Then she went to her aunt's house, whose affection for her, gained by giving presents, was such that far from betraying her niece, she would expedite her escape. Hence it was that under her eye, so to speak, she wandered that day where she liked, free from the vigilance of the others. When she complained about the late coming of her companion, she was soothed by the sympathy of her aunt. And with her eyes fixed all the time on the meadow beyond the river, fearing the return of her parents at any minute, she went out again to the church of Blessed Mary. On her way she met the reeve of the town accompanied by some citizens. And he took her by the mantle and entreated her to tell him whether she intended to run away. And she smiled and said: 'Yes'. 'When?' said he. 'Today', she replied. So when he let her go, she entered the church. And, falling on her face, she prayed with great sorrow in her heart: 'O Lord my God, my only hope, the searcher-out of hearts and feelings,[1] whom alone I wish to please, is it Thy pleasure that I should be deprived of my wish?[2] If Thou deliver me not this day, I shall be left in the world, anxious about worldly things and how

in seculo. sollicita que sunt mundi quomodo placeam viro.[1]
Illud autem te arbitro elegi tibi soli placere semper et adherere
semper* indissolubili. Quod utrum statueris apud te: in hoc
patebit si eicis me hac ipsa die de domo patris mei et de
cognacione mea.[2] ultra illuc non reversuram. Sanc⟨t⟩ius enim
michi est inde non egredi quam tanquam canis ad vomitum
reverti.[3] Tu autem vides quid michi magis expedit: et ego
nolo meam de me. sed tuam semper fieri voluntatem: sit
nomen tuum benedictum in secula.[4] Hiis dictis: surrexit et
abiit.

33. Et rursus ultra flumen intuens nec desideratum videns
adhuc: profecta domum inter ancillas matris sue tristicia
tedioque lassa rescedit. Et iam desperare cepit: cum ecce
subito quiddam in se quasi avicula viva et exultans. omnia
interiora eius suo plausu concussit. que senciebatur usque ad
guttur illius volitare. et huiusmodi verba formare. Teodora.
surge. Quid pigraris? Ecce Loricus adest. Hoc enim erat
puero vocabulum. Illa ad insolitam vocem attonita contremuit.
et utrum a considentibus audiretur circumspexit. Ut autem
vidit omnes intendentes operi suo: surrexit statim confidens
in Domino. Sumptisque clanculo vestimentis virilibus que
preparaverat sibi (f. 153rb) et eludens in sexum [virilem vestita
cap]pa talari exivit foras. Quod [cum vidis]set germana sua
Matildis [sci]licet properancius egredientem [nam eam]
cognovit de vestibus: secuta [est e ves]tigio sororem. Animadvertens hoc [Christi]na: finxit se velle templum beate Ma[rie]
semper virginis adire. Et dum iret [ecce una] de manicis
fustanii quod oc[cul]te sub cappa gerebat cecidit in terram
[sive] incuria gestantis sive industria nes[cio]. Qua visa
Matildis: ait. Quid est [hoc] Theodora unde verris terram?
At il[la] blande dixit ad eam. Cara michi [so]ror accipe.
regrediensque deferto do[mum] quoniam impedit me. Et
baiulavit illi bombicinum clavesque patris: dicens. Et has

* semper *sic* MS., *a corruption for* foedere?

[1] 1 Cor. 7. 34.   [2] Gen. 24. 40.   [3] Prov. 26. 11.   [4] Ps. 71. 17.

to please my husband.[1] My one desire, as Thou knowest, is to please Thee alone and to be united to Thee for all time without end. But whether this be Thy decision will become clear if today Thou drive me from my father's house and from my relatives,[2] nevermore to return. For it is better for me never to leave it than to return like a dog to its vomit.[3] But Thou seest what is more profitable for me: I wish not my will, but Thine to come to pass for ever. Blessed be Thy name for evermore.'[4] When she had said this, she rose and left the church.

And, scanning the meadow beyond the river once more and not seeing the man she longed for, she turned her steps homeward and sat down amongst her mother's servants, sad at heart and worn out with disappointment. She was already beginning to lose hope, when suddenly something inside her, like a small bird full of life and joy, struck her inward parts with its fluttering. And she felt it flying upwards towards her throat and forming these words: 'Theodora, arise. Why are you so slow? Behold, Loric is here' (for this was the boy's name). Astonished at the unusual voice, she trembled and glanced round to see if those sitting with her had heard it. And when she saw them all busy about their tasks, she jumped up immediately, full of trust in the Lord. And secretly taking masculine garb which she had got ready beforehand in order to disguise herself as a man, she went out swathed in a long cloak that reached to her heels. But when her sister Matilda saw her hasting out, for she recognized her from her clothes, she followed behind her. Christina, noticing this, pretended that she was going to the church of Our Blessed Lady. But, as she walked, one of the sleeves of the man's garment which she was hiding beneath her cloak slipped to the ground whether through carelessness or by design I do not know. And when Matilda saw it, she said. 'What is this, Theodora, that you are trailing on the ground?' But she replied with an innocent look: 'Sister dear, take it with you when you go back to the house for it is getting in my way.' And she handed over to her a veil and

pariter dulcis michi anima. ne si pater noster interim venerit.
et in qualibet [ar]charum suarum videre quippiam affecta-
[ve]rit non inveniens claves ad man[um] moleste ferat. Istis
Matildi persua[sis] paululum processit et quasi vellet ire
monasterium et mox ad pratum vertit gradum.

34. Premittensque sui noticiam [appo]sita manu fronti
digitoque erecto. comitem et equos habuit [pa]ratos. Quorum
unum arripiens: rubore perfusa substit⟨it⟩. Quid fugitiva
m[ora]ris? Quid sexum feminei vereris? [Vi]rilem animum
indue. et more viri [in] equum ascende. Dehinc ab[iecta
pusil]lanimitate: viriliter super equum [saliens] atque cal-
caribus eius latera [pungens] famulo dixit. Sequere me a
[tergo. timeo] ne si mecum equitaveris: de[prehensis] nobis
tu moriaris. Hora erat quasi tertia. et circa nonam pervenerunt Flamestedam: eo spacio plusquam XXX milibus pas-
suum traducti. Illic¹ a venerabili inclusa Alfuen suscepta
Christina cum gaudio. eadem die pro religionis ha(f. 153ᵛᵃ)
[bitu asperam indueba]tur tunicam que sericis ves[timentis
et] delicatis variarum pelliciarum [delic]iis in patris domo
consu[everat u]ti. Necnon in secretissimam amarissimam-
que cameram vix illi pre angustia sufficientem detrusa, [sed]
delectata pro Christo, multo tempore diligenter occultata
delituit. Statimque eadem die cepit de tricesimo psalmo
septimo leccionem quinque versus, quorum primus est:
Domine ante te omne desiderium meum.² Apta quidem
lectio conveniensque fortune legentis, et qua sepius eadem
repetendo, hinc illam gemebat infirmitatem et cecitatem,
illinc vim atque dolos suorum olim amicorum et proximo-
rum, qui querebant animam suam.³ Sed ante Dominum [af-
fir]mabat omne desiderium suum ab hiis [li]berari ut sine
timore serviret illi [in] sanctitate et iusticia coram ipso omnibus [die]bus vite sue.⁴ Interea parentes pu[elle] reversi de

---

¹ The hermitage of Alfwen should not be coupled with the Priory of Nuns 'St.
Giles of the Wood', founded there in the time of King Stephen by Roger de Toney
(Dugdale, iv. 299–302).   ² Ps. 37. 10.   ³ Ps. 37. 12.   ⁴ Luke 1. 75.

her father's keys, adding: 'And these too, sweetheart, so that if our father returns in the meantime and wishes to take something from the chest, he will not get angry because the keys are missing.' And when she had allayed Matilda's suspicions with these words, she sallied forth as if she were going towards the monastery, and then turned her steps towards the meadow.

And making herself known by raising her finger to her forehead, she got both her companion and the horses. And seizing hold of one of them, she paused, covered with embarrassment. Why delay, fugitive? Why do you respect your feminine sex? Put on manly courage and mount the horse like a man. At this she put aside her fears and, jumping on the horse as if she were a youth and setting spurs to his flanks, she said to the servant: 'Follow me at a distance: for I fear that if you ride with me and we are caught, they will kill you.' It was about nine in the morning; and about three in the afternoon they reached Flamstead, having covered over thirty miles in that time. There[1] she was welcomed with joy by Alfwen the venerable anchoress, and on the same day she put on the religious habit, and she who had been accustomed to wearing silk dresses and luxurious furs in her father's house was now covered with a rough garment. Hidden out of sight in a very dark chamber hardly large enough, on account of its size, to house her, she remained carefully concealed there for a long time, finding great joy in Christ. And on that very day she took for her reading five verses from the thirty-seventh psalm, of which the first runs: 'Lord, all my desire is before thee.'[2] A very suitable passage and one that described the situation of the reader; this she repeated often, lamenting at one moment her own weakness and blindness, at another the violence and guile of her parents, friends, and relatives, who were seeking her life.[3] But first of all she prayed to the Lord to deliver her from all these, so that without fear she might serve him in holiness and righteousness in his sight all the days of her life.[4] In the meantime her parents had returned from the hermitage, and when they

solitudine cum non invenirent filiam suam. neque domi [ne-
que inter] anchoretas Huntendonie, neque [in] monasterio
sancte Marie. cognoverunt [ea]m proculdubio fugisse. Sed
quo nescio fugisset penitus igno[rav]erunt. Miserunt ergo circumquaque per [plu]res vias quibus Huntendonia pa[tebat]
qui velociter illam prosequerentur [et apprehen]sam redu-
cerent cum contumelia interfecto quemcumque reperissent
[in] eius comitatu. Quibus furentibus [hiis h]uc illis illuc
Burhredus sponsus [esti]mans illam refugium habere penes
Rogerum heremitam, et ipse tendit sciscitatusque diligenter
ab uno clientum si quam illic sciat feminam; offert ei duos
solidos ut indicet illam. Cui ille indignando respondit:
Putasne tu quisquis es hora tali femi(f. 153^(vb))nam hic posse
reperiri? difficillime admittitur hic aliqua cum testibus eciam
tempore meridiano. Et tu queris hic [iuvenculam] antelucano? Hoc ille audito: properat Flamestedam. et loquens
cum venerabili Alfwen responsum tale recepit. Desine fili.
desine talem putare nobiscum. Nos non habemus in con-
suetudine sponsis fugitivis commodare latibulum. Taliter
homo delusus abscessit alia nequaquam simili causa peragra-
turus.

35. Ipso die Rogero post nonam de more sedenti ad mensam reficiendi gracia dixit puer: Non bene te noscit ille qui
ante lucem hodie speravit [hic] invenire puellam. Interrogavit. Quis erat. nescio inquid sed ab Huntendonia veniebat et querebat nescio[quam] puellam nobilem. que patrem
et sponsum suum fugit sicut michi dixit. Tunc suspira-
vit Rogerus et iussit mensam auferri ieiunusque secessit in
oratorium suum. ubi nocte ac die lamentis et fletibus in-
dulgens. et non manducans neque bibens. tandem merore
consumptus decidit? in lectum et dicebat. Scio. Domine
Deus omnipotens et districtissime iudex. quod requires animam illius de manu mea.[1] Equidem sciebam quoniam bo-
nam habebat voluntatem sed dum nolui subvenire roganti:

---

[1] Cf. Gen. 9. 5.

could find their daughter neither at home nor among the recluses of Huntingdon nor at the monastery of Our Lady, they came to the conclusion that she had run away. But where she had gone passed their comprehension. So they swiftly despatched search parties along all the roads that led to Huntingdon with orders to pursue and catch her and to bring her home in disgrace, killing anyone whom they might find in her company. Whilst some of them went raging in one direction, others in another, her husband Burthred, suspecting that she had taken refuge with Roger the hermit, went thither and, making careful inquiries from one of his disciples whether he knew of any woman there, offered him two shillings to disclose where she was. With indignation the man replied to him: 'Who do you think you are, expecting to find a woman here at this hour? It is with the greatest difficulty that a woman is allowed here even in broad daylight and accompanied. And you look for a girl here before daybreak?' Hearing this, he hurried off to Flamstead to speak with the venerable Alfwen and got this answer. 'Stop, my son, stop imagining that she is here with us. It is not our custom to give shelter to wives who are running away from their husbands.' The man, deluded in this way, departed, resolved never to go on such an errand again.

That very day, whilst Roger was sitting at his table to take his meal, about three in the afternoon his servant said to him: 'That fellow who came here today before dawn looking for a girl did not know you very well.' 'Who was it?' he asked. 'I don't know,' the servant replied, 'but he came from Huntingdon and was looking for some girl of noble family who, so he told me, had run away from her father and her husband.' Then Roger gave a sigh and ordered the table to be cleared, and went fasting into his chapel, where day and night, giving himself up to laments and tears, he neither ate nor drank until, worn out with sorrow, he sank on his couch and said: 'I know, O Lord almighty and most rigorous judge, that Thou wilt claim her soul at my hands.[1] For I knew that she had a good will, but I was unwilling to give her my

subintroductus aliquis astu diaboli aperte abduxit et perdidit
incautam. Nullam itaque requiem inveniens sibi. quamdiu
nesciret. quid de Christina gestum fuisset: sine intermissione
deprecabatur Dominum super indicio hoc.

36. Post dies aliquot unus de domo sua Wlfinus nomine.
perrexit sicut sibi mos erat loqui cum venerabili Alfuuen: et
ab ipsa doctus adventum et absconsionem Christine regressus
(f. 154ʳᵃ) enarravit domino suo Rogero. Qui ad audita resul-
tans gracias egit Domino et dixit Wlfuino: hodie revocasti
me ab inferis. Benedicatur dominus ex Syon: qui fecit celum
et terram.¹ [P]orro Sueno canonicus ut cognovit de abscessu
Christine. multum increpavit matrem eius. eo quod illam
effugasset. propter quam domui sue Deus benedixisset.
Ideoque scias inquid domui multa adversa futura precipue
dirum incendium. Que omnia iuxta sermonem hominis Dei
consequenter adimpleta sunt. Inter hec ges[ta] relatum est
domine Alfwen et per eam Christine. quod iuvenis cuius
ministerio fuerat abducta Christina. querebatur a parentibus
eius ad puniendum. vel eciam ad occidendum. Et ceperunt
amici super hoc contristari. Deumque pro liberacione hominis
deprecari: cum ecce quadam nocte astitit ille Christine pene
vigilanti decoro vultu valde. et increpavit eam de supervacaneo
timore querencium illam. atque hortatus est ad confidendum
in Domino protectore suo. Mane facto cum visionem aperuis-
set occultrici sue Alfwen. et monuisset securam fore. iuvenis
venit qui diceret illum more fidelium felici morte solutum
vinculis carnis. Cognoverunt ergo quoniam electorum adiun-
ctus est con[sorcio] qui et decorus apparuit: et ab hominum
metu prohibens in Domino [confide]re suasit.

37. Nichilominus et alia confortata fuit ibidem visione:

¹ Ps. 133. 3.

help when she asked for it: and now some fellow, at the instigation of the devil, having cunningly gained her confidence, has abducted and ruined her whilst she was off her guard.' And as he could find no rest as long as he was ignorant of what had happened to Christina, he prayed without ceasing to the Lord to give him a sign.

After some days, one of the servants of his house, named Ulfwine, set out, as was his custom, to take counsel with the venerable Alfwen: and hearing from her about the arrival and concealment of Christina, returned to tell the whole story to his master Roger. When Roger heard it, he broke out into joyful thanks to the Lord and said to Ulfwine: 'This day you have called me back from the grave. May the Lord who made heaven and earth be blessed out of Syon.'[1] Furthermore, when Sueno the canon found out about the departure of Christina he heaped reproaches on her mother for having driven out the one for whose sake God had blessed her house. 'Know, therefore,' he said, 'that your house will suffer much adversity in the future, especially from a terrible fire.' All of which was afterwards fulfilled according to the words of the man of God. Whilst all this was happening, it was told Alfwen, and by her to Christina, that the young man who had helped her to escape was being searched for by her parents in order that they might punish, or even kill him. And all her friends began to grieve at this and prayed to the Lord for the youth's safety. Then one night, whilst Christina was hardly awake, he stood by her side with a shining countenance and reproached her for her empty fears about those who were seeking her, and exhorted her to put all her trust in the Lord her protector. Next morning, when she revealed the vision to Alfwen who was hiding her, and declared that she would be safe, a young man came to say that the youth had passed away in a truly Christian death. They knew, therefore, that he who had appeared so beautiful and had advised her to trust in God, and to fear nothing from men, was now sharing the company of the elect.

In spite of this she had another vision there by which she

que facta ẻst. Videbat se super solidam stare terram. et ante
se campum patere latum et lutosum plenum tauris cornibus
ac vultu minacibus. Qui cum niterentur pedes suos eruere
de luto quatinus illam impeterent. totamque minutatim dis-
cerperent: in eisdem semper (f. 154rb) locis ipsos pedes [ten]
ebant: unde [stupefacta est] admiratione pariter et [terro]ri:
audita est vox huiusmo[di]. Si in loco tuo solide steteris
omnem istarum beluarum feritatem frustra [time]bis. Sin
autem abieris retrorsum eadem hora cades in potestatem
earum. Evigilavit. et interpretata est locum per significa-
tionem esse virginitatis propositum: Tauros: demones et
homines impios. Conceptaque grande fiducia magis sese in
amore sanctitatis accendi. minas vero querentium se moder
[acius] timuit. Interim latebre sue vita[que] tranquilla dia-
bolum exacerbabant. [lec]ciones ac psalmodia die noctuque
[cru]ciabant. Quanquam enim occultata [late]ret homines:
nequaquam latebat et demones. Qui ad deterrendam
[rever]endam ancillam Christi: bufones ir[rumpe]bant in
carcerem: eo quod averterent virginis obtutum. specie*
illa per omnem deformitatem. Ap[pare]bant subito teter-
rima. terribili[bus] ac spaciosis orbibus oculorum. se[debant]
hinc et hinc: spalterio vendicantes medium locum in gremio
virgi[nis] quod propemodum omnibus horis iacebat expan-
sum in usum sponse Christi. At cum illa nec se moveret nec
psalmodiam dimitteret: iterum a[bibant]. Unde magis credendum [est eos] fuisse demones. presertim qui[a deformita]te
tales apparentes et ins[pera]te comparentes videri non [po-
tuit unde] venerint vel quo devenerint [vel quo ex]ierint:
adeo carcer ille clausus [erat] et obstructus undique.

38. Exacto Christina biennio Flamestedam: necesse habuit
alio migrare. Quod dum parabatur quidam sonus quasi
virginei cantus (f. 154va) [a comitibus Ro]geri audiebatur
quando [Leofricus et socius] suus Acio debitas h[orarum
reddeb]ant laudes. Mirabantur [quid ess]et et delectati can-
tilena† non alternatim ut solebant sed am[bo si]mul eundem

---

* speciem *MS*.   † cantilene *MS*.

was consoled. She saw herself standing on firm ground before a large and swampy meadow full of bulls with threatening horns and glaring eyes. And as they tried to lift their hooves from the swampy ground to attack her and tear her to pieces, their hooves were held fast in the ground so that they could not move. Whilst she gazed on this sight with astonishment, a voice was heard saying: 'If you take a firm stand in the place where you are, you will have no cause to fear the ferocity of those beasts. But if you retreat one step, at that same moment you will fall into their power.' She woke up, and interpreted the place as meaning her resolution to remain a virgin: the bulls were devils and wicked men. And taking great confidence, she was inspired with a deeper desire for holiness, and had less fear of the threats of her persecutors. In the meantime her concealment and her peaceful existence irritated the devil: her reading and singing of the psalms by day and night were a torment to him. For although in her hiding-place she was hidden from men, she could never escape the notice of the demons. And so to terrify the reverend handmaid of Christ toads invaded her cell to distract her attention by all kinds of ugliness from God's beauty. Their sudden appearance, with their big and terrible eyes, was most frightening, for they squatted here and there, arrogating the middle of the psalter which lay open on her lap at all hours of the day for her use. But when she refused to move and would not give up her singing of the psalms, they went away, which makes one think that they were devils, especially as they appeared unexpectedly; and as the cell was closed and locked on all sides it was not possible to see where they came from, or how they got in or out.

After Christina had spent two years at Flamstead, it was necessary for her to go elsewhere. And whilst her departure was being prepared, the sound of virgins singing was heard by Roger's two companions, Leofric and Acio his friend, as they were rendering their due praises to God. They wondered what it was and, being enchanted by the melody, they did not sing alternately, as was their custom, but sang the

versum consona voce psallebant. Finito versu supprimebant
vocem. et a respondentibus subsequentem versum cum dulci
melodia recipiebant vicem. Sic aliquociens integer psalmus
inter viros et virgines finiebatur. Satagebant de significacione.
que postmodum oranti Rogero revelata est ex parte. Vocat
[ad s]e confestim Acionem et Leofricum [et] dicit eis: Pre-
parate vos et observa[te] diligenter quo digni inveniami[ni]
visitacione Dei. Certus quippe sum [qu]ia Deus visitabit in
proximo locum [is]tum. quiddam huc dirigendo quod [ille]
multum amat. Nescio fateor quid [illu]d sit. Scio tamen quod
carum est Deo [f]orte carius quam nos peccatores. [Pa]ucis
ab hinc evolutis diebus re[cordat]us Rogerus incommodita-
tum quas [spon]sa Christi pertulit Flamestede non so[lum]
pacienter sed et gaudenter. et perpen[dens] tum ex hiis tum
ex aliis eius virtu[tibu]s quam radicata et fundata erat in
[cari]tate Dei.¹ suam ei curam exinde non [defu]turam
statuit. ideoque propter mittens [ce]llam suam renitente
Alfwen ve[nire fe]cit. Non tamen consensit ipse [vide]re
faciem illius vel loqui cum [ea] sed per Acionem que non
haberet apud episcopum excusacionem que* accusabat [eum
ut] dissidii reum. Viderunt se tame[n eode]m die. quod contigit hoc or[dine]. Virgo Dei prostrata iacebat in o[rator]io
senis. demersa facie ad terram. Super quam vir Dei transibat
averso vultu ne videret eam. At ubi pertransierat respexit
ut videret quam apte Christi ancilla sese composuisset ad
(f. 154vb) orandum. quoniam hoc quoque censebat orantibus
esse observandum. et illa nichilominus eodem puncto sus-
pexit ad videndum incessum et habitum senis. in quibus credebat non nullum vestigium apparere tante religionis. Et ita
sese mutuo viderunt non sponte. sed nec fortuitu: ceterum
sicut postea claruit divino nutu. Si enim mutuo se non vidis-
sent: intra septum i[llius] celle neuter habitare cum altero

---

* que ... excusacionem *add. in marg.* que: qui *MS.*
¹ Eph. 3. 17.

same verse in unison. At the end of the verse they kept silent
and listened to the following verse being sung to a sweet
melody by the opposite choir. Quite often a whole psalm
would be sung completely by the men and the maidens in
this way. They spent much time trying to find out the meaning of this, and finally it was partially revealed to Roger in
prayer. He called Acio and Leofric to him immediately
and said to them: 'Get yourselves ready and make certain
that you are found worthy of the visitation of God. For I am
certain that God will soon visit this place, sending hither
something which He much loves. What it is I cannot tell.
All I know is, that it is something dearer to Him perhaps
than us sinners.' A few days later, whilst Roger was recalling
the discomfort that Christina suffered at Flamstead, not only
with patience but with joy, and judging from these and her
other qualities that she was deeply rooted and grounded in
the love of God,[1] he decided that he would no longer deny
her his assistance. And so he had her cell brought near his
in spite of Alfwen's opposition. All the same he would not
consent to see her or to speak with her, but only indirectly
through Acio, in order that there might be no excuse for
Alfwen to accuse him before the bishop of being a cause of
dissension. Nevertheless they saw each other the same day;
and it happened in this way. The virgin of God lay prostrate
in the old man's chapel, with her face turned to the ground.
The man of God stepped over her with his face averted in
order not to see her. But as he passed by he looked over his
shoulder to see how modestly the handmaid of Christ had
composed herself for prayer, as this was one of the things
which he thought those who pray ought to observe. Yet
she, at the same instant, glanced upwards to appraise the
bearing and deportment of the old man, for in these she
considered that some trace of his great holiness was apparent. And so they saw each other, not by design and yet
not by chance, but, as afterwards became clear, by the divine
will. For if they had not had a glimpse of each other, neither
would have presumed to live with the other in the confined

presumpsisset: non habitassent simul: non tantum arsissent
celesti desiderio. nec maneret eis* in celis tanta celsitudo.
Nempe calor qui succensus fuit Dei spiritu ardebat in singulis; scintillas suas iaculat[us] est in corda ipsorum altrin-
secus suo modo gracia mutue visionis. unde facti cor unum et
anima una[1] in caritate et in castitate in Christo non formida-
verunt convivere in eodem habitaculo.

39. Porro convivendo sicut ex duabus facibus coniunctis
flamma consurgit amplior: sic illorum sese mutuo incitancium
ad alciora cotidie sanctus excrevit amor. Ceterum quo fer-
vencius ad contemplandam speciem conditoris anehelabant.
eo felicius in summa gloria cum ipso simul regnant. Itaque
magnitudo profectus. provo[ca]vit illos. ad commorandum
simul. [Ca]ute tamen egerunt ne hoc fieret [notum] tam
propter scandala inferiorum [quam propter] rabiem querencium ancillam Christi. [Carcer erat iuxta] oratorium senis.
et domo illi con[tiguus qui] cum illo fecit angulum coniun
[ctione] sua. Is antepositam habens una[m tab]ulam pote
rat ita celari. ut de for[is] aspicienti nullum interius haberi
[per]suaderet. ubi tamen amplitudo plus palmo semis ines-
set. In hoc ergo carcere Rogerus ovantem sociam posuit. et
ligni robur pro hostio conveniens (f. 155[ra]) admovit. Et hoc
eciam tanti ponderis erat. quod ab inclusa nullatenus ad-
moveri sive removeri poterat. Hic igitur ancilla Christi co-
artata supra duram petram sedit usque ad obitum Rogeri. id
est .iiii. annis. et eo amplius. Latens illos quoque qui cum
Rogero simul habitabant. O quantas sustinuit illic incom-
moditates frigoris et estus. famis et sitis. cotidiani ieiunii.
Loci angustia non admittebat necessarium tegumentum al-
genti. Integerrima clausula nullum indulgebat refrigerium
estuanti. Longa inedia. contracta sunt et aruerunt sibi in-
testina. Erat quando pre ardore sitis naribus ebullire⟨n⟩t
frusta coagulati sanguinis. Hiis omnibus illi erat intollera-
bilius. quod exire foras non nisi sero licebat. ad alia quedam

---

* eis: eos *MS.*

[1] Acts 4. 32.

space of that cell: they would not have dwelt together: they would not have been stimulated by such heavenly desire, nor would they have attained such a lofty place in heaven. The fire, namely, which had been kindled by the spirit of God and burned in each one of them cast its sparks into their hearts by the grace of that mutual glance; and so made one in heart and soul[1] in chastity and charity in Christ, they were not afraid to dwell together under the same roof.

Furthermore, through their dwelling together and encouraging each other to strive after higher things their holy affection grew day by day, like a large flame springing from two brands joined together. The more fervently they yearned to contemplate the beauty of the creator, the more happily they reign with Him in supreme glory. And so their great progress induced them to dwell together. Yet they acted with circumspection in not letting this become known, for they feared scandal to their inferiors and the fury of those who were persecuting the handmaid of Christ. Near the chapel of the old man and joined to his cell was a room which made an angle where it joined. This had a plank of wood placed before it and was so concealed that to anyone looking from outside it would seem that no one was present within, since the space was not bigger than a span and a half. In this prison, therefore, Roger placed his happy companion. In front of the door he rolled a heavy log of wood, the weight of which was actually so great that it could not be put in its place or taken away by the recluse. And so, thus confined, the handmaid of Christ sat on a hard stone until Roger's death, that is, four years and more, concealed even from those who dwelt together with Roger. O what trials she had to bear of cold and heat, hunger and thirst, daily fasting! The confined space would not allow her to wear even the necessary clothing when she was cold. The airless little enclosure became stifling when when she was hot. Through long fasting, her bowels became contracted and dried up. There was a time when her burning thirst caused little clots of blood to bubble up from her

necessaria que natura postulabat. Nimirum instante necessitate nequibat ipsa sibi aperire et Rogerus de more tardabat.
ad illam venire. Itaque necesse fuit immobiliter eam in loco
sedere. torqueri et tacere.¹ Quia si Rogerum habere voluerat
voce vel pulsu vocari eum oportebat. Sed qualiter hoc faceret
abscondita que nec ausa fuit semisuspiria? Metuebat namque ne quis preter Rogerum adesset. qui vel anelitu spirantis
audito latebras suas deprehenderet. Et illa quidem mallet in
carcere mori. quam tunc temporis cuiquam externo patefieri.

40. Talia et alia tanto tempore pacientem: dura corripuit
morborum varietas. que de die in diem tantum invalescebat:
ut fieret eciam immedicabilis. At tamen cui nulla medicina
subvenire poterat humanitus impensa: vidimus post multos
annos divinitus inaudita gracia cura(f. 155ʳᵇ)tam. [Miseras
cotidiane adversitatis] anxietates portabat equanimi dulcedine
superni amoris: [ora]bat fortiter. illo petito tranquillit[atis]
tempore quando liberum habuit or[acio]ni seu contemplative meditacion[i] nocte vacare, quemadmodum ami[cus] dei
Rogerus eam informabat nunc [doctri]na, nunc exemplo.
Siquidem doce[bat] illam quedam pene incredibilia de [se]-
cretis celestibus, et exhibebat se talem [ut] solo corpore
videretur in terra. tota vero mente conversari in celo.² Forsitan hoc credat aliquis falsum. si non subiungo, quod michi
suffragetur testimonium. Ipsa de qua scribimus consocia
senis enarrante didici. quod ille tanta intencione solebat
orando suspendi [ut] diabolus invisibiliter incensus vi[si]bili
igne quodam tempore cucullam orantis dorso herentem in-
cenderet. et nec sic illum ab intencione remissiorem reddere
valeret. Quis igitur [pu]tas ille ignis intus in animo extitit
[qui] corpus exterius contra material[em] ignem insensibi-
le* fecit? Hoc igi[tur] credendum est Christinam quoque
non p[a]rum calescere. quando iuxta virum Dei st[a]bat in

---

* insensibilem *MS.*

¹ Cf. *Verba Seniorum*, i. 190 (*PL* 73. 801): 'Tu sede, tu tace, tu sustine'.
² Cf. Phil. 3. 20.

nostrils. But what was more unbearable than all this was that she could not go out until the evening to satisfy the demands of nature. Even when she was in dire need, she could not open the door for herself, and Roger usually did not come till late. So it was necessary for her to sit quite still in the place, to suffer torments, and to keep quiet,[1] because if she wished Roger to come to her, she had to summon him either by calling or knocking. But how could she do this from her hiding-place when she dared hardly breathe? For she was afraid that someone else besides Roger might be near and, hearing her breathing, would discover her hiding-place. And she would rather die in the cell than make her presence known to anyone at that time.

After suffering these and many other discomforts for a long time, she became subject to a variety of ailments, which gathered such strength from day to day that they became incurable. Yet she to whom no human medicine could bring relief was, as we saw many years later, cured by an unheard-of grace from God. She bore all these daily anxieties and troubles with the calm sweetness of divine love; she prayed earnestly in those moments at night when she was free to devote herself to prayer and contemplative meditation, just as her friend Roger had trained her, first by word, then by example. Indeed, he taught her things about heavenly secrets which are hardly credible, and acted as if he were on earth only in body, whilst his whole mind was fixed on heaven.[2] Someone may think perhaps that this is an exaggeration if I do not add a proof to confirm what I say. She of whom we are writing and who was the old man's companion has told me that once when he was rapt in prayer his concentration was so intense that the devil, invisibly incensed visibly set fire to the cowl that clung to his back as he prayed, and even so could not distract him. What think you then must have been the fire that burned inwardly in his spirit when it rendered his body insensible to the material fire that burned without? It should therefore be believed that Christina also was no less on fire when she

oracione. Nulla dies preteriit, q[uo] non illam ob hoc in oratorium suum [con]duxit. O quantas illic fundebant lacrimas
celestis desiderii. quam preciosis saginabantur deliciis interni
gaudii.

41. Prius erat metus, et ille grandis. qui sepius illorum
[corrum]pebat gaudium. ne Christina [cum illo] aliquo casu
reperta raperetur a[uctorita]te episcopi. et traderetur voluntati
[sponsi] sui. quos per se et per quoscumque hos[tis] antiquus
illis sociare poterat. rece[nti] semper furore ad indagacionem
eius incessanter agitabat. Proinde multum super hac re Christi misericordiam flagitabat. (f. 155ᵛᵃ) Nec frustra. Quippe
dominice annunciacionis die Christina supra petram [suam]
sedente et de insania queren[cium se] sollerter cogitante:
intravit [ad e]am speciosus forma pre filiis [homi]num¹ ob-
serato aditu. crucem ferens [aur]eam in dextera manu ad
cuius [int]roitum expavit virgo. quam ille [bla]nde confortavit tali alloquio. Ne timeas inquid. non enim veni quo tibi
metum augerem: sed ut securitatem ingererem. Tolle igitur
crucem istam. ac tenens firmiter non inclines eam ad dexteram
neque ad sinistram. Tene semper recta linea sursum versus.
et memento quoniam ego ipse tuli eandem primitus. Nec non
omnes qui volunt ire Ierusalem: necesse est hanc portare
crucem. Hiis dictis: crucem [e]i baiulavit. promittensque
quod post modicum ab ea resumeret. ab [ocu]lis eius evanuit.
Quod ut ex or[din]e enarravit Christina viro Dei Rogero:
intellexit ille significacionem [et] cepit flere pre gaudio.
dicens. Benedictus deus. qui suis semper adest humilibus.
Et ad virginem. letare mecum. ait anglico sermone. [my]n
sunendaege dohter. quod latine dicitur. mea dominice diei
filia. eo quod ceteris omnibus quas Christo genuerat aut
nutrierat. Christinam plus amaret: quantum dominica dies
reliquis septimane feriis honorabilitate pre[staret]. Letare
inquid. vestra tribu[lacio] gracia Dei terminanda est. in
proxi[mo . . .] est. Est enim interpretacio cru[cem quam] in

¹ Ps. 44. 3.

stood by the side of the man in prayer. No day passed without his taking her into his chapel for this purpose. O how many tears of heavenly desire did they shed: on what rare delicacies of inward joy were they feasted!

At first they were haunted by the fear, and a deep one at that (which spoilt their joy), that if by chance Christina were found in his company she might be snatched away on the orders of the bishop and handed over to her husband to do as he liked: for the old enemy did not stop importuning these two, and any others he could associate with them, to discover where she was. Therefore she prayed much for Christ's mercy on this matter. And not without effect. For on the day of Our Lord's annunciation, whilst Christina was sitting on her stone and giving anxious thought to the senseless behaviour of her persecutors, the fairest of the children of men[1] came to her through the locked door, bearing in His right hand a cross of gold. At His appearance the maiden was terrified, but He put her fears at rest with this comforting assurance: 'Fear not', He said: 'for I have not come to increase your fears, but to give you confidence. Take this cross, therefore, and hold it firmly, slanting it neither to right nor left. Always hold it straight, pointing upwards: and remember that I was the first to bear the same cross. All who wish to travel to Jerusalem must carry this cross.' Having said this, He held out the cross to her, promising that after a short time He would take it back again from her. And then He vanished. When Christina recounted this experience to Roger, the man of God, he understood its meaning and began to weep for joy, saying: 'Blessed be God, who succours His lowly ones at all times.' And he said to the maiden in English: 'Rejoice with me, myn sunendaege dohter', that is, my Sunday daughter, because just as much as Sunday excels the other days of the week in dignity so he loved Christina more than all the others whom he had begotten or nursed in Christ. 'Rejoice with me,' he said, 'for by the grace of God your trials will soon be at an end. For the meaning is this: the cross which you have received as a token will shortly be taken

promissione accepisti su[m]endam a te post modicum. Evenit sicut homo Dei locutus est.

42. Post biduum. idest .vi. kalendas aprilis. qua die redemptor mundi resurrexit a mortuis:[1] venit ad (f. 155vb) cellam viri Burhredus cum duobus fratribus suis: altero canonico. altero laico. humiliter rogans ut graciam indulgencie consequetur ab eo. Cognovit enim et confessus est se graviter in illum offendisse. et Theodoram ancillam Christi maxime. et ad hoc venisse nunc ut absolvat eam a sponsaliis. seipsum quoque tradat gubernandum imperio senis. Ita sibi pronunciavit esse preceptum ab imperatrice mundi. genitrice Dei Maria. que nudius tercius ei terribiliter in visu noctis apparuerat: et de supervacua persecucione sacre virginis dure increparat. Rogerus autem considerans personas que cum illo aderant nimis esse privatas: obtulit ei prudenter ac dedit inducias. dum et ipse sibi melius consuleret. et ille testes alios exhiberet. Adveniente termino Burhredus rediit. et sponsam suam sicut preceptum acceperat absolvit: dexteram suam in dextera Rogeri ponendo fidemque ac confirmacionem huius absolucionis faciendo coram hiis sacerdotibus. Burhredo scilicet qui desponsaverat illos et Robert decano Huntendoniensi[2] et Radulfo Flamestedensi: et coram quinque Rogeri coheremitis. Ab hinc homo Dei factus securior. collecta spe ex multitudine graciarum quas probaverat inesse Christine, cogitabat illam heremi sue post se heredem relinquere. Unde et sermonem habuit aliquando cum illa. Que tametsi crederet hoc supra vires esse non statim contradixit. sed nec assensum prebuit. fecit autem sicut faciebat semper et hoc et totam sui curam iactavit in Domino[3]. et in Maria virgine. Quocirca res quedam mirabilis. et mirabilibus mirabilior accidit. Nam cum aliquando lacrimis in oracione maderet pre desiderio celestium: subito rapitur (f. 156ra) ultra nubes usque ad

---

[1] i.e. 27 March, the date usually assigned in medieval calendars for the resurrection.

[2] See p. 66, n. 1.

[3] Ps. 54. 23.

from you.' And it happened as the man of God had foretold.

Two days later, that is, on the 27th of March, the day
on which the Redeemer of the world rose from the dead,[1]
Burthred came to Roger's cell with his two brothers, one a
canon, the other a layman, humbly asking to be granted
pardon. For he was aware, and he admitted it, that he had
gravely sinned against him, and especially against Christ's
handmaid Theodora. And now he came, he said, to release
her from her marriage vows and to submit himself to the
guidance of the old man. So, he declared, had it been en-
joined upon him by the queen of the world, Mary mother
of God, who two nights before had appeared to him in a
terrifying vision, harshly reproaching him for his needless
persecution of the sacred maiden. Roger, considering that
the two persons who accompanied him had little public
standing, wisely offered and obtained a few days' respite
whilst he himself thought over the matter and whilst Burthred produced other witnesses. At the end of the period
Burthred returned and according to the injunction which he
had received, released his wife, placing his right hand in the
right hand of Roger and promising and confirming her release in the presence of the following priests, namely Burthred who had married them, Robert, dean of Huntingdon,[2]
and Ralph of Flamstead,[3] and before five hermits who lived
with Roger. After this the man of God felt more safe: and
taking heart from the manifold virtues which he had proved
Christina possessed, he conceived the idea of leaving her as
successor to his hermitage. On this point he sometimes spoke
with her. And though she feared that this would be beyond
her capacities, she did not at once refuse, nor did she give her
consent: she acted in her usual manner and placed both
this and the charge of herself in the hands of the Lord[3] and the
Virgin Mary. Wherefore a wonderful thing, more wonderful
than any wonder, happened. For once when she was at prayer
and was shedding tears through her longing for heaven, she
was suddenly rapt above the clouds even to heaven, where

celum ubi conspicata reginam celesti in trono sedere vidit et
angelos illi gloriosos assistere. Quorum splendor solare iubar
tantum superabat quantum splendor solis quicquid in astris
rutilat. Nec tamen lumini quo circumdabatur illa que genuit
altissimum potuit comparari lumen angelorum. Quantum
igitur credas extitit ipsius facies clara que longe choruscabat
super ista omnia? Cum tamen vicissim intenderet. nunc in angelos nunc in dominam angelorum miro modo facilius pene-
trabat candentis obtutus splendorem circumfusum domine
quam qui circumfulgebat angelos. cum infirmitas humane
visionis habeat egrius inspicere clariora. Cercius igitur vidit
vultum illius quam angelicum. Cuius pulchritudinem cum
avidius intueretur [et] intuendo iocunditate delectaretur.
con[vertit] se regina illa ad unum astantium angelorum et
dixit ad illum: Interroga Christinam quid querit, quia dabo
illi quod pecierit.

43. Porro Christina ante reginam prope stetit, et loquentem ad angelum manifeste audivit. Procidensque ad terram
deorsum. uno [intui]tu vidit immensum mundum. At [ante]
omnia cellam Rogeri oratoriumque [eius] respiciebat. quod
nimis can[didum at]que nitidum sub se positum appa[re]bat.
[Et dixit]: utinam detur michi locus [iste ad habitandum].
Respondit imperatrix: [vere] dabitur et si plus vellet [illi]
ovancius daretur. Ex hoc itaque [cognovit] quod ad incola-
tum habi[tacul]i Rogero successura sit. Deinceps Rogerus
erat apud Deum et homines in magna sollicitudine de pro-
videnda heredi sue tutela cum necessariorum ope. Tandem
recordatus Eboracensis archiepiscopi[1] ⟨Turstini⟩. erat enim
talium fautor (f. 156rb) studiorum. mandavit q[uid de Chri-
sti]na vellet fieri. Turstinus [petiit] secretum virginis colloquium. Misit itaque senex et accersit ad se G[odeschal]dum
de Catendonia[2] et uxorem eius. homines sibi familiarissimos
atque [nobi]lissimos qui ad arbitrium Rogeri laudabiliter
vivebant sub lege coniugii. Locutus est in auribus eorum

---

[1] Thurstan, archbishop of York, elected 1114, consecrated 20 Oct. 1119, died
6 Feb. 1140.　　　　[2] Caddington lies two miles to the north of Markyate.

she saw the queen of heaven sitting on a throne and angels in brightness seated about her. Their brightness exceeded that of the sun by as much as the radiance of the sun exceeds that of the stars. Yet the light of the angels could not be compared to the light which surrounded her who was the mother of the Most High. What think you then was the brightness of her countenance which outshone all the rest? Yet as she gazed first at the angels and then at the mistress of the angels, by some marvellous power she was better able to see through the splendour that encompassed the mistress than through that which shone about the angels, though the weakness of human sight finds brighter things harder to bear. She saw her countenance therefore more clearly than that of the angels; and as she gazed upon her beauty the more fixedly and was the more filled with delight as she gazed, the queen turned to one of the angels standing by and said: 'Ask Christina what she wants, because I will give her whatever she asks.'

Now Christina was standing quite close to the queen and clearly heard her speaking to the angel. And falling downwards to the ground, she saw in one flash the whole wide world. But above all else she turned her eyes towards Roger's cell and chapel which she saw beneath her, shining brilliantly, and she said: 'I wish to have that place to dwell in.' 'She shall certainly have it,' replied the queen, 'and even more would gladly be given if she wanted it.' From then on, therefore, she knew that she would follow Roger as the tenant of that place. Consequently Roger was anxious both before God and men to provide a patron and the necessities of life for his successor. At length he bethought him of Archbishop Thurstan of York,[1] for he was a helpful promoter of such holy vocations. He sent to him therefore to ask what he thought should be done about Christina. Thurstan asked to have a private interview with the maiden. So the old man sent for Godescalc of Caddington[2] and his wife, people very close to his heart and of good family, who lived a happy married life under Roger's direction. He explained to them

quomo[do] vel qua causa oporteret Christinam ducere Redburnam.[1] Spondentibus illis et accipientibus licenciam abs-
cedendi. dixit homo Dei: Ite securi quoniam orabo pro
vobis, et fortasse non penitebit vos laboris quem pro Deo
et ipsius ancilla suscipitis. Abierunt ergo. uno tantum equo
contenti. Et factum est nitente iumento contra ascensum
per devia nemoris. sella solutis cingulis versata dilabitur ad
terram cum sessoribus suis. Illi quid facerent? Nox erat.
equus aufugerat. ipsi sine comite ac senio graves. nec si dies
esset sequi valentes. Tandem ipsa quoque sella derelicta.
quia nequiverunt tollere. pedites et palpitando per tenebras
[prout] potuerunt ceperunt ambulare. Sed cum gravaret eos
labor, contristati sunt dicentes: Ubi est promissio Dei? Non-
dum sermone completo. [ecce] equus infrenatus et insellatus
astitit iuxta illos ut agnus mansuetus. ad unum precisum
truncum qui vi[debatur] illic preparatus. ut servis Dei [ac-
commoda]ret ascendendi ministerium. [Quo] viso. Deo ac
famulo eius Rog[ero gracias] egerunt et ascenso iumento [ad
do]mum suam usque profecti sunt. [Et mane] facto rever-
tens Godeschaldus ad Rogerum susceptam ab eo Christinam
duxit privatim Redburnam ad archiepiscopum. Qui seorsum
diu locutus est cum illa et per ipsam discens [quid fieri]
oportuit (f. 156ᵛᵃ) . . . ex illa hora accepit eam [in su]a.[2] Promittensque illi quod post[modum] executus est: scilicet im-
muni[tatem] coniugii. confirmacionem voti. [pro] sponso
suo licenciam ducendi aliam uxorem per apostolicum: remisit
[ea]m. Permansit igitur Christina cum Roger[ro u]sque ad
obitum illius in heremo. [Tr]anslato autem eo ad celestia ubi
post tantos labores requiesceret in pace secura. necesse fuit
Christinam alio migrare ad declinandum furorem episcopi
Lincolnie. Cum igitur diffugiendo prius aliis latuisset in
locis: postremo commen[d]avit eam archiepiscopus cuidam

---

[1] Redbourn is some 4 miles from Markyate along the Roman road towards
St. Albans and London. It is the site of the cell of St. Albans which owned the only
surviving copy of Christina's life. This passage is taken from the *Gesta Abbatum*,
i. 100, where the corresponding excerpt from the *Vita* occurs.

[2] John 19. 27.

in what way and for what reason he wished them to con-
duct Christina to Redbourn.[1] When they had accepted the
charge and received permission to depart, the man of God
said to them: 'Go with all confidence because I shall pray
for you, and you will not, perhaps, have cause to rue the
trouble which you are taking for God and His handmaid.'
They departed, therefore, mounted on only one horse. And
it fell out that as the beast was labouring up a steep incline
through the woody paths the girths broke and the saddle
fell to the ground with the riders on it. What were they to
do? Night had fallen: the horse had run away; they were
burdened with age and all alone: even had it been daylight,
they could not have caught up with it. At last, leaving the
saddle where it was, because they could not carry it, they
began to walk on foot, groping their way in the darkness as
best they could. But when they grew weary, sadness overcame them and they complained, 'What has happened to the
promise of the man of God?' The words were hardly out of
their mouths, when a horse, saddled and bridled stood beside
them, quiet as a lamb, near a fallen tree trunk which seemed
put there on purpose to help the servants of God to mount.
When they saw it, they gave thanks to God and his servant
Roger and, mounting the beast, set off for their house. Next
morning Godescalc returned to Roger, took Christina from
him and led her secretly to the archbishop at Redbourn.
With her he talked privately for a long time and, learning
from her what needed doing, he took her from that time into
his keeping,[2] and made a promise which later on he fulfilled: namely, the annulment of her marriage, the confirmation of her vow, and permission for her husband to marry
another woman by apostolic indult. Then he sent her back
home. Christina remained therefore with Roger in his hermitage until his death. But when he had gone to heaven,
where he rested in peace after his many tribulations, it was
imperative that Christina should go elsewhere to avoid the
anger of the bishop of Lincoln. Therefore after she had first
taken various hiding-places, the archbishop commended her

clerico [si]bi familiari et amico. cuius nomen necessario sileo.
Erat autem hinc religiosus inde potens in seculo. quo utroque
freta munere: tucius habitabat Christina cum illo. Et certe
in inicio nullum cogitaverunt ad invicem: nisi castum [et]
spiritualem amorem. Sed hoc diu non [pat]iens diabolus
castitatis inimicus [de] ipsorum securitate et domestica con-
ver[sac]ione nactus oportunitatem. laten[ter] prius surrepsit
et callide. et post pau[lo] heu fortiter illos aggressus est impugnare. Et ignita iacula mittens tanta virtute institit. quod
viri fortitudinem penitus expugnavit. virginis autem et variis
titillacionibus carnem. cogi[tac]ionibus impetivit animum.
nunquam [tamen] ab ea prevaluit extorquere con[sensum].
Et multas quidem per hospitem [cui se s]ubdiderat: pessi-
mas artes atque [insidi]as adversus illam exercebat. [Quan]-
doque miser homo instigatus ve[nieba]t nudus ante illam
ardens et [a]mens. ac tam nefando genere se agens: quod a
turpitudine non possum illud prodere ⟨ne⟩ vel scribendo
cera⟨m⟩ vel eloquendo aerem ipsum polluam. Quandoque
procidens adorabat eam usque ad ter(f. 156ᵛᵇ)ram obsecrans
ut respiceret ac miseraretur suam miseriam. Illa vero ad-
oranti exprobrabat irreverenciam ordinis ipsius. et obsecran-
tem amovebat duris increpacionibus. Cumque laboravit et
ipsa incendio miserabili. prudenter tamen simulabat se nichil
tale pati. Unde nonnunquam virum illam non feminam esse
dicebat quem virago virtute virili predita recte effeminatum
appellare poterat.

44. Vis scire quam viriliter ipsa se continuerit in tam
grandi periculo? Violenter res[pu]ebat desideria sue carnis.
ne propria mem[bra] exhiberet adversum se arma iniquitatis.[1]
Protracta ieiunia. modicus cibus isque crudarum herbarum.
potus aque ad mensuram. noctes insomnes. severa verbera.
Et quod prestat his omnibus ... contribula[ciones que] laci-
vientem carnem lacerabant [et] edomabant. Deum in[voca]-

[1] Rom. 6. 13.

to the charge of a certain cleric, a close friend of his, whose name, I am under obligation not to divulge. He was at once a religious and a man of position in the world: and relying on this twofold status Christina felt the more safe in staying with him. And certainly at the beginning they had no feelings about each other, except chaste and spiritual affection. But the devil, the enemy of chastity, not brooking this for long, took advantage of their close companionship and feeling of security to insinuate himself first stealthily and with guile, than later on, alas, to assault them more openly. And, loosing his fiery darts, he pressed his attacks so vigorously that he completely overcame the man's resistance. But he could not wrest consent from the maiden, though he assailed her flesh with incitements to pleasure and her mind with impure thoughts. He used the person she was lodging with to play her many evil tricks and wiles. Sometimes the wretched man, out of his senses with passion, came before her without any clothes on and behaved in so scandalous a manner that I cannot make it known, lest I pollute the wax by writing it, or the air by saying it. Sometimes he fell on his face at her feet, pleading with her to look pityingly upon him and have compassion on his wretchedness. But as he lay there she upbraided him for showing so little respect for his calling, and with harsh reproaches silenced his pleadings. And though she herself was struggling with this wretched passion, she wisely pretended that she was untouched by it. Whence he sometimes said that she was more like a man than a woman, though she, with her more masculine qualities, might more justifiably have called him a woman.

Would you like to know how manfully she behaved in so imminent a danger? She violently resisted the desires of her flesh, lest her own members should become the agents of wickedness against her.[1] Long fastings, little food, and that only of raw herbs, a measure of water to drink, nights spent without sleep, harsh scourgings. And what was more effective than all these, . . . trials which tore and tamed her lascivious body. She called upon God without ceasing not to

bat assidue qui non sinat illam post virgin[ita]tis votum et
thori contemptum tam* [inter]minabiliter interire. uno tantum successu respirabat. quod scilicet presente p[atrono]
temperancius urebatur. in cuius [absen]cia sic estuabat intus:
ut de se p[uta]ret incendi posse vestimenta c[orpori] suo
adherencia. Si sibi sic esset [ipso pre]sente forsitan ut ipsam
an[cilla] non posset se continere. Il[li cum] aliquando per-
geret ad monast[erium] malignus spiritus suus videl[icet
clericus] apparuit ambulans ante [se in specie] cuiusdam
inmanis ursi: val[de ferocis] atque deformiter hispidi. [ut
impedi]ret eam ab ingressu monasteri[i. Ni]chil enim suas
tam retundebat sagit[tas] quam cum in oracione et lacrimis
sese virginea mactaret humilitas. Illa [vero] non retrahente
gradum absorbuit ibidem terra desperantem ini(f. 157ʳᵃ)
micum. Hoc [unum] . . . ex eius viscatis virgo reporta-
vit: quod plusquam binis ebdomatibus elanguit.

45. Nec tamen intermittebat impudicus clericus sollicitare languentem ea [intensitate] qua sollicitaverat valentem.
Usque dum dormienti nocte qua[dam apparuerunt] ei
terribiles hii tres [sancti] Iohannes evangelista. Benedictus
institutor monachorum. et Maria Magdalene. Quorum
Maria. ipsam enim presbiter colebat ac venerabatur specialiter. torvis illum respiciens oculis dure increpabat super
impia persecucione electe sponse regis altissimi. Pariterque
comminabatur quia si eam ultra molestaret: omnipotentis
iram et eternum interitum non evaderet. Qui visione territus
et a somno excitus: mutata mente virginem adiit et quid
viderit vel audierit aperiens veniamque delicti ab ea petens
et obtinens: de cetero emendavit. Verumtamen nec sic nec
ulla racione: deferbuit estus in virgine. Quo circa multo
tempore consumpto in iugi conflictu adversus infatigabilem
hostem. abominata ferale hospicium. rediit ad felicem ab
ipsa celi regina datum sibi solitudinis locum. ubi die ac
nocte procumbens in oracione. flendo. gemendo. rogabat
ab infestacione liberari. Cuius stimulos invita pertulit et in

---

* tam: ? dittograph of contemptum.

allow her, who had taken a vow of virginity and had refused the marriage bed, to perish for ever. Only one thing brought her respite, the presence of her patron, for then her passion abated: for in his absence she used to be so inwardly inflamed that she thought the clothes which clung to her body might be set on fire. Had this occurred whilst she was in his presence, the maiden might well have been unable to control herself. One day as she was going to the monastery, the cleric, her evil genius, appeared to her in the form of an enormous wild, ugly, furry bear, trying to prevent her from entering the monastery, for nothing repelled his attacks so effectively as the prayers and tears of the lowly ascetic maiden. But as she proceeded on her way the earth opened a pit for her despairing foe. . . . One result of this was that she was ill for a fortnight or more.

And yet the abandoned cleric did not cease from molesting the sick maiden with as much importunity as he had done when she was well. At last one night there appeared to him three saints, John the evangelist, Benedict the founder of monks, and Mary Magdalen, threatening him in his sleep. Of these Mary, for whom the priest had particular veneration, glared at him with piercing eyes, and reproached him harshly for his wicked persecution of the chosen spouse of the most high king. And at the same time she threatened him that if he troubled her any further, he would not escape the anger of almighty God and eternal damnation. Terrified at the vision and wakened from sleep, he went to the maiden in a changed mood and, revealing to her what he had seen and heard, begged and obtained her pardon: afterwards he changed his way of life. Nevertheless neither this nor anything else was able to cool the maiden's passion. And so, after a long time had been spent in constant warring against her tireless adversary, disgusted with that deadly lodging, she returned to the pleasant place in the wilderness bestowed on her by the queen of heaven; and there day and night she knelt in prayer, weeping, and lamenting, and begging to be freed from temptation. Even in the wilderness she un-

solitudine. Tunc benignus filius virginis respexit humilitatem ancille sue.[1] et contulit ei refrigerium inaudite gracie.
Ipse namque in forma parvuli venit inter brachia probate
sibi sponse. et per integrum diem mansit cum illa. non modo
sensibilis. sed eciam visibilis. Accipiens itaque virgo puerum
in manibus: gracias agens astrinxit sibi ad pectus. Et in-
estimabili de(f. 157rb)[lectacione] nunc et virginali illum in
suo tenebat sinu. nunc intra se immo per ipsam cratam
pectoris [apprehen]debat intuitu. Quis eruc[tabit memo]ri-
am abundancie suavitatis[2] qua [leta]batur mancipium ex hac
dignacio[ne] sui conditoris? Ex tunc ille lib[idinis] ardor ita
extinctus defecit. quod nun[quam] postea reviviscere potuit.
P[er] idem tempus interiit Lincolniensis ep[iscopus][3] accer-
rimus Christine persecutor. qui diut[ur]nam perpessus ultio-
nem subitanea morte vitam finivit. et alios a persequendo
Christi virgines exemplo suo deterruit.

46. Mansit igitur ancilla Dei tucior. in solitudine. pacem-
que diu desideratam amplectens secum retractabat quibus
misericordiis de quantis angustiis liberavit eam Christus.
Et obstupescens ad magnitudinem gracie: libera[to]ri suo
cotidie cum lacrimis offerebat hostiam laudis.[4] Hoc tunc
eius rarum gaudium. hoc erat omne studium. Dei laudibus
vacare. et in graciarum actione persistere. Interea disposuit
palam facere Dominus. quanti fuisset apud se meritum illius.
Erat quedam femina Cantuarie. non ignobilis genere. parentibus suis cara. post autem vilis et abiecta propter infirmitatem que* dicitur gutta [ca]duca. quam pro quodam temerario
ausu iam adulta incurrit et duobus annis feria tercia ad
horam terciam cum horrore pertulit. T[ercio] miseriarum
suarum anno venit [ad illam] missa a Deo beata martir et
vi[rgo Mar]gareta. et per visum monuit quod [cito] iret ad
amicam Dei Christinam [que non] longe a monasterio sancti
al[bani de]gebat in heremo. et aquam [quam] ipsa manibus

* que: quod *MS.*

---

[1] Luke 1. 48.   [2] Ps. 144. 7.
[3] He died 10 Jan. 1123 whilst riding with the king in his 'deer-fold' at Woodstock, and
was buried before the altar of St. Mary in the cathedral of Lincoln.   [4] Ps. 115. 17.

willingly felt its stings. Then the Son of the Virgin looked kindly down upon the low estate of His handmaid[1] and granted her the consolation of an unheard-of grace. For in the guise of a small child He came to the arms of his sorely tried spouse and remained with her a whole day, not only being felt but also seen. So the maiden took Him in her hands, gave thanks, and pressed Him to her bosom. And with immeasurable delight she held Him at one moment to her virginal breast, at another she felt His presence within her even through the barrier of her flesh. Who shall describe the abounding sweetness[2] with which the servant was filled by this condescension of her creator? From that moment the fire of lust was so completely extinguished that never afterwards could it be revived. About the same time the bishop of Lincoln,[3] Christina's most persistent persecutor, died; after suffering long punishment his life was cut short by sudden death, and by his example he deterred others from persecuting the virgins of Christ.

The maiden therefore remained in her solitude free from care: she took advantage of the peace which she had so long desired to meditate on the mercy with which Christ had delivered her from so many perils. And being astonished at the greatness of the grace, she offered a sacrifice of thanksgiving[4] every day to her deliverer. This then was her one joy, her only purpose, to spend her time in praising God and in giving thanks. In the meantime the Lord decided to make known how great her merit was in His sight. There was a woman of Canterbury of good family. She was dear to her parents, but owing to an infirmity called the falling sickness, which she had contracted through her rash fault when she was already grown up, she had become a nuisance to them and had been cast out: this sickness she endured for two years every Tuesday at nine o'clock. In the third year of her misery there came to her, sent by God, the blessed martyr and virgin Margaret, who in a vision admonished her to go to God's friend Christina, then dwelling in the hermitage not far from St. Alban's monastery, and to drink water which

et ore benedixerat [in] nomine summe trinitatis [sumeret].
(f. 157ᵛᵃ) et pristinam sanitatem recuperaret.

47. Nec mora mulier surrexit. et ad Christinam spe
adiuta celeriter pervenit. Cui primo suam indicavit culpam.
deinde miseriam. [tercio] loco revelacionem. Postremo petit
relevacionem. Illa vero recusante atque dicente hoc suum
non esse. nec illam ad se missam. sed forte somnio delusam
fuisse: perstitit improba mulier in precibus. adiungens sibi
presbiterum Alfuuinum. et non nullos alios qui affuerunt.
Quibus diu multum rogantibus ne graciam Dei que presto
erat ad subveniendum. illa non obtemperando contumaciter
averteret: non adquievit antequam spopondissent quod presbiter celebraret missam et reliqui se⟨cum⟩ in commune fla-
gitarent super hoc Dei misericordiam. Hoc iccirco fecit ut
non sibi sed illorum meritis videretur prestita gracia sanitatis.
Igitur feria iiiᵃ mane conveniunt simul in oratorium omni-
busque Deum invocantibus: Christina benedixit aquam. ac
dedit muliercule ad potandum. Et factum est in canone
misse. venit quidam inter eos decorus aspectu et venerabilis
amictu. qui libellum gestans in manu. pergensque ad mulierem ante faciem eius stetit. et libellum aperuit. Intellexit
itaque Christina que sola ex omnibus hoc [po]tuit videre.
quia Christus misso apostolo [suo]¹ sanaverat† mulierem. et
hoc ei [aperuit exp]leto officio. Illa vero quanquam [fidem
h]abuisset tamen adhuc dubita[ns] usque ad plenam terciam
in ora[torio] cum trepidacione sustinuit. Ni[chilo]minus
usque ad meridiem perman[sit] [ibi]dem. Tunc videns quia
trans[ierat] hora sua. cognovit perfecto* quod [erat sana]ta.
Et flens uberrime pre gau[dio roga]vit omnes ad agendum
gracias (f. 157ᵛᵇ) salvatori suo. Et [promisso] ab illa quod
nemini diceret vivente Christina quomodo sanata fuisset
dimiserunt eam a se.

48. Porro Christina ipsa que celitus procurabat salutem
aliis. non minimis tamen laborabat infirmitatibus quas ex
diversis calamitatibus [sustinuer]at: quas pridem tolerabat.

---

* perfecto *sic MS. for* profecto ?   † sanaverit *MS.*

¹ The Apostle mentioned was probably St. John the Evangelist, who was invoked
in cases of epilepsy, though St. John the Baptist was more commonly associated with
it, hence the name *mal de Saint Jean.*

she had blessed with her hands in the name of the Blessed Trinity. She would then receive back her former health.

Buoyed up by hope the woman arose without delay and came swiftly to Christina. To her she first confessed her fault, then her wretchedness, thirdly the revelation, finally she asked for a cure. Christina, however, refused and said that this was not her affair, that she was not sent to her, but that perhaps she had been deluded by a dream. The bold woman persisted in her entreaties, enlisting the help of Alfwyn, the priest, and some others who were present. And though they pleaded with Christina for a long time not to be obstinate and refuse the grace of God which was at hand to help, she would not agree until they had promised that the priest should celebrate Mass whilst the others should join with her in praying for the mercy of God on this matter. This she did to ensure that the grace of recovery should be attributed to their merits, not to hers. On the morning of the Tuesday, therefore, they gathered together in the chapel and all prayed to God whilst Christina blessed the water and gave it to the woman to drink. And during the canon of the Mass, a handsome figure of venerable mien, bearing a book in his hands, came towards the woman and stood before her and opened the book. And Christina, who was the only one of those present to see it, realized that Christ, having sent His apostle,[1] had cured the woman: and when Mass was over she told her so. Willing to believe, but full of doubt, the woman stayed in the chapel trembling until nine o'clock. Indeed, she stayed there until midday. And then, seeing that her hour had passed [without a relapse], she knew for certain that she was cured. And weeping copiously for joy, she asked them all to give thanks to her redeemer. And on her promising that during the lifetime of Christina she would tell no one how she was cured, they sent her away.

Christina, moreover, who obtained cures for others from heaven, suffered from grievous ailments which she had contracted through the various trials which she had endured.

Et indies accedentibus novis non decessere priores. Que
cum essent omnes inmedicabiles: nam humana industria
quicquid artis habebat in curam illarum nequicquam tem-
ptaverat: novissime divinitus contra spem novo genere sunt
curate. Et prius quidem quam dignanter Christus eam
sanaverit per genetricem suam de una tantum. sed molestis-
sima passione. deinde quam sublimiter de reliquis omnibus
simul missa sibi corona de celo in designacione⟨m⟩ virginalis
integritatis: fideliter accipe. Igitur passio quam paralysin
vocant: illam invasit que ab imis partibus usque supremum
capud repens tocius corporis alteram medietatem sibi vendi-
cavit. Ex morbo adhuc recenti tumebant iam atque rubebant
gene pacientis. Contrahebantur palpebre. turbabatur oculus.
sub ipso oculo videres cutem ita sine intervallo moveri: ac si
eam intus latens avicula iugi volatu percuteret. Quamobrem
probati medici ei* missi sunt. et studium suum antidotis.
diminucione sanguinis. aliisque medicandi generibus in eam
solerter exercuerunt. Ea vero que sperabant ei fore in salutem: in contrarium omnino sunt conversa. Quippe morbus
ille quem perimere debuerant econverso hiis irritatus et ex-
acerbatus in tantum illam absque remissione (f. 158ra) quinque continuis diebus afflixit. ut quod fuerat ei sanitas respectu
egritudinis ante medicamenta: hoc eidem fuerint ipse egri-
tudines respectu passionis que post est subsecuta. Ut autem
nichil deesset vel tempori ad perfectionem. vel dolori ad
gravedinem: senior quidam misit ei lectuarium quod vino
desperatum† et sic potatum: funditus omnem. ut ipse asseruit. extirparet et expelleret ab ea passionem. Sed ut Dei
sponsa divinam solummodo prestolaretur opem. tantum
prevaluit dolor extremus reliquis quantum primi cessere
secundis. Hunc tota die sexta sustinuit adeo validum: ut
sub omni momento putaretur ultimum exalatura spiritum.
At nocte insecuta nutu Dei qui septimo die requievit.[1] et‡
cum evigilasset se sibi redditam immo nobis deo gracias reperit. Nam quacumque hora desereret carnis sue angustias

---

* eo *MS.* † desperatum *MS. for* distemperatum. ‡ *sic MS.*

[1] Gen. 2. 2.

And as time went on new ones were added to the old. And as they were all incurable (for everything known to human science had been tried in vain), she was cured in the end, quite unexpectedly, by divine power. But first, listen carefully how appropriately Christ cured her of only one malady, and that the worst, through His Mother, and then how sublimely He cured her of all the rest altogether, by sending her a crown from heaven to signify her virginal integrity. The malady, which they call paralysis, attacked one half of her body, spreading from her lower limbs to the top of her head. As the result of a recent illness the cheeks of the patient were already swollen and inflamed. Her eyelids were contracted, her eyeball bloodshot, and underneath the eye you could see the skin flickering without stopping, as if there were a little bird inside it striking it with its wings. For this reason experienced physicians were sent to her and to the best of their power they practised their craft with medicines, blood-letting, and other kinds of treatment. But what they thought would bring relief had quite a contrary effect. Indeed the malady, which they ought to have cured, became on the contrary so irritated and inflamed, that she suffered from it for five whole days without ceasing, so that what her health had been in comparison with her sickness before treatment, now her sickness became in comparison with the maladies that followed. And that nothing should be lacking either in time for her perfection or in pain for her suffering, a certain old man sent her a tablet, which, dissolved in wine and drunk, would, he asserted, eradicate and expel that malady from her. But in order that the spouse of God should put her trust only in divine help, her final suffering was as much greater than all the rest as the second was greater than the first. So violent was it on the sixth day that at any moment she was expected to breathe her last. But on the following night, by the will of God (who rested on the seventh day),[1] when she woke up, she found herself restored to health and, thanks be to God, to us. For no matter at what hour she was released from the prison of her flesh,

carcerales cui dubium erat quod veniente sponso non statim
introiret cum eo ad nupcias? Senciens facilitatem palpebra-
rum. acumen oculi qui caligaverat. detumuisse genas. ceterorumque* subiecti corporis alleviacionem. quod tamen adhuc
pre admiracione minus credidit: accersitis puellis et allato
lumine comprobavit. Postera die convenientibus omnibus in
unum: initus est sermo de tam repentina sanitate domine.

49. Tunc una ex illis ait vidisse se prima vigilia noctis
per somnium quasi quandam magne auctoritatis matronam
adesse splendidissimo vultu. velatam caput niveo amictu:
distincto per latum aureis intexturis. necnon aureas habente
fimbrias in utroque capite. Et cum cedisset ante lectum
egrote: proferre pixidem in qua lectuarium attulerat insolite
(f. 158rb) fragrancie. Quod cum delicatissime prepar⟨ar⟩et.
ut cibaret illam: omnes simul eam corripere. dicendo cum
lacrimis. Noli domina noli lectuarium et laborem tuum per-
dere. quia vidimus illam quam curare satagis per simile
lectuarium quo utebatur heri vix mortem evasisse. Illa vero
pro nichilo ducere ignorancium verba. et propter quod
venerat sicut ceperat lectuario porrecto sanare languidam.
Hanc graciam curacionis illa⟨m⟩que revelacionem visionis eo
cum maiori gratulacione tunc retractabant. alterutrum et cu-
rata d[omina] et contuita famula. quod nec ista noverat visionem illius. nec illa sanitatem istius: antequam ad invicem
didisciscent. Vides ergo quam facile quam apte virtus Dei
per suam virginem matrem curavit suam virginem filiam
celesti medicamine. cui iudicavit indignum quicquid adhiberi
potuit a mortali homine.

50. Restat nunc aperire. ut a cetera morborum suorum
liberata sit multitudine. Siquidem plures erant numero.
Quorum singuli preponderabant paralysi. Quibus cotidie
minitantibus vitam tollere pacienti. illa mori nollet. nisi prius
sacrari meruisset. Porro venerunt ad illam frequenter non
ignobilium monasteriorum magni patres tam de remotis Anglie finibus quam de transmarinis amplitudinibus cupientes

---

* ceterorumque: ceterarumque *MS.*

who could doubt that her Spouse would come and lead her with Him to the nuptials? Feeling a movement of her eyelids, sight in her eye which had been blind, the swelling gone from her cheeks, and relief in the other limbs of her body, and hardly believing it through surprise, she called her maidens together and corroborated the fact with a lighted candle. On the following day, when they had come together, they began to talk about the sudden cure of their mistress.

Then one of them said that in the first watch of the night she had seen in a dream a woman of great authority, with a shining countenance, whose head was veiled in a snow-white coif, adorned across the breadth of it with gold embroidery and fringed on each end with gold. And when she had sat down before the patient's bed, she took out a small box in which she had brought an electuary of unusual fragrance. While she was daintily preparing to give it to her, all of them with tears in their eyes warned her, saying: 'Do not waste both your lozenge and your labour, lady, because we saw the woman you are trying to cure barely escape death after taking a similar electuary yesterday.' But she took no notice of what they were saying, and, carrying out the errand on which she had come, gave the lozenge to the sick woman and cured her. The patient who was cured and the maiden who had seen the dream discussed both cure and vision with all the greater joy, because before their talk the one was unaware of the vision, the other of restoration to health. You see how easily and how appropriately God cured His virgin daughter with heavenly medicine through His virgin Mother, deeming anything employed by mortal man to be unworthy of His spouse.

It now remains to reveal how she was released from her many other maladies, for they were not few. Each one was worse than the paralysis. As they threatened to cut short her life at any moment, she had no wish to die until she had been professed. Furthermore, she had frequent visits from the heads of celebrated monasteries in distant parts of England and from across the sea, who wished to take her away with

illam secum abducere. et corporali quoque presencia ipsius
loca sua fulsire vel exaltare. Maxime autem pontifex eboracensis desudabat ut honoraret eam aut preficeret virginibus
que sub nomine suo congregate fuerunt Eboraci.[1] aut trans-
mitteret ultra mare Marciniacum[2] vel certe ad Fontem
Everaldi.[3] Illa vero preelegit nostrum monasterium. tum
quia egregius athleta Christi Albanus in eo requiescit cor-
poraliter. quem (f. 158va) pre ceteris sibi dilectis martiribus
amabat specialiter. tum quia Rogerus heremita fuerat inde
monachus et in eo sepultus. tum quia te super omnes sub
Christo pastores in terra fortissime diligebat sicut [iugi] experimento probasti. tum quia in nostra congregacione nonnulli erant quorum animas omnibus aliorum locorum cariores
habebat. de quibus aliquot ipsa fecerat in ea monachos. Et
senciendum quod ipse benignissimus patronus noster Albanus [elegit] eam a domino quam in exco[lendo] et pro-
vehendo familiam suam haberet in terra cooperatricem et
postmodum in celo felicitatis eterne consortem.

51. Quocirca statuit in hoc monasterio professionem suam
facere et benediccionem optate sacracionis per episcopum
accipere. Sed intra semetipsam multum estuabat. ignorans
quid sibi faciendum. quid dicendum foret. quando sacra-
turus eam episcopus de virginitate sua requireret. Recor-
dabatur namque quos impetus cogitacionum quam ignotos
carnis sue stimulos sustinuerat nec audebat se profiteri de
tantis procellis integram evasisse. et si nusquam meminerit
se neque actu neque voluntate lapsam fuisse. Tandem convertit se toto corde ad castissimam Dei genitricem rogans
et petens ut ipsius interventu caperet ambiguitatis sue* certi-
tudinem. Dum autem in hoc studio erat: concepit quandam
fiduciam consequendi licenciam rei. quod eciam sperabat
fore circa festivitatem Assumpcionis genitricis Dei. Unde
nullam in animo potuit habere requiem donec videret hanc
festivitatem. Que quo magis appropinquabat eo magis anxia

---

* *lege* vice.

[1] The convent of St. Clement, founded between 1125 and 1135; Dugdale *Monasticon Anglicanum*, iv. 323; W. Farrar, *Early Yorkshire Charters*, Edinburgh, 1914, i. 278.

[2] Marcigny-les-Nonnains, founded in 1080 by St. Hugh of Cluny. It housed two kinds of nuns: those living in community and those living as recluses in separate cells: see the Life of St. Hugh of Gilo, edited by Huillier as an appendix to *Vie de S. Hugues*, Solesmes, 1888.

them and by her presence add importance and prestige to their places. Above all, the archbishop of York tried very hard to do her honour and to make her superior over the virgins whom he had gathered together under his name at York,[1] and if not, send her over the sea to Marcigny[2] or at least to Fontevrault.[3] But she preferred our monastery, both because the body of that celebrated martyr of Christ, Alban, rested there (whom she loved more than the other martyrs revered by her), and because Roger the hermit came from there and was there buried: also because, as you have learned by experience, she revered you more than all the pastors under Christ, and because there were in our community certain souls whom she cherished more than those of other monasteries, some of whom owed their monastic vocation to her. And it should be borne in mind that as our blessed patron St. Alban had her from the Lord as co-operator in building up and furthering his community on earth, so he had her afterwards as sharer of his eternal bliss in heaven.

For these reasons she decided that she would make her profession in this monastery and would receive her consecration from the bishop. But inwardly she was much troubled, not knowing what she should do, nor what she should say, when the bishop inquired during the ceremony of consecration about her virginity. For she was mindful of the thoughts and stings of the flesh with which she had been troubled, and even though she was not conscious of having fallen either in deed or in desire, she was chary of asserting that she had escaped unscathed. At last she turned to the most chaste Mother of God with her whole heart, pleading with her and asking her to intercede for release from this uncertainty. Whilst she was thus occupied, she began to feel more confident about gaining permission, and she hoped it would come about the feast of the Assumption of the Mother of God. For this reason she had no peace of mind until the feast day actually arrived. The nearer it

[3] Fontevrault, founded by Robert d'Arbrissel *c.* 1100 for women who had previously lived under his direction as recluses.

desiderio Christina tarditatem illius increpabat. Tandem
venit. nec statim satis(f. 158ᵛᵇ)factum est expectanti. Preterivit prima. preterivit secunda. preterierunt sex pariter
solemnitatis dies. in fideli tamen postulacione non tepuit
ullatenus. immo iugiter crevit et devocio. et spes.

52. Septima die quod est .xii. kalendas Septembris ante
lucem circa gallicinium surrexit et stetit ante lectum suum.
Iam enim hora transierat qua nocturna cantica celebrare
consueverat. Quod sic evenisse credens pigricia puellarum:
circumquaque omnes firmiter dormientes vidit. Ipsisque et
quicquid est auditu sensibile circumquaque contra solitum
alto silencio demersis. dum virgo staret et obstupesceret:
O ineffabilis pietas divine dignacionis. ecce circumsteterunt
illam iuvenes eximii decoris. Plures quidem aderant. sed illa
tres tantum discernere poterat. Hii salutantes eam. ave in-
quiunt virgo Christi. Ipse dominus omnium Ihesus Christus
mandat salutes tibi. Hoc dicto propius accesserunt. et hinc
et hinc stantes coronam quam secum attulerant. posuerunt
super caput eius dicentes. hanc tibi mittit unicus filius altissimi regis. et scito quod una es de suis propriis. Speciem
miraris et opus. que nequaquam mirareris si nosses artem
opificis. Erat quippe sicut ipsa asseruit. cuius species candore
nivem. splendore solem transcenderet. cuius forma describi.
cuius materia sciri nequiret. A parte posteriori pendebant
albe due tanquam vitte instar episcopalis mitre. descendentes
usque ad renes eius. Stetit itaque Christina inter angelos
ad se missos coronata a gallicinio noctis. quousque dies in-
caluit post ortum solis. Tunc enim angelis sese recipientibus
in celum: illa secum remansit. indubitanter agnoscens per
celestem coronam quod Christus eam mente et corpore
(f. 159ʳᵃ) virginem usque servaverat. Preterea se repperit ita
sanam ut infirmitatum quibus ante laboravit. nec minimam
quidem deinceps sentiret molestiam.

53. Commotus ex hiis demon et in nova bella prorumpens

approached, the more anxiously did Christina complain about the delay. At last it came, but her hopes were not immediately fulfilled. The first day passed; so did the second; so in the same way passed six days of the festival. She was unwearying in her entreaties; indeed, her devotion and hope increased as the days went by.

On the seventh day, that is 21 August, about cock-crow and before the dawn, she got up and stood before her couch. The hour had passed at which it was usual to sing the nocturns. Thinking that this was due to the laziness of the nuns, she noticed that, contrary to custom, all of them were fast asleep, and the world about them was sunk in deep silence. Whilst the virgin was standing still in astonishment (o ineffable kindness of divine condescension), behold, there gathered round her youths of extraordinary beauty. There were several present, but she could see only three. Addressing her, they said: 'Hail, virgin of Christ. The Lord of all, Jesus Christ Himself greets you.' And when they had said this, they approached nearer and, standing round about her, placed on her head a crown which they had brought with them, adding: 'This has been sent to you by the Son of the Most High King. And know that you are one of His own. You marvel at its beauty and the craftsmanship: but you would not marvel if you knew the art of the craftsman.' It was, as she averred, whiter than snow and brighter than the sun, of a beauty that could not be described and of a material that could not be discovered. From the back and reaching down to her waist hung two white fillets, like those of a bishop's mitre. Thus crowned, Christina stood in the midst of the angels who had been sent to her from cock-crow until the day grew warm after the rising of the sun. Then, as the angels withdrew to heaven, she remained alone, knowing for certain from the heavenly crown that Christ had preserved her chaste in mind and body. Furthermore, she felt so strong in health that never afterwards did she feel the slightest twinge from those maladies which had afflicted her earlier on.

Disturbed by these events, the demon launched out into

tam in intendendis (?) horribilibus: et immundis tormentis
amicam Ihesu Christi crebrius exagitavit. ut per plures annos
cum fessa sopori membra locaret. in lecto nec latus vertere
nec quoquam respicere presumeret. Videbatur enim sibi
quasi comprimendam vel nefaria demonis arte ad obscenitatis
queque ludibria se fore trahendam. Sed dum diutina hac
defatigacione virginis animus ad pravitatis non valeret deflecti consensum: falsis eam. quia veris non potuit infamacio-
nibus frangere molliens. inaudita incredibiliaque per virosas
membrorum suorum linguas. venenosus ipse serpens usque-
quaque machinabatur dispergere. Iam quisque sed quorum
erat mens perversa. malicia dictante hostisque fallentis versucia instigante. malum quod profundius fingere poterat dis-
seminare gaudebat. Se glorios⟨i⟩orem reputans. quisquis
urbanius de Christina falsidico nosset ore garrire. Sed inter
hec ancilla Christi gloriam suam habens testimonium consciencie[1] sue se ipsam pietati redemptoris. causam vero suam
divino committebat examini. Et ne salvatoris tramitem de-
siliret pio pro maledicentibus orabat[2] animo. Perpendens
demon. quia quicquid moliretur in iaculis fidei scuto[3] Christina propelleret. et quod amore Dei possessam mundialis
amor pervertere nequivisset: impudens audaxque preliator.
ut nil intemptatum relinqueret. per spiritum blasphemie
virginem impugnare non metuit. Illa fretus fiducia ut si fidem illius qualibet posset ob(f. 159rb)nubilare macula. venit
[fraude ut mal]icie sue macula virginis animum [ob]velaret.
Horrenda de Christo. de ipsius sancta genitrice detestanda
suggerebat nec [audi]ebatur. impetebat. sed profugabatur.
[ur]gebat sed obruebatur. Sed nec inauditus siluit. nec pro-
fugatus evanuit. nec ob[rutus] recessit. Nova namque semper
et exqu[isitio]ra resumens temptacionum tela. tanto instancius virginem impugnabat. quanto gravius a virgine tenera
se vinci doleret. Inventam in oratorio solam aliquando tam

---

[1] Cf. Rom. 2. 15.   [2] Cf. Luke 6. 28.   [3] Cf. Ephes. 6. 16.

new warfare, so terrorizing the friend of Christ with horrible
apparitions and unclean shapes that for many years afterwards, whenever she composed her weary limbs to rest,
she dared not turn upon her side nor look about her. For it
seemed to her that the devil might stifle her or inveigle her
by his wicked wiles into committing some unseemly wanton-
ness. But when he was foiled in his unwearying attempts to
debauch her mind, the poisonous serpent plotted to break
her steadfastness by creating false rumours and spreading
abroad unheard-of and incredible slanders through the bitter
tongues of his agents. Everyone with a perverse mind,
prompted by malice and goaded on by him who was always
a liar, took pleasure in disseminating every imaginable evil
of her, each one thinking himself to be the more admired,
the more wittily he fabricated lying tales about Christina.
The maiden of Christ, sustained in the midst of all this by
her good conscience,[1] committed herself to the loving care of
her Redeemer, and submitted her case to the judgement of
God. In order not to transgress our Lord's precept, she
prayed for them that reviled her.[2] The demon, seeing that all
his schemes were nullified by Christina's faith,[3] and that one
possessed, as she was, by the love of God could not be turned
aside by love of this world, to employ every stratagem in
his bold and ruthless warfare assaulted her with the spirit
of blasphemy. He was confident that if he could cloud her
faith with the slightest darkness, [he would win the fight].
He came by stealth and put evil thoughts into her mind. He
suggested horrible ideas about Christ, detestable notions
about His Mother. But she would not listen. He attacked
her, but was put to flight. He pressed his assaults, but was
routed. Even so he would not be silenced; when put to
flight, he would not disappear; when routed, he would not
retreat. Taking new and more elaborate weapons of temptation, he assaulted the virgin all the more intensely, as his
resentment grew to find a tender virgin more than a match
for him. When she was all by herself in the chapel he molested
her with such sordid apparitions, terrified her with such

informibus impetivit monstris. tantis minarum terruit asperis.
ut quilibet alius in amenciam facile rueret.

54. His et aliis ancilla Christi exagitata intus turbabatur
et quasi se derelictam a Domino metuens. quid ageret quo
se verteret. quove fugiendo hec demonum machinamenta
devi[ta]ret ignorabat. Tandem ad se reversa ex parteque
respectu clemencie roborata ecclesiam adiit. et quantis in talibus solebat suffusa lacrimis. totam se superne pietatis expo-
suit obtutibus. Recogitansque quia nil impunitum relinquit
Deus. et re[vol]vens si quo suo forte commisso tanta tamque
gravia sibi mala ingruerent. corpore prostrato. erecta mente.
Ihesum [su]per hiis interpellabat attencius. supra se [tem]-
ptari formidans. si moretur auxilium. cum nullius vires Deus
temptacionem excedere permittat.[1] Et ecce dum protensius
oracioni insisteret. dum cordis [inten]cio[ni] nullus obsisteret
pulvis: d[um terram] ipsam transcensa tota transferret[ur
in celum] audivit sed quibus auribus [nescio vox au]ditur
divina: Ne formides im[petus es]tuancium temptacionum
horrore[sque demonum] ⟨.⟩ cordis enim tui clavis in m[anu
mea est] seramque mentis tue cet[erique corporis] custodio
nec patebit cuiquam ingre[ssus] nisi mee disposicionis arbitrio. Nulla (f. 159ᵛᵃ) [interfu]it mora. sic se liberatam a
cunctis hiis sensit doloribus; ac si nullum eorum aliquando
vel semel sensisset: sed et reliquo tocius vite sue cursu [quo]-
ciens spiritualis huius clavis memo[raba]tur, a quacumque
temptacione a [quovi]sque gravabatur dolore, ut promissio-
[nis] fidem in ancilla sua Christus firmaret, [vel] celerrime
divinum senciebat levamen. In camino tamen paupertatis
tribulabatur adhuc Christi virgo illarum egens rerum qua-
rum egestas virtutes non minuit sed accumulat. Noluit enim
dilec[tus] et dilector sponsus et dominus su[a]m mercedem
presentem pro relictis: sibi quantocius centuplicare. ne
spiritualis amor exteriorum affluencia vel in modico defer-
veret. Sed nec ipsa facile vel necessaria sumebat ab aliquo.
nisi que vel puritatis amor. vel sancte pietatis viscera dele-
garent. Cum vero secretorum ille conscius oportunum censuit ut illi et in hiis subveniret: hoc modo disposuit.

---

[1] 1 Cor. 10. 13.

harsh threats that any other person would easily have gone out of his mind.

Harassed by these and other matters, the handmaid of Christ was inwardly disturbed and feared that God had abandoned her; she knew not what to do, where to turn, or where to go to avoid the machinations of the devil. At length, pulling herself together and taking courage from the remembrance of past mercies, she entered the church and, bathed in tears as was her wont, placed herself in the loving presence of God. But when she recalled that God leaves no sin unpunished, she wondered whether these many and grievous ills might not have come upon her through her own fault: she fell prostrate on the ground, raising her mind to God and praying earnestly about it, for she was afraid that if help was not quickly forthcoming, she would be tempted beyond her strength, though God allows no man to be tempted beyond his strength.[1] And behold, whilst she was praying and nothing distracted her attention, whilst she was rapt from earth to heaven, she heard (but with what ears I know not) the divine words: 'Be not afraid of these horrible temptations, for the key of your heart is in my safe keeping, and I keep guard over your mind and the rest of your body. No one can enter except by my permission.' Immediately she felt relief from all these trials, just as if she had never felt them at all; and during the rest of her life, as often as she was assailed by temptation or wearied with suffering, she remembered the key and as confirmation of Christ's promise to His handmaid she instantly experienced divine consolation. Yet she was still tried in the crucible of poverty, lacking those things the absence of which increases rather than lessens virtue. For her beloved and loving spouse the Lord did not wish to give her a hundredfold reward here for the things she had forsaken, lest earthly affluence should cool her spiritual love. She on her side would not receive what she needed from anyone unless it was prompted by spiritual love and holy compassion. But when He who knew her secrets thought it opportune to come to her aid even in these matters, this is the way He did it.

55. Erat in confinio heremi ipsius persona quedam nobilis
et potens utriusque sciencie gracia preditus abbas sancti
Albani dominus Galfridus. Hic in inicio prelacionis sue licet
in ordinis rigore et possessionum ampliacione domum sibi
commissam strenue gubernaret: ex parentum tamen nobilium
confluencia ridenteque fortuna plus iusto forsitan ceperat
insolescere ac suo sensui quam monachorum. quibus vero
religiosis pre[erat consiliis] magis credulus existere. [Huic
nulla] cum virgine Christi adhuc erat [cognitio] nisi quam
communis perferebat fa[ma. pri]mo namque sua per plurimum [nec acta] nec faciem nec familia[ritatem] cognoverat.
Disposuerat ta[men] subtilis ille rerum provisor et virgi[nis]
inopie per virum illum occurrere virique mores per suam
virginem ad se funditus revocare. cuius rei hoc primum fuit
(f. 159vb) inicium. Proposuerat aliquando abbas [mag]num
quid se facturum unde non [sine] capituli sui perturbacione
Deum intelligebat offendi. Sed quoniam magnanimus erat a
proposito facile nequibat deflecti. Tumidum etenim iter in-
gressus pertinaciam sepius subrogabat constancie. Propositum tamen ali[ter]* necdum cuiquam communicaverat

56. Vixerat autem in ecclesia sancti Albani sub prefato
abbate vir quidam magni testimonii notus ac familiaris Christi
virgini de qua loquimur Alveredus nomine. qui iam con-
summatus in bonis[1] vitam non amiserat sed mutaverat. Hic
visibiliter apparens Christine. et ut lucis amicus. speciosam
in manu accensamque gestans candelam taliter orsus est.
dicens. Domnus abbas Gaufridus absque capituli consultu.
tale quid. expressitque causam. statuere disponit. nec sine
piaculo. Deum enim in hoc si fecerit offendit. Per te res fiat
queso ne illud faciat. Hoc tibi enim ex Deo mandatum in-
dico. Hiis completis disparuit. Recogitans itaque virgo. secum cepit revolvere. utrumne mandatum expleat an desistat.
Si enim inquid explevero. michi forsitan erit incredulus. sin

* *Sic MS.: an pro alteri?*

1 Cf. Sap. 4. 13.

There was in the neighbourhood of that hermitage a certain noble and powerful person, versed in both kinds of knowledge, abbot Geoffrey of St. Albans. At the beginning of his prelacy he governed the house committed to him with strictness and kept it flourishing in possessions; but as fortune smiled upon him through the support of noble relatives, he began to grow more haughty than was right and relied more on his own judgement than on that of his monks, over whose religious counsels he presided. This man was quite unknown to the maiden of Christ except by common repute. She had never seen him nor had she any acquaintance with him. Nevertheless, it was through this man that God decided to provide for her needs and it was through His virgin that He decided to bring about this man's full conversion. And this was how it began. The abbot at one time had decided to carry out a project which he knew could not be accomplished without the annoyance of his chapter and offence against God. But as he was a man of great spirit, it was not easy to turn him from his course. When embarked on a high-handed course, he often allowed obstinacy to lend a hand to determination. His proposal, however, had not yet been shared with anyone.

Now there had lived in the monastery of St. Alban under the aforesaid abbot a certain man of great authority who was known and was friendly to the virgin of whom we are speaking: his name was Alvered, who, being perfected in good things[1], had not lost his life but changed it. He appeared in visible form to Christina, and carrying in his hand a burning candle, as befits a friend of light, began to speak thus: 'The Lord Abbot Geoffrey, without consulting the chapter, has decided on a course of action (and he explained the matter), which is not without danger, for if he carries it out he will offend God. I beg of you not to let him do it. This is the injunction I bring you from God.' And having said this, he disappeared. Thinking this over, the virgin began to consider whether she should fulfil the command or not. 'If I do it,' she said, 'perhaps he will not believe me. But if I do not, then I fear to incur the wrath of God.' The fear of God

autem: divinum incurrere formido iudicium. Vicit tamen
viri discrimen timor Dei. accersitoque quem habebat familiari. mandavit abbati que viderit. que audierit. et quomodo
pro tempore potuit ne faceret dis⟨s⟩uasit. Ille pro sompnio
mandatum reputans commotus intumuit. ac ne sompniis
crederet ancille Christi remandavit. Admiratus tamen virgini
esse revelata que solo tantum corde conceperat. [In]solentis
illa mandato percepto. nota recurrit ad confugia. ieiuniis.
vigiliis. et oracionibus De[um] (f. 160ʳᵃ) supplicans [ut quia]
illi suadere non valebat abbas a proposito per aliam aliquando
revocaretur personam. Nec aspernatus est dilecte sibi virginis p[reces]. Quid plura? Venit nox. in cuius crastino
ceptum complere pertinaci cum obstinacione vir predictus
affirmaverat. Corpori requiem indulturus. lectum peciit. In
prima autem noctis vigilia vidit plures nigras horridasque
circumstare personas. Que* facto impetu eum de lecto ex-
cuciunt. impellunt. suffocant. ac diversis excruciant modis.
Cumque iam expiraturus penis undique cingeretur. dever-
tens obtutus vidit predictum Alveredum oculis vultuque
similem indignanti. Neuter tamen alteri primum locutus est.
Sed inter angustias resumens vires. quid inquid domine
iubes ut faciam? Cui Alveredus. quasi fremebundus. Tu
bene ait nosti. mandatum enim habuisti nec a malo cessare
disposuisti. Sancte ingeminat ille. sancte Alverede miserere
mei. et a malo cessaturi. et mandatis abhinc illius prompcius
obtemperaturi. Quibus dictis subtrahitur Alveredus. tortori-
busque remotis tormenta cesserunt.

57. Mane facto neque enim differendum censuit. vera
namque fuerant flagella. convocat in partem quas familiari-
ores in ecclesia personas habebat. eisque rem ex ordine pandit. propositumque spondet dissolvere. Deus in commune

* Qui, *MS*.

overcame her fear of man, and, calling one of her close companions, she sent word to the abbot what she had seen
and heard and tried her best to dissuade him from doing
what he intended. He grew angry, considering the message
as a piece of nonsense, and sent the man back to the virgin
with the advice not to put her trust in dreams. Nevertheless
he was astonished that the virgin should be aware of something that was only in his own mind. When she received
the haughty abbot's message she had recourse to her usual
remedies, pleading with God in fastings, watchings, and
prayers that, as she could not persuade him, the abbot should
be diverted from his course by some other person. Nor did
God spurn the prayer of his beloved virgin. To be brief.
The night came after which the man already mentioned had
decided in his proud obstinacy to carry out the business he
had begun. He went to bed prepared to take some rest. But
in the first watch of the night, he saw several black and terrifying figures standing about him: who attacked him, threw
him out of bed, struck him, suffocated him, and in various
ways tormented him. When he was almost at his last breath,
as a result of the sufferings that encompassed him, turning his
gaze he saw the aforesaid Alvered, his eyes and countenance
blazing in anger. At first neither spoke to the other. But
plucking up his courage amidst the trials, the abbot said:
'What, my lord, do you wish me to do?' To whom Alvered
replied in an angry manner: 'You know well. For you have
received a message and yet you have made no move to with-
draw from your evil course.' 'Holy Alvered', he repeats,
'holy Alvered, have pity on me: I will not continue on my
evil bent and from now on will obey her messages promptly.'
At these words Alvered withdrew and as the torturers also
withdrew, the torments ceased.

Next morning he thought there should be no delay, for
his weals had been real. He called together on one side those
persons in the monastery who had his confidence and explained the matter to them in detail and promised to put an
end to the project. God was praised by them all, the holiness

laudatur. virginis sanctitas predicatur. eiusque monitis et mandatis ab abbate deinceps effectuosius obtemperatur. Memor itaque abbas promissi nec flagellorum immemor. ancillam Christi visitare maturat. debitum pro mandato. gracias pro liberacione referens. Spondet prohibita vitare. complere mandata. Loci illius se futurum adiutorem. tantum illam (f. 160ʳᵇ) apud Deum mereatur interventricem. Hec sunt tua Christe magnalia. qui graciam tuam uberius diffundere. et quibus ipse per quos disponis consulere prevales. Abhinc enim virgo tua per abbatem ⟨ab⟩ exteriorum attenuacione: abbas iam tuus per virginem ab interiorum aggravacione levatur. Denique vir ille famulam Christi postea frequentare. exhortaciones audire. monita suscipere. de incertis consulere. prohibita refugere. increpaciones sustinere. Et quoniam in agendis seculi admodum erat industrius. nec in regendis animabus minus sollicitus. multa sibi sepius ex hiis ingruebant que* quietem quam summopere querebat turbare videbantur. Que fastidiens. et ancillam Christi ac si asilum suum adeundo consulens. responsum illius pro divino suscipiebat oraculo illud recolens evangelicum. Non vos estis qui loquimini. sed spiritus patris vestri qui loquitur in vobis.[1] Desolatus siquidem consolatus abibat. fluctibus seculi exestuans. refrigeratus. Sed sub umbra illius quem desiderantes inveniunt[2] recedebat. ab amore tepens divino illa consulta se calere gaudebat.

58. Senciens itaque virgo Christina cor abbatis ad uberiores reddendos fructus habile. et quoniam mediante tantilla tot malorum eversor. et tot sanctorum executor. fieret studiorum. multo eum excoluit affectu. miroque sed sincero dilexit amore. Sic enim eam sanctus imbuerat spiritus ut nichil carn[ale vel] diligere nosset vel affectaret. Eratque amor mutuus. sed cuiusque pro modo sanctitatis. Illam ipse in

*que: qui *MS*.

[1] Matt. 10. 20.   [2] Cant. 2. 3.

of the virgin was spoken highly of and from that time her warnings and exhortations were implicitly obeyed by the abbot. Mindful therefore of his promise and not unmindful of his punishment, the abbot made haste to visit the virgin, acknowledging his debt to her for the message and thanking her for his deliverance. He promised to avoid everything unlawful, to fulfil her commands, and to help her convent in the future: all he asked was her intercession with God. These changes were wrought by Thee, o Christ, who in the outpouring of Thy grace art able to succour Thy friends through whomsoever Thou choosest. Hence Thy virgin was relieved of material poverty, whilst Thy abbot was freed from the burden of spiritual troubles. Ever after the man often visited the servant of Christ, heard her admonitions, accepted her advice, consulted her in doubts, avoided evil, bore her reproaches. And as he was very businesslike in worldly affairs and not less careful in his zeal for souls, this entailed much activity which seemed to disturb the peace which he so much desired. Growing weary of it, he went to the handmaid of Christ for advice as to a place of refuge and received her answer as if it were a divine oracle, mindful of the words of the Gospel: 'It is not ye that speak, but the Spirit of your Father which speaketh in you.'[1] If he went discomfited, he returned comforted; if weary of the vicissitudes of the world, he returned refreshed. He withdrew under the shadow of Him whom lovers find,[2] and when he grew cold in divine love, he was glad to realize that, after speaking with her, he grew fervent.

The virgin Christina, seeing that the abbot was ready to undertake greater tasks and that through the intervention of so lowly a person as herself he had overcome evil and was now bent on doing good, cherished him with great affection and loved him with a wonderful but pure love. For she was so imbued with the Holy Spirit that she neither knew nor wanted to like anything of this world. Their affection was mutual, but different according to their standards of holiness. He supported her in worldly matters: she commended

exterioribus sustentabat. ipsum illa suis sanctis precibus attencius Deo commendabat. Nec minus immo amplius de ipso quam de se sollicita. tanto studio eius invigilabat saluti (f. 160ᵛᵃ) ut quod dictu mirum est v[ix vel propius] vel remocius degens facto aut verbis Deum offendisset. quin illa per spiritum idem in instanti sciret. Nec dissimulabat cum terro[re] presentem arguere. quando senciebat absentem gravius deliquisse. meliora reputans amici vulnera.¹ quam inimici blandimenta. Quod ex presenti patebit exemplo.*

59. Dehinc si quando aliqua peccandi temptacione pulsaretur. habens eam quasi presentem quam vix aliquid de se latere sciebat: forti fidei clipeo temptacionem facile repellebat. Et quoniam flagellat Deus omnem filium quem recipit.² flagellavit abbatem illum egritudine gravi. ad mortis usque desperacionem. Et licet spes eius non esset in homine. set tamen spes eius multa in Deo per hominem. ancillam scilicet Dei Christinam. Unum erat enim remedium et illud magnum si ante mortem presenti virgini se posset commendare. Illam itaque proposuit invitandam. Presto sunt nuncii. preparantur et equi in crastino profecturi. Nichil horum Christine absconditum. Venerat autem ad eam vix pridie vir modestus ac religiosus eius autem commonachus. dicens eam. infirmantem abbatem necessario visitaturam. At illa: Addidisci inquit lilia [s]ine modo non esse deferenda. Ecclesio[la]m itaque suam ingreditur Deum lacrimo[sis] vincit precibus. ut sibi per graciam suam de abbatis valetudine [visu] atque audictu certum quiddam† innotescat. Erat enim ferens [colobatum?] quociens clausulam egredi[e]batur heremi.* Ecclesiam egressa: ad ipsius [   ]atur maceriam sentitque se transduci super conclave. videtque suum illum pro quo laboraverat uno in loco sedentem. caputque suum super baculum quem egritudinis causa ferre solebat reclinantem. (f. 160ᵛᵇ) . . . ne ecclesie monachos . . . dominum scilicet . . . Euisand' duasque Christi virgines Margaretam ipsius Christine sororem sancte simplicitatis et admirande h[onestatis] virginem. et [Ad]am que Margaretam quesivit

---

* Part of the text seems to be omitted.   † quiddam: quidem *MS.*

¹ Cf. Prov. 27. 6.   ² Heb. 12. 6.

him to God more earnestly in her prayers. If anything, she was more zealous for him than for herself and watched over his salvation with such care that, surprising to say, the abbot, whether near or far away, could not offend God, either in word or deed, without her knowing it instantly in the spirit. Nor did she make a secret of reproving him harshly in his presence, when she knew that in his absence he had sinned, thinking that the wounds of a friend are better than the flattery of an enemy.[1] This will be made clear from the present example.

Hence, whenever he was urged by temptation to sin, remembering that she was present (knowing scarcely anything escaped her) he repelled the temptation with the shield of faith. And as God scourges every one whom He receives,[2] He scourged that abbot with a grave malady even to the point of death. And though he put no trust in man, yet his hope was firm in God through man, that is, through the handmaid of Christ, Christina. One remedy he had left, and that not small, to commend himself to the maiden before he died. So he decided to invite her. Messengers and horses were got ready to set out on the morrow. Nothing of this escaped Christina. Almost the day before, one of his monks, a grave and religious man, had come to her saying that she ought to visit the abbot who was sick. She said: I have learned that one should not carry lilies without reason. So she went into her little chapel and prayed tearfully to God that a sure answer both by sight and hearing should be given her about the abbot's health. For she wore a short sleeveless tunic (?) whenever she left the enclosure of the hermitage. Coming out of the chapel she . . . the wall and felt herself carried over the chamber and saw him for whom she had prayed sitting in a corner and resting his head on a staff which he carried with him on account of his illness. [And she saw] the monks [of Saint Alban's] monastery . . . and two nuns, Margaret the sister of Christina, a virgin of admirable simplicity and uprightness and Ada (?), who had sought Margaret as a companion on visiting her mother, who was staying at West-

consociam [   ]sanda matrem apud Westmonasterium com-
morantem redibat et. ad visitandum quasi iam obiturum abbatem venerat. His attencius oblectata Cristina vocem abbatis
audivit in hec verba: Utinam placitum esset domino Christo
dominam meam Christinam scire quia hic considemus. Ap-
plaud[amus] respondent et monachi. Reversa ad se Christina. instancius post matutinas orat Dominum ut cito abbati
sue misericordie conferat levamen. Non negligens pius in-
dultor precibus ancille sue sanitatem confert abbati. leticiam
conventui ecclesieque sue fidelem conservat ministrum. Senciens itaque vir venerabilis se convalescere. voluit venire
virginem post matutinalem sinaxim servans a destinandis
nunciis itineris relaxacionem. Et quoniam plurimum virginis
vellet affatu consolari: voluntatem tamen presidens vicit
racio. In ipso crastino diluculo venit prefata .M. ad sororis
sue gratum habitaculum. Post oracionem dicto benedicite ut
mos est. nil autem loquendo:[1] imperat Christina sorori ut
taceat. replicansque quomodo viderit abbatem quid ab illo
audierit. cuncta ex ordine. et de considentibus: attestatur
.M. veritati miratur factum. glorificatque Deum qui virtu-
tem operatur in sanctis. Post recuperatam valitudinem non
immemor beneficiorum eius rediit abbas ad vere diligendam
sibi virginem. appetens dulci eius colloquio amplius ad
superna spirare. Nec frustratur voto. Accedens autem .M.
seriatim intimat abbati qualiter consessus eorum verbaque
prescripta sorori sue Christine spiritu (f. 161ra) docenti
fuerint revelata et quomodo ab ipsa didiscerit.

60. Veneratur ille virginem et [in ea] divinum quid solito
amplius in eadem amplectitur: frequentabat eciam ab hinc
multa cum devocione ipsius colloquium itineris labori fructu-
ram preferens itineris. Vix tamen aut nunquam illam adibat.
quin per spiritum eius presciret adventum et alicui de sociis
revelaret. Quoniam enim ad superna eum toto senciebat

---

[1] The reference is to the monastic custom of saying *Benedicite* before entering
upon any conversation. As soon as the Superior, or whoever was addressed, had
answered *Dominus*, the conversation could begin.

minster: and she was on the return journey to see the abbot who was dying. And with great delight she heard the abbot's voice saying: 'O that it would please our Lord Christ that my lady Christina knew we were sitting here together.' 'We agree', replied the monks. Christina came to herself and after matins prayed earnestly to the Lord to give quick and merciful relief to the abbot. Without delay the loving hearer of her prayers gave back health to the abbot, joy to the community, and a faithful servant to the church. The venerable man, feeling his strength returning, wished to pay his respects to the maiden. After the office of Matins . . .. And though he greatly desired the consolation of the virgin's company, yet reason prevailed over desire. On the following morning at daybreak Margaret, whom we have already mentioned, came to her sister's dwelling place. After a prayer, having said *Benedicite,* as the custom is, without saying anything else,[1] Christina ordered her sister to be silent, and related to her everything in detail: how she had seen the abbot, what she had heard from him, and what those seated had said. Margaret acknowledged the truth of it, marvelled at what had been done, and gave glory to God who works in His saints. After the abbot had recovered his health, not unmindful of her benefits, he returned to his beloved maiden, wishing to gain some spiritual profit from her sweet conversation. Nor was his wish unfulfilled. Margaret came to him, and told the abbot everything in detail, how all their words had been revealed to her sister Christina in the spirit and how she had learned everything from her.

He had a deep respect for the maiden and saw in her something divine and extraordinary. From that time forward he sought her company with great assiduity, thinking little of the fatigue of travelling in comparison with the profit gained from the journey. Nevertheless, he hardly, if ever, went to her without her knowing beforehand of his coming and revealing it to one of her companions. For as she became aware that he was making every effort to become more

tendere conatu, tanto circa eum sollicitabatur studio, ut in
suis quas fere continuabat lacrimosis precibus illum sibimet
in divina sepius preferret presencia. Et ut ipsa fatebatur.
nullus eorum erat quos multum habebat in Christo familiares. pro quo tanta devocionis et precum instancia Deo posset
supplicare. Unde factum est. ut incursiones demonum in-
sidiasque paratas sepe previdens. sepe diu interpellando per-
vertens dilectum suum. ex hinc enim sic eum vocare solebat.
in tranquillo figere laborabat statu.

61. In crastino vero Pentecostes convocatis tribus de
secum morantibus puellis. iam enim crescente fama Christine crescebat numerus puellarum. predixit eis precordialem
suum ipso die affuturum. Monuit honeste cuncta componere.
religiose se habere. ne religionis amicus quicquam quod sibi
displiceret offenderet. Credule ille. spem enim sumebant de
preteritis. mandatis parent domine. Moratur abbas. Proposuerat enim nullum adventus sui cuiquam fieri indicium.
nisi forte virginem latere potuisset. Celebratur missa. nuncius
abbatis nullus precedit. Respectant se invicem virgines facti
moram admodum admirantes. Hoc solum sibi certum erat.
Christinam (f. 161rb) nec falli posse nec fallere. Cum ecce
preveniens nuncius. omnes de adventu letificat abbatis. Ad-
venit vir venerandus. colloquium dulce et salutare tractat
cum virgine. Interque loquendo. nunc scio ait subitum nostrum vos adventum latuisse. Advocat illa cum quibus de hiis
prius contulerat. M. scilicet sororem et secretorum suorum
consciam et iubet ut edicant quid de eius audierint adventu.
Fatentur verum. veritatis obtemperantes amice. Laus Dei in
commune resonat. spiritus* sancti gracia diffusius[1] eo die
sentitur.

62. Diu siquidem in nota est† heremo conversata. priusquam ab episcopo virginee humilitatis. et humilis virginitatis sacratum susciperet signum. Monebatur autem a multis

---

* spiritus+quidem est *MS.*   † est+in, *MS. expunct.*
[1] Cf. Rom. 5. 5.

spiritual, she was so zealous on his account that she prayed for him tearfully almost all the time and in God's presence considered him more than herself. And, as she admitted, there was none of those who were dear to her for whom she could plead to God with such devotion and instant prayer. Hence it came about that she often foresaw the assaults and snares which the demons had prepared and by assiduous prayer often warded them off from her beloved (for this was what she used to call him), and laboured to establish him in a state of peace.

On the morrow of Whitsunday, having called together three of the maidens who were living with her (for with her growing reputation the number of her maidens grew), she foretold that her beloved would come on that day. She ordered them to put everything in good order and to behave devoutly lest the friend of devotion should find anything that displeased him. Believing what she said (for past events gave them confidence), they obeyed their mistress. The abbot was long in coming. For he had decided to tell no one of his visit, so that, if possible, the maiden might not know. Mass was said: no messenger came from the abbot. The maidens looked at one another, very surprised at the delay. Only one thing was certain: Christina could not have misled them or have made a mistake. Suddenly the arrival of a messenger gladdened their hearts at the abbot's coming. The venerable man arrived, and had an edifying talk with the maiden. Whilst they were speaking, he said: 'This time I know my sudden coming took you by surprise.' She called to her her sister Margaret who knew her secrets, and the others to whom she had spoken on this matter and ordered them to say openly what they had heard about his visit. They admitted it was true, obeying the friend of truth. Praise to God rose from all: and the grace of the Holy Spirit was felt more abundantly[1] that day.

She dwelt for a long time in the hermitage which we know before she received from the bishop the consecration of her virginal humility and humble virginity. By many wise and

magna sapientibus et religiosis ipsisque familiaribus et ami-
cis suis. ut collum iugo subderet et animi votum sacracionis
dignitate firmaret. esseque congruum. ut sponsa Christi
proposito. Christi sponsalibus insigniretur. Differebat illa.
incertum habens si maneret in loco utpote que remotas
olim disposuerat petere terras si forte civitas incognita latebras alicubi pro Christo fovere potuisset. Tandem divinitus
inspirata ac crebris supplicacionibus. et humili dulcedine
memorati abbatis devicta assensum prebuit suggerentibus.
Die itaque festo Sancti Mathei.[1] qui et ipse primus virginum
consecrator[2] describitur. ab Alexandro episcopo Lincolnie[3]
virgo Christo consecratur.

63. Quarto autem ipsius sacracionis anno circa octabas
epiphanie. gravi febrium abbas vexatur dolore. Ex misera-
cionibus enim suis Deus que multe sunt[4] disposuit eum
flagellis ad coronam cedere. quem prius ad coronam* dignatus est flagellare. Remocius (f. 161ᵛᵃ) discedit ab abbate
sullevamen gravis invalitudinis. Mandat tamen probate pa-
trone ut quemadmodum in ceteris et in hac sibi subveniat
necessitate. Intrat illa notum asilum. corpus prosternitur.
manant lacrime. cordeque clamante. preces a Domino. sani-
tasque suscipitur ab egroto. Iamque toto conceptu spiritu⟨s⟩.
precum sentit efficaciam. voce sibi celitus in hunc modum
delapsa: Scias pro certo carissimum tuum te proxima .vᵃ.
feria gaudenter visitaturum. Tunc enim erat dies dominicus.
Que mox oratorium egressa. redituro sic dicit nuncio. Quam
tocius reverteris illo die cum huc properantes ad talem de-
veneritis locum. dicito ex me domino tuo: Cras in ollam can-
didi dimittentur lapilli. Urbanum sane proverbium quod in
prosperis agendorum dicitur successibus. Tanquam diceret:
Tunc sospitate suscepta tuus ad me maturabit dominus. Cui
ille certum se de domini sui suspicans infirmitate. Hoc inquit

---

* coronam, *an pro* correctionem?

[1] 21 Sept.

[2] Cf. *The Apostolic History of Pseudo-Abdias*, vii. 13, ed. M. R. James in *The Apocryphal New Testament*, Oxford, 1953, p. 467.

[3] Consecrated 22 July 1123, died 1148.   [4] 1 Paralip. 21. 13.

religious persons, and close connexions and friends, she was encouraged to put herself under obedience and to confirm her vow by solemn consecration, saying that it was fitting that as her vow had made her a spouse of Christ, she should be marked out by due ceremony. She put it off, uncertain whether she would remain in that place, since earlier on she had made up her mind to retire to some distant country where a town off the beaten track might provide a hidden refuge. At length, inspired by God and persuaded by the frequent pleadings and humble sweetness of the abbot already mentioned, she gave her consent to their suggestion. And so on the feast of St. Matthew,[1] who is said to have been the first consecrator of virgins,[2] the virgin of Christ was consecrated by Alexander, bishop of Lincoln.[3]

In the fourth year of her profession, about the octave of Epiphany, the abbot was troubled with severe pains and fever. Out of his great compassion[4] God arranged to beat him with scourges for his benefit, whom previously He had scourged for his punishment. She who was the soother of his grave infirmity was far distant from the abbot. However, he sent a message to his faithful protectress, asking her to come to his aid in this crisis as she had in others. She went to her usual refuge: prostrated on the ground, wept tears and, as her heart cried out for him, her prayers were heard by the Lord, and the sick man's health was restored. And already in her inward being she felt the efficacy of her prayers as a voice came from heaven saying: 'Know for certain that your beloved will come joyfully to see you five days from now' (Thursday). It was then Sunday. Coming quickly from the chapel, she said to the messenger, who was about to depart: 'Return as quickly as you can: when you both reach such a place on the day you are coming here, tell your master from me: "Tomorrow white stones will be thrown into the pot."' A charming proverb which is quoted when success is assured. As if to say: 'At that time, when your master has recovered his health, he will hasten to me.' But he, convinced of his master's ill-health, answered: 'Mistress, this cannot be. For he is

domina fieri non potest. Tanto enim febrium estu. tanto
vicissim frigoris laborat contractu ut vix iacere. ne dum
equitare valeat. Vade replicat illa. vade. et certus de ipsius
salute. sicut iniunctum est. tibi facito. Illud summopere pre-
cans ne vel leve cuiquam verbum super hiis ante destinatum
proferas locum. Suscipiens ille mandatum. cavens prohibitis
revertitur. dominumque convalescentem. sed de profeccione
nichil loquentem invenit. Dissimulat audita donec probetur
exitus. Die vero denunciato illucescente: paratis equis et
sociis festinatur ad virginem. prefato approximatur loco.
ubi tunc demum Christine mandata suo nuncius defert
domino. Obstupefactus ille. Novitne. inquit. virgo tam celerem meam sospitatem hodiernumque profectum? Novit respondit talibus manifestat (f. 161vb) indiciis. de preteritis vir
prudens presencia confirmans et salvatoris clemenciam et
virginis circa se securam veneratur sollicitudinem.

64. Quadam autem nocte nativitatis dominice dum inter
matutina officia tanto puerperio prona mente intenderet. et
intendendo ad illius se desiderium magis ac magis accenderet:
occurrit ei sicut et semper in talibus dilecti ac familiaris sui
memoria. Cumque pro illo quam pro se modo quodam plus
esset sollicita: ecce vox ad eam dicens: vis illum pro quo
sollicitaris. quove modo sit cernere? Illa vero respondente
sed opto: vidit abbatem .G. de illo enim sermo est: rubea
indutum cappa. cuius facies non simplici candore sed candori
mixto rubore prefulgidam. humanum vultum transcendere
videbatur et gloriam. Cuius aspectu refocillata Christina.
tanto ab hinc eam sibi devinxit amore ut nullius gracia.
nullius odio. ipsum esse sibi familiarissimum. exigente racione predicare desisteret. Nec sine multorum livido dente.[1]
Erant enim quam plurimi qui similis vite sanctitatem assequi
volentes. similem Christine quem in abbatem exercebat
amorem assequi cupiebant. Sed ab amore decidentes. ob-
loquiis pascebantur. Cumque post biduum: tercio scilicet

[1] Horat. *Epod.* 5. 47.

suffering with hot fever and at times with pinching cold, that he can scarcely lie in bed, much less ride a horse.' 'Go', she replied: 'go and, assured of his recovery, do what I have told you. But above all, I beg you not to breathe a word of this until you reach the place I have mentioned.' Accepting his orders and taking care not to disobey, he returns and finds his master already convalescing, but saying nothing about making a journey. He keeps secret what he has heard until it is proved by facts. Early on the day which had been foretold, horses and retinue were prepared and he hastens to the maiden. They reach the spot aforementioned, and then at last he gives Christina's message to his master. He is astounded. 'Did the maiden know', he asks, 'that my recovery would be so sudden and that I should make the journey today?' 'She knew', he replies: 'she made it known with such and such signs.' The prudent man, confirming the present from the past, was aware both of the Saviour's mercy and the maiden's safe care of him.

One Christmas night when she was meditating deeply during matins on this great birth, and in her meditation became more and more inflamed with desire for it, there came to her, at such moments, the remembrance of her beloved friend. And as she was in some way more anxious for him than for herself, a voice came to her saying: 'Would you like to see him for whom you are anxious, and how he is?' And when she answered: 'I would', she saw Abbot Geoffrey (for it is of him we are speaking) vested in a red cope, his countenance shining not with a simple brightness but with brightness mixed with ruddiness, transcending human beauty and glory. At this sight Christina was encouraged, and from that time she became so deeply attached to him that no favour nor malice could prevent her from calling him her closest friend when reason demanded it. Nor did this happen without the wagging of spiteful tongues.[1] For there were several who wished to reach the same holiness of life and to gain the same affection from her as did the abbot. But falling out of favour, they veiled their disappointment by speaking

ipsius natalis dominici die ad eam visitandam vir sancte
dilectionis Alexander. qui et ipse eiusdem ẏppo*prior erat
ecclesie venisset. inquisitus de hiis alba cappa indutum re-
spondisset abbatem: recole cercius quod verum est ait virgo.
quia rubea cappa indutum ea nocte presens ego conspexi.
Ille sic fuisse non sine admiracione memorans Christum in
Christina devocius glorificavit. Quomodo autem hanc visionem viderit. cum ipsa bene sciret. ab ea usque presens nullo
modo (f. 162ʳᵃ) potuimus elicere.

65. Dehinc vir ille spem omnem subtrahens seculo figens
in Christo totus sudat in utile. terrenis animo renuncians.
supernis inhians. in hoc tamen consolari gestiens. sed si
nesciente seculo. seculi divicias Christi posset erogare pau-
peribus.¹ Iam siquidem iniustum adimens questum. iuste
possessa iustis expendebat donariis. Quod enim in seculi
fastu prius dispergere. nunc inclusis. heremitis. ceterisque
necessitatem pacientibus quo latencius poterat impertiri
satagebat. apostolico dignus testimonio. tanquam nichil
habens et omnia possidens.² Quod totum gracia⟨e⟩ Dei. vir-
ginisque sancte deferebat sollicitudini. Tantumque a se sed
qualis fuerat alienatus est: ut qui prius mundi gl⟨orie⟩ de-
sudaverat. nunc pro tocius mundi machina nec in modico
Deum offenderet. unum tamen erat quod artius precupiebat
rescire de virgine. Cuius scilicet puritatis studio. quarumve
prerogativa virtutum tanta fuerit donata gracia. ut occulta
vel remocius acta. mox spiritu docente presenserit. Sepe
enim nunc cum de nuper gestis vel secretis suis quicquam
illi propalare disponeret nec me latet respondebat illa. edice-
batque seriatim quod se dicturum pararat. Unde multa recogitans animo secum plura revolvens excogitabat qualiter
super hac convenire causa valeret. Si enim tepide negligen-
ciam. si autem improbe temeritatem formidabat. hiis simili-
busque curis sepius concussus. dies in vesperam. noctesque
fere ducebat insompnes.

---

* *i.e.* hypo.

¹ Regula S. Benedicti, cap. 4.   ² 2 Cor. 6. 10.

ill of her. And after two days, namely on the third day after Christmas, when Alexander who was the sub-prior of the same church came to visit her, being asked about it, he replied that the abbot had been vested in a white cope: the maiden said: 'Think carefully again if that is really true, because on that night I was there and saw him vested in a red cope.' Then he recalled with some astonishment that this was so, and glorified Christ devoutly in Christina. How she saw this vision (though she herself well knows) we have never been able to elicit from her up to the present.

From that time forth the abbot withdrew all his hope from the world and fixed it on Christ; he laboured wholeheartedly on what was useful, manfully renouncing the things of the earth and longing for those of heaven. Nevertheless one consolation gladdened him that, unknown to the world, he could bestow his earthly riches on the poor of Christ.[1] Indeed, far from seeking unjust gain, he lavished his just possessions on worthy aims. What he had expended formerly on worldly ostentation, now he sought to bestow as unostentatiously as possible on hermits, recluses, and others who were in need, thus deserving the apostle's commendation 'as having nothing and possessing all things'.[2] All this he attributed to the grace of God and the watchful care of the maiden. And he became so changed a man from what he once was, that he, who had striven formerly for material glory, would not now offend God in the slightest way for all the world. There was one thing above all which he wished to learn about the maiden: and that was, by what practice of purity or what prerogative of virtue such grace was given her that by the prompting of the Spirit she soon knew his deeds beforehand whether done secretly or far away. When he spoke of such, she would reply: 'I know all about it', and would then tell him in detail what he was going to say. Wherefore giving it much thought and turning it over in his mind, he wondered how he could find out about it. For if he went about it lackadaisically he feared negligence; if boldly, rashness. Puzzled by these and similar problems, he passed whole days until evening, and spent many sleepless nights.

66. Una vero nocte vidit floridam se pre manibus herbam tenere cuius succus repellendis admodum valeret langoribus. Quam si forcius premeret minus eliceret de succo: si vero dulcius et modestius: votum exequeretur (f. 162ʳᵇ) compressor. Nec mane distulit. quin comitante viro religioso Evisando* ad heremum sibi proficisceretur dilectam. At inter eundum† conferens de sompnio: herbam Cristinam. florem vero virginitatis interpretatur honorem. Quam nullius improbitatis impetu. sed dulci blandoque affatu disseruit percunctandam. Quod pluries postea experti sumus. Revelavit cuncta Christine. Summo etenim mane. auditis que Dei sunt exit ecclesiam. ecclesieque contiguam herbis consitam deambulat areolam. ac quam primum forte offendit herbam camillamⁱ surripit. et pie manibus deferens. venientique abbati quasi eum gratulatura procedens. hec inquid herba non est quam hac nocte in visione vidisti? Ostendit et herbam. Hoc enim sibi vocis delapse revelacione‡ didicerat. Audita mirantur abbas et ⟨Evisandus⟩, ille visionem. uterque verba per viam collata referunt. glorificantes Deum qui que sapientibus velet prudentibus revelare dignatur parvulis.² Sicque misericors Deus et curas inquisitoris expl⟨e⟩vit. et virginem dilectam dilecciorem exhibuit abbati.

67. Accidit iterum eundem dilectum suum in antelucano vigilanter lecto suo sedere et quibusdam profuturis intendere. Circumducens itaque oculorum orbes vidit manifeste. neque enim somnium erat. vidit inquam eandem ancillam Christi. suo assistentem capiti similem sollicite qualiter se erga [Deum] in suis haberet secretis: vidit [illam] inter notas sed verbum cum illa nullum conferre poterat. Stupore tamen perfusus et gaudio. noctem reliquam magnum habuit emolumentum. Mane facto cum surrexisset advocari fecit quandam parentem suam Leticiam nomine die ipso ad virginis heremum profecturam. Erat autem et ipsa sanctimonialem ducens vitam. Vade (f. 162ᵛᵃ) inquid. et dic dilecte domine tue. quia

---

* Evisandus *MS*.   † eundem *MS*.   ‡ reuelacionem *MS*.

ⁱ Or *Camelina sativa*, i.e. Gold of Pleasure, a plant producing a kind of oil.
² Matt. 11. 25.

One night, however, he saw himself holding a flowering herb in his hands, the juice of which was very efficacious for driving away maladies. If he squeezed it strongly, little juice came out, but if gently and quietly he would get what he wanted. Next morning he hastened to accompany a religious man, Evisandus, on a visit to the hermitage which he loved. And in discussing the dream as they went, the herb was interpreted as Christina, the flower as the honour of her virginity; he said she should be approached not on impulse, but gently and kindly. This we often experienced later on. He told everything to Christina. For at a very early hour, after having heard the divine Office, she came out of the church and walked in a little enclosure near-by filled with flowers, and plucked the first flower, camilla,[1] which she found. And taking it reverently in her hands, she went towards the abbot as he approached and as if about to greet him said: 'This is the flower, is it not, which you saw in your vision during the night?' And she showed him the plant. For she had been told this by a voice which came to her from above. The abbot and Evisandus were astonished at what they heard; the first recounted his vision, both of them their conversation on the way, and glorified God who reveals to the lowly what he hides from the wise and prudent.[2] In this manner God in his mercy solved the problems of the inquirer and made the loved maiden more lovable to the abbot.

Again it happened that her beloved was sitting awake on his bed in the early hours of the morning and thinking about certain things that would be useful, and as he turned his eyes this way and that, he saw clearly (for it was no dream), he saw clearly, I say, the handmaid of Christ near his head like one anxious to see how he bore himself towards God in his innermost thoughts: he saw her but could not speak with her. However, filled with surprise and joy, he spent the rest of the night with profit. When morning came, he rose and summoned to him one of his relatives named Lettice, who was going that day to the hermitage. She also was leading the life of a nun. 'Go', he said, 'and tell your beloved

manifesta est sollicitudo sua de me. Vere enim quia vigilando vidi. quod ⟨h⟩ac nocte visitaverit me. locumque tempus et horam annexuit. Estimabat enim hoc Christinam latere. Adveniens Leticia illa Christi virgini mandatum cepit iniunctum exsolvere. Ad primum itaque verbum. ne amplius respondit illa. Mandansque sororem beate memorie virginem .M. voluit enim eam vocare ne forte suspicioni esset Leticie: precepit ei. Dic inquiens audiente Leticia quid ego tibi primo diluculo. de illo intimavi somnio. Et illa. Dixisti domina. inquid pro certo ⟨h⟩ac nocte. tali loco et hora. ad eum visendum sua venerit puella. Sic enim se humilitatis gracia vocare consuerat. Et adiunxit.* quod si tale quid in tempore beati Gregorii accidisset: mandasset illud memorie. quamvis res parva sit et memoria parum digna. Respondique non parum quid esse. sed mirabile: posterisque memorabile. Audiens hec prefata Leticia. edificata plurimum Deum glorificavit in sanctis:[1] A Domino factum est istud et est mirabile in oculis nostris.[2]

68. Visitat de hinc vir misericordie deditus amplius locum. virginis frequentat colloquium. providet domui. et dispositor efficitur agendorum. Intendit ille virgini ministrare subsidia. Desudat illa virum accumulare virtutibus. tanto studio Deum precibus flectit [ut hi]is inherens. presens aliquando presentem nesciat virum. Post perceptam enim eucharistiam. vel in ipsa misse celebracione communicabat. nam et mense Christi fere quociens abbas Verbi divina celebrat misteria. sic mente excedebat Deo.[3] ut terrena nesciens. solius faciem creatoris intenderet contemplari. Quo cognito. abbas in hoc aiebat: multa mea gloriacio si in presenti mei oblita sibi me (f. 162vb) presentes. ob cuius presencie dulcedinem hic me presentem sentire non prevales.

69. Iam ancilla Christi mentem vigiliis. corpus exercens

sic MS. pro adiunxisti?

[1] Cf. 2 Thess. 1. 10.　　[2] Matt. 21. 42.　　[3] Cf. 2 Cor. 5. 13.

mistress, that her anxiety for me is obvious. For as I lay
awake, I saw her visiting me last night' (and he mentioned
the place, time, and hour). For he thought that Christina
knew nothing of it. When Lettice came, she began the message to the maiden of Christ. And at the first word, she
replied: 'No more'. And sending for her sister Margaret,
the virgin of blessed memory (for she wished to call
her, for fear Lettice might be suspicious), she gave her
an order: 'Tell me in Lettice's hearing what I mentioned to
you early this morning about that dream.' And she replied:
'You said for certain that last night at such a place and hour
his daughter had been to see him' (for this was the way she
used to call herself out of humility). 'And you added that if
such a thing had happened in the time of blessed Gregory
he would have preserved it for posterity, even though it was
a small thing. I said it was not small but something marvellous and worthy to be remembered by those who come after
us.' On hearing this the aforementioned Lettice was greatly
edified and glorified God in His saints:[1] 'This is the Lord's
doing and it is wonderful in our eyes.'[2]

Henceforward the man devoted to good works visited the
place even more: he enjoyed the virgin's company, provided
for the house, and became the supervisor of its material
affairs. Whilst he centred his attention on providing the
virgin with material assistance, she strove to enrich the man
in virtue, pleading for him so earnestly with God in prayer
that, whilst occupied in it, she became unaware of the man's
presence. After receiving the eucharist or even during the
celebration of mass (for she communicated at the table of
Christ as often as the abbot celebrated the divine mysteries),
she was so rapt[3] that, unaware of earthly things, she gave
herself to the contemplation of the countenance of her
Creator. Knowing this, the abbot used to say: 'Great is my
glory in this, that though for the moment you are forgetful
of me, you present me to Him, whose presence is so sweet
that you fail to realize that I am present.'

Now the handmaid of Christ, disciplining her mind by

ieiuniis. Deum precibus pulsat accumulacius. nec desistendum censet donec de dilecti vere salutis noticia satisfaciat animo. Puritatis preces Deus attendit maturius. qui priusquam invocetur: dicit exaudiam.[1] Quod visionis huius ostendere dignatus est indicio. Vidit siquidem Christina se in camera quadam. materia arte. et odore gratifica. duabus venerandis et admodum speciosis. albisque indutis assistere personis. Que collateraliter stantes. nulla stature vel decoris differencia discrepabant. In quorum humeris columba. sed et ipsa speciem excedens aliarum columbarum. quiescere videbatur. Vidit et exterius abbatem volentem ad se sed non valentem ingredi. Innuens autem illi oculis et capite postulabat suppliciter. ut in divina presencia. sese studiosius astantibus commendaret personis. Nec distulit virgo consuetis amico: succurrere precibus. Annisu enim quo prevalebat. affectu quo profundebatur. Devocione qua ⟨m⟩ novit. ut dilecti misereretur Dominum interpellabat. Nec mora. conspicatur columbam alarum* applausu cameram pervolitare ac intuentis oculos dulci pascere intuitu. Quo viso cultrix Dei roborata non destitit a precibus donec m[emo]ratum virum. vel possidere columbam. vel possessum cerneret a columba: ad se autem reversa manifestius intellexit columbam sancti spiritus graciam designare. qua perfusus abbas non nisi ad superna [pos]set amplius respirare. Unde nimio [exul]tans gaudio iam illum non ut [. . . ter]reni. sed ut celestis glorie concivem et consortem excolebat. et venerabatur et arciori sancte dileccionis amplectabatur sinu. Quos enim singultus. que suspiria (f. 163ra) quos fletus. considentes et de supernis tractantes effuderunt quis edisseret? Quantum quod transit vilipenderent. quantum quod permanet. appeterent. quis edicet? Aliorum ista sint. meum est simplicem virginis vitam simpliciter describere.

70. Habebat hec eadem virgo fratrem carnis. Gregorium monachum sancti Albani. ob cuius morum venustatem. fidei-

---

* columbam aliam suam *MS.*, *an pro* alarum?

[1] Isa. 65. 24.

watching, her body by fasting, stormed God in prayer and would not cease until she was satisfied in her mind about the sure salvation of her beloved. God listens more attentively to the prayers of the pure in heart, and even before He is invoked says: 'I hear'.[1] This He designed to show in a vision. For Christina saw herself in a kind of chamber, pleasing in its material, design, and atmosphere, with two venerable and very handsome personages clothed in white garments. Standing side by side, they differed neither in stature nor beauty. On their shoulders a dove far more beautiful than other doves seemed to rest. Outside she saw the abbot trying without success to gain entrance to her. Giving her a sign with his eyes and head, he humbly begged her to introduce him to the persons standing at her side in the divine presence. The virgin lost no time in coming to her friend's aid with her usual prayers. For with all the energy of which she was capable, with all the love she could pour out, with all the devotion she knew she pleaded with the Lord to have mercy on her beloved. Without delay, she saw the dove glide through the chamber with a fluttering of its wings and delight the eyes of the onlooker with its innocent gaze. When she saw this, God's servant took courage and would not stop pleading until she saw the man already mentioned either possessing the dove or being possessed by the dove: and when she came to herself, she understood clearly that the dove meant the grace of the Holy Spirit, and that the abbot, once filled with it, would be able to aspire only to things above. Filled with joy at this, she cherished him and venerated a fellow and companion of heavenly not earthly glory, and took him to her bosom in a closer bond of holy affection. For who shall describe the longings, the sighs, the tears they shed as they sat and discussed heavenly matters? Who shall put into words how they despised the transitory, how they yearned for the everlasting? Let this be left to someone else: my task is to describe quite simply the simple life of the virgin.

This same virgin had a brother, Gregory, a monk of St. Albans, whom she cherished with extraordinary affection for

que constanciam. eum miro diligebat affectu. Secura namque carnalium erat amoris parentum. nisi quos aut morum
honestas. aut ingenitus aliquis probitatis commendaret conatus. Hic itaque .G. paululum temporis ex iussu abbatis sui
cum sorore moratus. divinum inibi servicium celebrabat.
Appropiante vero die quo eum Deus de huius vite dispone-
bat erumnis eripere: langore corripitur. scilicet eo qui vite
ultimum clausit diem. Cui plurimum compaciens soror. erat
enim quasi singularis suo tempore bonorum amatrix. ad nota
precum recucurrit subsidia. Deum sedulo interpellans ut
sue miseracionis dignacione. quid de fratre disposuerat sibi
revelare dignaretur. Precum differtur effectus. sed earum
non languente constancia. languida fratris complexio mortem
intentare videtur. Unde tristior effecta Christina Christum
suum uberioribus pro fratre deflectit lacrimis.* donec in
hec† verba vocem sentiret delapsam. Scias quod eum affectat
domina. Modicoque facto intervallo. adiecit vox eadem. Et
te scilicet affectat. Certa itaque de fratris obitu nec de proprio
transitu et eo citaciore diffidens. gracias refert Domino. et
quod exaudiri meruerit magis tamen quod utrosque a domi-
narum domina vocandos ⟨di⟩dicerit. Ergo fratrem adiens
quod a do(f. 163rᵇ)mina celi vocaretur insinuat. Et annectit.
Si nobilis aliqua seculi prepotensque matrona in suum te
dum esses ⟨in⟩ seculo vocaret obsequium. multimode sollici-
taveris gratum te suis exhibere conspectibus. Quanto magis
cum te nunc celi vocet Domina. quecumque sibi placita
sunt pro posse dum licet debes exequi? Hiis auditis .G. carnis celerem credens mortem. tanto securius Christi se muni-
vit sacramentis. quanto cercius quod dissolveretur accepit.
Perceptoque viatico ac‡ cunctis que ad id obsequii pertinent decenter completis. presente abbate et conventu sancti
Albani. inanimis ad ecclesiam illam delatus est. Non sine

---

* lacrimas *MS.*   † in hec *bis, expunct.*   ‡ ac *sup. lin.*

the charm of his manners and the staunchness of his belief.
Unless their goodness and innate propensity to holiness commended them, her family relatives shared little of her affection. This Gregory then, having with his abbot's permission
stayed a short time with his sister, used to say Mass there.
But as the day approached on which God had disposed to
snatch him from the cares of this world, he was seized with
that sickness which was to end his life. His sister, having great
compassion on him (for she stood out above all others in
those days in loving the good), had recourse to her usual
remedy—prayer—and pleaded with God to reveal to her in
His mercy what plans He had in mind for her brother. The
result of her prayers was long in coming, but their constancy
never flagged, even though her brother's flagging health
seemed to forebode death. At this Christina grew more sad
and for the sake of her brother moved Christ with floods of
tears until she heard a voice from heaven saying these words:
'Thou mayest be sure his lady loves him.' And after a brief
space the same voice added: 'And she loves you also.' Convinced therefore of his death, and no less convinced that her
own passing was not far off, she gave thanks to God both
because she had deserved to be heard, but more because she
had learned that both of them would be summoned by the
queen of queens. So going to her brother, she intimated to
him that he would be summoned by the Mistress of heaven.
And she added: 'If some noble and powerful lady in the
world had called you to her service while you were in the
world, you would have taken great care to appear gracious in
her eyes. Now that the Mistress of heaven calls you, how much
more should you fulfil her behests to the best of your ability
while you can!' When Gregory heard this, believing that his
death was near, he fortified himself with the sacraments of
Christ so much the more composedly as he felt the more certain
that he would die. And after he had received the viaticum, and
all those things which concern the burial had been decently
arranged, he was borne unconscious to the church in the
presence of the abbot and the community of St. Albans, not

multorum humanitatis lacrimis in spe bona flatum reddidit
ultimum. Quodque prius vivens admodum optaverat. Mortuo tumulando soror utraque Christina scilicet et Margareta
presens astitit.

71. In anno quo primum ad regnum Anglie rex est
Stephanus electus:[1] ex consulto prudentum. destinandos ad
Papam romanum Innocencium .ii. ut scilicet a tanto patre
ipsa eius confirmaretur electio procurare disposuit nuncios.
fit et in huius allegacionis execucione. primus vel inter primos
eligitur abbas sancti Albani Gaufridus. Mandatur ad curiam
regis auditurus edicta. Festinat ad virginem illius oracionum
se piis commendaturus suffragiis. De regis confer⟨t⟩ mandato:
cause tamen adhuc ignarus. Illa mestior solito. Vade ait. vade
Dei comitatus gracia. Noveris iter istud non omnimodis prosperandum. Neque enim talem sencio te. qualem in divina
solebam presencia. Regis aditur curia. regale super allegacionis negocio decretum auditur. nec refellitur. Mestum iter.
Sed itineris mestior causa. Redit domum. profectionis preparaturus expensas. Revisit iterum suum penetrale divinum.
ac iniunctum (f. 163ᵛᵃ) pandit obsequium. Tristem se fatetur.
Et tristicie lacrimas prodit testes. Interulas ab ea duas expetit.
non ad voluptatem sed ad laboris relevandum sudorem. Orat
tamen ut Deo propensius pro ipso supplicans. eius super his
rescire satagat voluntatem. Illa dilectum adiens secretum.
vultum suffusa lacrimis. cor attrita suspiriis. diem nocti continuat in precibus. auditque vocem in hec sibi verba delapsam.
Ecce maceria. viditque maceriam. in qua dilectus suus* ac si
vivus incementatus est. Cui quam diu fuerit firmiter innisus
Dei protectio sibi nusquam deerit. Interulas autem quas ad
laboris sui preparasti levamen. egenis quam tocius impertire.
gracius enim in itineris missione Christus sibi procurabit
levamen. De oraculo itaque certa divino. neque enim rudis

---

* suus *sup. lin.*

[1] i.e. A.D. 1136.

without the tears of many mourners. Full of hope, he breathed
forth his last and, what he had most hoped for earlier in life,
both his sisters, Christina and Margaret, were present at his
burial.

In the year when Stephen was first elected king of England[1] he decided on the advice of wise counsellors to send
ambassadors to Pope Innocent II at Rome in order to obtain
from this supreme authority the confirmation of his election.
For the fulfilment of this embassy the first or among the
first to be chosen was Abbot Geoffrey. He was summoned
to the king's court to get his orders. He hastened to the virgin to commend himself to her holy prayers. He discussed
the summons of the king, not yet knowing the reason. She,
sadder than usual, said: 'Go, go with the grace of God. But
be assured that this journey will not succeed. For I do not
feel about you as I used to do in the divine presence.' He
went to the king's court: he heard the royal decree on the
matter of the embassy, and did not refuse. The journey was
grievous, but the reason was not less grievous than the
journey. He returned home to arrange his expenses for his
going. Once again he visited his divine refuge and discussed
the task imposed on him. He admitted his sadness, and
shed tears as a proof of his grief. He begged for two under-
garments from her, not for pleasure but to mitigate the
hardship of the journey. Nevertheless he asked her to pray
to God more earnestly for him, asking that His will on this
matter might be made known. She went to her beloved
privacy with her countenance bathed in tears, her heart torn
with sighs, and, as she continued praying day and night,
heard a voice coming to her from above: 'Behold the wall'.
And she saw a wall, in which her beloved friend was, as it
were, cemented alive. 'As long' (it continued) 'as he is firmly
fixed in it, the protection of God will never desert him. But
the garments which you have prepared for his comfort, give
as quickly as possible to the poor, because Christ will obtain
for him more gracious comfort on his journey.' Certain that
it was a divine promise (for she was not ignorant of these

erat in istis. lacrimas in gaudium. suspiria vertit in devo-
cionem. Rediens interim de curia vir venerabilis Thomas[1]
cuius supra meminimus. quem ad sullimiores regni personas
super allegacionis indulgencia transmiserat abbas. et eo non
invento iam ad regem. de rege Romam profecturus abierat.
denunciat virgini dilectum suum. nullum remanendi reper-
turum consilium. unam omnium voluntatem. ut iniunctum
compleat mandatum. At illa desistas inquid queso super hiis
pavere. Hec enim talia michi dicta sunt. hec ostensa. Credulus
ille utpote secretorum eius bene conscius ⟨.⟩ cur exclamat non
illum prosequor. et ut redeat satago? Nequaquam respondit
virgo. Certum quidem illum est ab itineris labore dimissum.
sed iustum censeo. ut cum munere divino regia munificetur
gracia. Dando siquidem interulas complevit mandatum. re-
tinendo dilectum firmavit promissum. leve rata dispendium
texta fila dis(f. 163vb)pergere. ut quem vera contexuerat
caritas.[2] a tanto posset labore retinere.

72. In anno itidem tercio regni eiusdem regis .S. a Papa
Innocencio .ii. ad urbem generale convocatur consilium.[3]
Huius convocacionis apostolici. circumquaque deferuntur
apices. nec minus in Anglia. In qua tunc forte consilium iure
tenebat legatus romanus. Hostiensis episcopus Albericus.[4]
Mandato itaque Pape percepto quid faciendum sit com-
muni consilio tractatur. Et quoniam in discrimine visum est
sub bellorum procinctu dimissa patria omnes ecclesiarum
Anglie pastores alpium ardua transpetere: eliguntur quidam
et illi prudenciores. sua et ceterorum allegacione functuri.
Inter quos primos primus eligitur abbas Gaufridus. Nec
multum remittitur.* utpote qui dilectus in curia. familiares
suos revisere cupiebat. Gaudebat tamen virginis in hoc assensum comprobare. Non enim autumabat de tanto negocio
Christine cum Christo cessare colloquia. Adveniens itaque

---

* remittitur, *Sic MS. leg.* renititur.

[1] Thomas has not been mentioned earlier in this text. It appears, therefore, that
something has been omitted. This gives rise to the suspicion that the Tiberius text is
an abbreviated version of the original *Life*.

[2] This mention of garments woven by Christina fits in well with the later report
of her having sent embroidered mitres and sandals to Pope Adrian IV.

[3] i.e. A.D. 1139.   [4] Alberic, cardinal bishop of Ostia, 1138–48.

matters), she turned her tears into joy, her sighs into devotion.
In the meanwhile, the venerable Thomas,[1] whom we have
mentioned above, and whom the abbot had sent to the highest personages in the realm for release from the embassy, not
finding him with the king, was on his way to Rome. Returning from the court, he assured the virgin that no reason
could be found for deferring her beloved's departure;
all were of the same mind, that the abbot should carry out
his orders. But she said: 'Have no further fears on this point.
This is what has been told me, and this is what I have seen.'
He believed her, for he knew her secrets, and exclaimed:
'Why should I not follow him and persuade him to return?'
'By no means', replied the virgin. 'It is certain that he has
been relieved of the burden of the journey. All the same I
think it is only right that the king's favour should be repaid
with a divine gift.' So in giving away the garments, she fulfilled the command, whilst He, in keeping back her beloved,
confirmed the promise. And she counted it little loss to dis-
pose of the woven stuff so long as he, whom true charity had
woven,[2] was prevented from embarking on so onerous a task.

In the third year of the reign of the same King Stephen a
general council was convoked in Rome by Pope Innocent II.[3]
Apostolic letters ordering this convocation were dispatched
everywhere, England included. At that time the Roman
legate, Bishop Alberic of Ostia,[4] was rightfully holding a
council. When the papal mandate was received, a general
discussion took place as to what should be done. And since
it seemed dangerous that in times when war was imminent
all the prelates of England should leave the country and
make the difficult crossing of the Alps, certain ones, and they
the more prudent, were chosen to undertake an embassy for
themselves and the rest. Among these the first to be chosen
was Abbot Geoffrey. Nor did he much object, for as he was
popular at the papal court he looked forward to seeing his old
friends again. Nevertheless, he wanted to have the virgin's
confirmation of his decision. For he did not think that Christina would cease from praying to God about so important

quantulum hilarius Romam se pro suo regnique negocio
fatetur destinandum. Nec posse desistere. Presertim cum
Pape mandatum perurgeret. Illa sicut semper non preceps
in respondendo. corde solum reclamat agendis. Tandem
suspiria contrahens. perge ait cum Domino. certum enim
michi est quia sive in eundo. sive in remanendo. in te divina
complebitur voluntas. In oracionibus namque constituta vidi
ambitum quemdam de lignis candidissimis. et hiis perspicuis
circumseptum ostio fenestrisque carentem ad modum claustri
sed rotundum. cuius interioris herba pratelli communium
virorem excedebat herbarum: delectata super his vidi te
sollicitudinis mee causam. infra ambitum iocunde satis et
cum quadam amplec(f. 164ra)tenda dulcedine consistentem.
Cumque sollicitarer adhuc ne forte vel suffodiendo vel
alia qualibet arte qua evaderes haberes: dictum est michi.
huius quem cernis ambitus Deus solus claviger est. nec iste
poterit quoquam egredi nisi divine disposicionis apericione.
Quare de Ihesu Christi roborata clemencia infra illum te
detentum ambitum detineri et ab hac profectione confido.
Oxenefordiam tamen ille ubi tunc regia morabatur maiestas.
ipsa regi eterno supplicatura vota precum ad idem iter properat. Tractabatur apud regem et cum rege terreno ut abbas
proficiscatur. tractat illa cum Deo et cum rege celesti. ut
idem a profectione retrahatur.* Vicit que victoriosius diligere
novit. victoriosius novit diligere que causarum omnium
effectum a Deo studuit impetrare. superna namque pro-
vidente gracia. contra conatus multorum. contra vota omnia†
apostolici legati littere super abbatis revocacione ad archiepiscopum Cantuariensem Tetbaldum[1] diriguntur. Iam iamque
qui prius quasi destinandus erat ad iter. nunc cum ceteris
remansuris de destinandis miscet colloquia. Sentitque plus

---

* retrahatur *sup. lin.*   † omnia *in marg. MS.*

[1] Theobald, archbishop of Canterbury, 8 Jan. 1139 to 18 Apr. 1161.

a business. Coming to her, therefore, in a happy frame of mind, he told her that he was being sent to Rome on business concerning himself and the realm. He could not refuse, especially as the papal mandate was urgent. She, as usual, was slow to reply, but in her heart she did not approve of the undertaking. At last, checking a sigh, she said: 'Go forth in the Lord. For I am certain that, whether you go or whether you stay, the divine will in you will be fulfilled. For when I was at prayer I saw a kind of enclosure surrounded by high fences which were transparent: it resembled a cloister without door or windows, but it was round, and the grass in the garth was greener than ordinary grass. Overjoyed at this, I saw you, the cause of my anxiety, within this enclosure, standing happily enough with an enviable degree of pleasure. And when I was still anxious how you would get out, whether by digging or any other way, it was said to me: "This enclosure which you see has but one doorkeeper, God: and that man cannot come out except by divine intervention. On this account, strengthened by the mercy of Jesus Christ, I am confident that you are kept within that enclosure and prevented from setting out on your journey."' He, on his part, hastened to Oxford, where the king's court was being held, she to the eternal King to pray about the same journey. At the king's court and with the earthly king discussions were held about the abbot's departure. With God and the celestial King she discussed how the same man might be prevented from departing. She who knew how to love to supreme advantage gained the day. She knew how to love to supreme advantage because she made it her practice to pray to God in every case for a just outcome. For by divine providence, contrary to the efforts of the majority, contrary also to everyone's expectation, letters were sent by the apostolic legate to the archbishop of Canterbury, Theobald,[1] recalling the abbot. And he who previously had been fated to set out on the journey now joined with the others who were to stay behind in discussing who should go. And he had to admit that the virgin's pure heart had

apud Deum virginis posse puritatem quam potentum seculi factiosam vel prudentem calliditatem.

73. Eodem anno prefatus rex .S. ex quorumdam satellitum suorum consilio. sed perverso. in curia sua consistentes. duos cepit episcopos. Rogerum scilicet Saresberiensem et Alexandrum Lincolniensem.[1] eo quod suspectos eos haberet. utpote prudencia. castris pecunia. parentibusque munitos. captosque custodie illorum nec dignitati nec ordini congrue deputavit. Interpellatus pro hiis a Cantuariensi archiepiscopo Tetbaldo et a quibusdam suis suffraganeis spopon(f. 164ʳᵇ) dit ecclesiasticam se super eorum captura subiturum censuram. Condictoque tempore apud Wyntoniam conveniunt.[2] Hinc rex cum obtimatibus et satellitibus suis. hinc archiepiscopus. episcopi abbates fere tocius Anglie. cum multo clero religioso. in presencia Romani legati Wyntoniensis scilicet episcopi Henrici[3] de tanto negocio tractaturi. Convenitur rex de sponsione subeunde censure. sed abiurat nullum in hiis ⟨a⟩ se subeundum iudicium. nisi ⟨sibi⟩ sueque parti sit consonum. Attemptatur regis clemencia nec ostenditur. ecclesiastica proponitur censura. Sed contempnitur. Quid plura? Discidium regni sacerdociique hostiles moliuntur ecclesie inimici. cum ecce rex quorundam profundioris astucie consilio se senciens pregravari. ne presens anathematis multaretur baculo. Romam appellare compellitur. Cumque utrinque Romam transmittendi disponerentur nuncii: ad ecclesie ius exequendum cum ceteris quibusdam venerandus abbas predictus electus est Gaufridus. dignus omnium arbitrio qui iura sciret ecclesie conservare. Quid ageret? Reniti non erat consilii. Negocium suscipere: gravis erat discriminis. Interminatus namque fuerat rex rerum omnium proscripcionem qui contra se romanum arriperent iter. Hinc iam fractus corpore laborem viribus preponderare cernebat. Hinc pauperum

---

[1] 24 June 1139: Wm. of Malmesbury, *Historia Novella*, § 469; cf. *Gesta Stephani* (ed. K. R. Potter, 1955), § 35.

[2] 29 Aug. 1139: *Historia Novella*, §§ 470–7.

[3] Henry of Blois, bishop of Winchester, 17 Nov. 1129 to 8 Aug. 1171.

more power with God than the factious and shrewd cunning
of the great ones of this world.

In the same year, the aforesaid King Stephen, on the
wicked instigation of some of his favourites, took into custody
two bishops who were attached to the court, namely Roger
of Salisbury and Alexander of Lincoln,[1] because he suspected
them of being too powerful in wisdom, castles, wealth, and
relatives: and put them into prison, which was out of keeping with their position and ecclesiastical status. On being
called to account for this action by Theobald, archbishop of
Canterbury, and by some of his suffragans he gave his word
that he would answer to the judgement of the Church on
their capture. At the appointed date they met at Winchester.[2]
On one side was the king with his barons and followers, on
the other the archbishop, bishops, abbots of almost the whole
of England, with a concourse of clergy to discuss so important a matter in the presence of the Roman legate, namely
Henry, bishop of Winchester.[3] The king was cited on his
promise to undergo sentence: but he refused to submit to
any judgement on these matters unless it were favourable to
himself and his party. The king's mercy was requested, but
refused: ecclesiastical censure was threatened, but despised.
In short the enemies of the church attempted to bring about
a split between the king and the clergy: when suddenly the
king, feeling that he was being overborne by the machinations of certain people whose cunning was abnormally deep,
was compelled to appeal to Rome in order to avoid the sentence of immediate excommunication. And when both sides
had arranged to send representatives to Rome, the aforesaid
venerable abbot Geoffrey was chosen with several others to
uphold the rights of the Church, being judged, in the opinion
of all, as best capable of preserving the rights of the Church.
What was he to do? To refuse was bad policy. To accept the
charge was very dangerous. For the king had threatened
with confiscation of their property all those who went to
Rome to contest his will. On the one hand he perceived that
in his state of health the task was beyond his strength. On

quorum cure pius provisor desudabat flexus gracia. iter
arripiendum eorum perpendebat dispendium. Verumtamen
unum erat sibi solacium. et illud solidum. divinum de hiis
inquirere consilium. Parvipendebat enim omnem mundi
gloriam. divine vel in modico preponere voluntati. Matu-
rans itaque ad dulce sibi notumque remedium. domini
famulam dico Christi Christinam. Mandata denunciat. man-
datorumque discrimen. Orat. supplicat instat. ut pro cause
magnitudine Deum propencius (f. 164va) interpellet volen-
temque virginem fletibus magis concitat. Discedit abbas.
nullius nisi laboris itineris certus. Illa causam miserata dilecti. sed et plusquam corporis anime verens detrimentum.
illum solum propter quem cuncta reliquerat. horum agendorum invocat provisorem. Interea dum oracionis fieret proten-
cio sicut solebat in exstasi rapta. vidit se salvatoris assistere
presencie. illumque suum pre cunctis familiarissimum intra
brachiorum suorum girum pectori suo constrictum inclu-
sisse. Sed dum timeret ne forte sicut vir muliere robustior
et de se quoquomodo posset excutere: videt salvandorum
subventorem Ihesum manu pia suas manus non consertis
digitis. sed aliis aliis superpositis iunctas constringere ne
minus in manuum iunccione quam in lacertorum fortitudine
ad retinendum dilectum robur sentiretur. Hiis ita perceptis
non modico gestiens gaudio uberes reddit gracias. et quod
amici curam noverit exemptam. maxime tamen quod et
sponsi dominique sui viderit presenciam. Nec enim mora.
Dei disponente clemencia omnes destinati laboriosi missio-
nem senserunt itineris.

74. Post aliquod tempus iterum mandatur abbas ad
curiam: regie nescius voluntatis. Verebatur tamen ne quo-
rumlibet factiosa falsatorum versucia in aliquo contra se*
regis animus moveretur. Erat enim rex quandoque plus

* se *sup. lin.*

the other, if he undertook the journey, he had to consider the cost to those poor folk, for whose material care he had lovingly laboured. There was, nevertheless, one consolation left to him, and that well founded: to seek the divine will on these matters. For he did not care to place the glory of this world even in the slightest degree before the divine will. Hastening therefore to his sweet and known remedy, I mean the servant of the Lord Christ, Christina, he told her his orders and the danger attending the orders. He begged, pleaded, implored her, seeing the importance of the case, to intercede with God most earnestly, and moved the already sympathetic virgin with his tears. The abbot departed, certain only of one thing, the burden of the journey. She, deploring the position her friend was in, but fearing more the danger to his soul than to his body, invoked Him who watches over these matters, and for whom she had abandoned all things. Whilst her prayer was as usual prolonged, she was rapt in ecstasy and saw herself in the presence of her saviour; and she saw him, whom she loved above all others, encircled with her arms and held closely to her breast. And whilst she feared that, since a man is stronger than a woman, he would free himself from her grasp, she saw Jesus, the helper of the saved, closing her hands with His own loving hand, not by intertwining her fingers with His but by joining them one over the other: so that by joining her hands no less than by the power of her arms she should feel greater strength in holding her friend back. When she noticed this, gladdened not a little, she gave effusive thanks with joy both because she knew that her friend was relieved of trouble, and also because she was aware of the presence of her spouse and Lord. And within a short time by the disposition of God's mercy, all those who were being sent abroad heard of their dismissal from the difficult journey.

After some time the abbot was summoned once more to the court, ignorant of what the king wanted. All the same he was afraid that the king's heart might be turned against him because of the plots and lies of others. For the king was

lenocinantibus quam vera dicentibus credulus. In eundo
vero divertit ad virginem. eius se precibus commendaturus.
Nulla pavebat adversa. ipsius prius interventu munitus.
nimirum quam tociens in tantis subventricem probaverat.
Itaque in conferendo primum enim semper de hiis que ad
Deum sunt conferre solebant. vado ait abbas ad curiam de
reditu nescius: utpote (f. 164vb) regiam verens levitatem.
Erat tunc dies dominicus. Quid fluctuas ait virgo? Quid
dubitandum cui tutamen prestat omnipotens? vade securus.
regis enim animum propicium invenies. proxima quinta feria
multa es hilaritate reversurus ad me. Progreditur ille cum
gaudio. adit curiam. ad nutum succedunt omnia. dieque
pretaxato gracias relaturus dilectricem suam letus revisit.
Ita namque sese agendorum immerserant cause: ut nec prius
venire posset. tametsi vellet nec amplius necesse esset im-
morari.

75. Erat enim mirum de illa sed venerandum. quia sepius
inter colloquendum rapiebatur in exstasim. videbatque que
sibi videnda sanctus monstrabat spiritus. nichil senciens.
nichil sciens eorum que circa se vel fiebant vel dicebantur.
Habebat enim certa quedam signa cum exaudiebatur. pro
quibus Deo supplicare propensius intendebat. Videbat enim
aliquando Evianum sed non mortalem cum levi attactu du-
orum digitorum indicis scilicet* et medii†: per faciem eius
ad os usque descendere. aviculam aliquando infra cratam
pectoris cum levi alarum applausu volitantem cernebat. Cum
vero mens eius liberius evolaret: aliquando unum tria sepius
videbat lumina equo splendore luceque radiancia. ita ut crederet se alicui de dilectis suis si presentem haberet. eadem
lumina posse monstrare. Quodlibet istorum signum vidisset:
erat de postulatis certus exauditus. Neque enim phantastice
erant visiones iste sive per sompnium. sed vero intuitu cerne-
bantur ab ea. illo scilicet quo spirituales frui merentur oculi.
Sepissime eciam cum vel vigiliarum protelacione vel aliqua
corporis fessa valitudine. sopore plus (f. 165ra) solito de-
tineretur. horaque matutinorum appropinquaret. tanta cum

* scilicet *in marg.*   † medium *MS.*

sometimes more inclined to believe flatterers than those who
spoke the truth. But on his way there he turned aside to
commend himself to the prayers of the virgin. When he was
supported by her he feared no difficulties, for he had very often
experienced her help in so many ways. And so, whilst they
were talking (for they always spoke of the things of God
first), the abbot said: 'I am going to the court, but of my
return I know nothing, for I fear the fickleness of the king.'
It was then Sunday. 'Why are you troubled?' said she. 'Why
hesitate if the Almighty is your protection? Go in confidence,
for you will find the king favourable towards you, and you
will return happily to me next Thursday.' He departed with
joy: he went to the court and everything turned out as he
desired. And on the day foretold he revisited his friend to
thank her. For he could not come before, however much he
might wish it, because he had been immersed in business,
and there was no reason to stay longer.

There was one thing about her which was wonderful and
to be revered. Often, whilst she was speaking, she was rapt
in ecstasy and saw things that the Holy Spirit showed her.
At such times she felt and knew nothing of what went on
about her or what was spoken. When the matters for which
she earnestly prayed to God were granted she received certain signs. Sometimes she saw Evianus (though not in the
flesh) lightly caress her face and mouth with his first and
middle finger: at other times she felt a little bird fluttering
gently with its wings within her breast. But when her mind
roamed freely, sometimes she saw one, more often three
lights shining with equal brilliance and splendour, so much
so that she felt that, had any one of her friends been present,
she could show these same lights to them. Whichever of
these signs she saw, it meant her prayer was granted. For
these visions were not imaginary or dreams: she saw them
with the true intuition enjoyed by the mystics. Very often
also when she slept more soundly than usual as a result of long
vigils and bodily exhaustion, as soon as the hour for matins
approached, she awoke so easily that you would scarcely

levitate excitabatur ut vix crederes sonitum ab alio posse deprehendi. Tantum autem Christus suam zelabat ancillam: ut si qui eam infestarent aut cita corrigerentur penitencia: aut incommodo corporis aliquo multarentur. ita ut audiremus de illis aliquem cecitate* percussum. alium absque viatico viam universe carnis ingressum. alios invidia tabescentes omnem fere qua prius claruerant religionis oppinionem amisisse.

76. Sed numquid inter hec tua Zabule tela iacula contunduntur: Numquid quia iam de Cristina desperas. ne Christine causa plures inficias desperare cogeris? Nequaquam. Generacio namque prava et perversa¹ que Christum Ihesum in Beelzebul demonum infamabat expulsorem.² que Christi discipulis quia mulieres circumducerent derogavit:³ ipsa de† Christi bono odore⁴ per Cristinam resperso. quia sano caruit olfactu franganciam non sensit. fumum etenim admisit. Unde propria compulsi malicia. et demonis instimulantis urgente invidia. multis crebrisque dilectricem Christi Christinam exacerbare studebant susurriis. detraccionibus venenosis. verborum iaculis. illam infamare cupientes. que fame meritum summo studio mortalibus occultabat. Hinc eam alii sompniatricem alii animorum translatricem. alii quasi miciores secularium agendorum prudentem procuratricem appellabant. Scilicet quod divini erat muneris. seculari prudencie conantes imputare. Alii autem aliter loqui nescientes‡ eidem abbati carnali devinctam amore summurmurabant. Ita sub unius Ihesu Christi munitam presidio. quasi divisi unusquisque de se. plures per suos insectabantur demones. Quibus illud erat quantulumcumque licet improperiosum (f. 165ʳᵇ) remedium. sed§ quia virginem in nullo deflectere valebant. id solum efficerent ut multi sinistra falso de illo sentirent. Essetque sicut Christi bonus odor bonis in vitam. ita Christi bonus odor malis in mortem.⁵ Christi tamen ubique bonus odor. Hinc iam primum vulgus verborum novitate lasciviens rumoribus percutitur. De hinc

---

* cecitatem *MS.*   † de *sup. lin.*   ‡ nescientes+ac vix *expunct.*
§ sed *MS.*; ? scilicet ut.

¹ Cf. Matt. 17. 16.   ² Matt. 12. 24.   ³ 1 Cor. 9. 5.
⁴ 2 Cor. 2. 15.   ⁵ 2 Cor. 2. 16.

believe that anyone else could have heard a sound. But so jealously did Christ watch over His handmaid that if any molested her, they were visited with swift punishment or afflicted with some bodily ailment, so that we heard that one was stricken with blindness, another had died without the sacraments, others were eaten up with envy and lost all the reputation for holiness which they had once enjoyed.

But amidst all this, o Satan, were your darts blunted? Because you despaired of Christina, were you forced, because of Christina, to despair of poisoning others? By no means. For a depraved and perverse generation[1] which accused Christ Jesus of casting out devils in the name of Beelzebub,[2] which despised the disciples of Christ because they took women about with them,[3] that same generation, because it lacked good sense, did not perceive the good savour of Christ shed abroad by Christina,[4] taking notice only of the smoke. Hence, a prey to their own malice, yet urged on by the envy of the devil, they spent their time in pursuing Christina, the lover of Christ, with gossip, poisonous detractions, barbed words, trying to take away the good name, which she had most carefully tried to hide from men. Hence, some of them called her a dreamer, others a seducer of souls, others, more moderately, just a worldly-wise business woman: that is, what was a gift of God they attributed to earthly prudence. Others who could think of nothing better to say spread the rumour that she was attracted to the abbot by earthly love. In this way, though divided amongst themselves, each one according to his own devil persecuted her, fortified as she was by the protection of Jesus Christ. To all these there was but one satisfaction, insulting though it was: namely, if they could not deflect the virgin from her path, at least to make many people believe scandal about her falsely. And as the good savour of Christ is life for the good, so the good savour of Christ is death to the bad.[5] But the savour of Christ remains good everywhere. Hence it was that the common folk, who revel in anything unusual, were assailed with rumours. Thenceforward some who bore the habit of

quidam habitum religionis preferentes. invidie iaculo con-
fodiuntur. Isti nec vera nec verisimilia garriunt. illi que
confinxerunt quodam veritatis velamento palliare nituntur.
ita ut alium Ieronimum aliam cerneres Paulam.[1] si non ista
virgo virginis illa mater fuisset. Priusquam se invicem in
Christo diligerent. abbatis nota probitas et sancta virginis
castitas per plures Anglie partes excolebantur. Cum vero
utrosque mutua sed in Christo dileccio ad bonum magis
accenderet. subversor abbas peccatrix virgo diffamabatur.
Nec mirum. verebatur enim inimicus eorum Zabulus tamen
utriusque ex alterutro profectum. ac per eos tantam ecclesie
Dei conferendam utilitatem. unde quod inter eos excellen-
cioris erat causa profectus. credi volebat gravioris causam
esse defectus. Sed eius in contrarium versa sunt argumenta.
Multi enim quorum quosdam et nos vidimus.* quibus eam
infamare fuerat pro deliciis. ad veritatis viam reducti. culpam
confitentes. veniam consequebantur. sed [qui] prius falsi
criminatoris vice fungebantur. postea veritatis eam inhabi-
tantis assertores veri fiebant. Eorum autem si qui rerum
adhuc ignari de ipsius opinione animo fluctuarent. eos mani-
festis Deus revocabat indiciis. Quod hoc monstrari poterit
exemplo.

77. Erat secus civitatem Londonie in monasterio Ber-
mundesie[2] vir vite venerabilis vere monachus (f. 165ᵛᵃ) et
nominis sui certam gerens ethimologiam Simon dictus ipsius
loci secretarius: et inter primos eiusdem monasterii vite
sanctitate. et morum probitate conspicuus. Hic virginem
prefatam multo colebat studio. diligebat affectu. predicabat
amore. utpote cuius familiaritatis dulcedine. sepius in se
sancti spiritus perfusiorem senserat graciam. Susurratoribus
vero atque oblatratoribus eius ita oppositus erat ut a primo
verbo omnem eorum quos audiebat contunderet conatum.
Sed quoniam omni iuste cause Deum patrocinari debere

---

* vidimus+viam reducti *expunct.*

[1] A reference to the relationship between St. Jerome and St. Paula, a widow and
mother of St. Eustochium. She presided over a convent of nuns founded by St.
Jerome at Bethlehem.

[2] The Cluniac House founded by Aylwin Child, a citizen of London, in 1082:
Dugdale, *Monasticon*, v. 85–95.

religion were pierced by the lance of envy. Some of them gossiped about things neither true nor having the appearance of truth, others tried to veil their fictitious tales under an appearance of truth, so that listening to them you might think one was Jerome, the other Paula,[1] had not one been a virgin and the other the mother of a virgin. Before they had become spiritual friends, the abbot's well-known goodness and the maiden's holy chastity had been praised in many parts of England. But when their mutual affection in Christ had inspired them to greater good, the abbot was slandered as a seducer and the maiden as a loose woman. This is not surprising, for the devil, their enemy, feared the advantage they would gain from one another and the great usefulness that would accrue through them to the Church: and so what was the cause of their extraordinary progress he wished to be considered as the cause of their falling away. But all his attempts were turned to his own disadvantage. For many of these people who took pleasure in soiling her reputation returned (as we ourselves have seen) to the path of truth, confessed their fault, and obtained pardon: whilst those who played the part of the false accuser afterwards became the true assertors of the truth that dwelt in her. Some of those who were ignorant of the state of affairs and were left in uncertainty God recalled by manifest evidence. This can be proved by the following example.

In the monastery of Bermondsey[2] near the city of London there was a man venerable in his way of life, a true monk, living up to the meaning of his name Simon, who was sacrist to that house and who on account of his holiness and the strictness of his life was a leading member of that community. This man had great respect for the virgin just mentioned: he cultivated her friendship, and spoke affectionately of her, since through being accepted into her familiar circle he had felt a greater outpouring of the Holy Spirit. He was so antagonistic to tale-bearers and detractors that he silenced them as soon as they opened their mouths to speak. But as he knew that God defends just causes, he decided that he would

didicerat. ei qui cordis renumque scrutator est[1] supplicare
deliberavit. ut qui secretorum est conscius. quicquid est de
Christina. sibi revelare dignaretur. Corpus ob hoc ieiuniis
macerabat. animam vigiliis affligebat ⟨et⟩ fletibus. pavimento
decumbebat. consolari nesciens donec responsum susciperet
a Domino. Neque enim non pro crimine ducebat. falso
crimen obici Cristine. Nec posse fieri ut in Cristine falleretur
amore. Volens itaque Deus et ipsius labori finem imponere
et veritatis amico quod verum erat pandere. quadam die dum
idem vir venerandus Simon altari astans missam celebraret
sue postulacionis non immemor. mirum dictu ipsam Cristinam videt altario consistere. Obstupefactus in hoc: neque
enim virgo cellam egredi. sed nec [ad] altare illud mulier
quelibet facile [vale]bat admitti: non multa sine admiracione
rei prestolabatur exitum. Cum illa. Scias inquid carnem
meam omnis corrupcionis immunem. Et hiis dictis evanuit.
Ille vero animo gestiens et tantum gaudium vix mente
concipiens: missam quidem oportune finivit. sed diligende
virginis desiderium finire nequivit. Repertoque uno sancti
Albani monacho qui tunc forte Ber(f. 165ᵛᵇ)mundeseyam
venerat. Quid viderit. quid audierit. quid super Cristine
causa certum habuerit. abbati Gaufrido per eundem man-
dare monachum curavit. Pie et iuste disponente Domino. ut
quia monachus ille unus erat ex oblocutoribus. in hoc mandato condisceret quid de Cristina sentire deberet. Ut si de
illa sinistrum quid ulterius dispergeret. consciencie reus et
iudicis graviori se pena multandum non ambigeret. Ipse
tamen venerandus Simon. monachum illum talem fuisse
nesciebat. Cumque abbas mandatum Simonis percepisset:
multiplices Domino gracias reddidit. quia quod per se verum
rescierat. alii misericorditer revelavit.

[1] Cf. Ps. 7. 10.

beg Him, who is the judge of thoughts and desires[1] and the knower of all secrets, to reveal to him the truth about Christina. For this reason he afflicted his body with fasting, his mind with watching and tears: he slept on the bare ground and would accept no consolation until he received some answer from the Lord. For he considered it a crime to make false accusations against Christina, and he could not believe that he had been led astray in his affection for Christina. God therefore wished to put an end to his troubles and to show him, as a lover of the truth, the true state of affairs; and so one day whilst the same venerable man Simon was at the altar celebrating Mass, mindful of his prayer, he saw, with surprise, Christina standing near the altar. He was astonished at this for the virgin could not have come out of the cell and it was hardly possible that any woman would be allowed to approach the altar. Not without amazement he awaited the issue. Then she said: 'Thou mayest be sure that my flesh is free from corruption.' And when she had said this she vanished. Filled with gladness and hardly able to contain himself for joy, he finished the Mass in due course, though he was not able to put as quick an end to his affection for the virgin. Finding one of the monks of St. Albans, who by chance had come to Bermondsey at that time, he sent a message to Abbot Geoffrey through that same monk telling him what he had seen, what he had heard, and what he knew about the case of Christina. And as that monk was one of those who slandered her, the Lord in His kindness and justice had arranged that through this message he should become aware of what he ought to feel about Christina; so that if he should spread false rumours about her in future, he should not be left in doubt that he was acting against his conscience, and that he would be visited with the heavy punishment due to tale-bearers. But the venerable Simon was quite unaware that the monk was such a one. And when the abbot received the message from Simon he gave thanks to God because He had mercifully revealed to others what he already knew himself.

78. Cristina vero versuciis demonum frangi nesciens. quippe quas graves iam ac multiplices sepe iam nunc fidei scuto colliserat. revolvit quid Deo novum offerat. quatinus abbatem vero illustraret lumine. et obtrectatorum quibus compaciebatur desisteret procacia. Itaque non consumente. sed illuminante illustrata lumine proponit per omnem noctem dominicam cereum lumen in ecclesia sua munus offerre. Propositum gratum firmatur a sororibus. propositi causam ignorantibus. Tunc dies erat sabbati. Irritatus demon in virginis constancia quam* proprio nullo suorum conatu valebat interius deflectere: monstruoso corpore sumpto deflectere pertemptat exterius. Nocte itaque sequenti id est illu⟨ce⟩scente dominica.† in monasterio constituta Christina cum ad matutinalem synaxim cetere se prepararent: vident corpus sed sine capite. verum enim caput Deum amiserat: secus ostium oratorii in claustro sedere. Quo perviso perterrite sicut se puellaris habet timor. omnes prone circa pedes domine consternantur. Videres (f. 166ra) aliam si posset sinum eius intrare conantem. aliam se illius pallio velantem. aliam genua constringere. aliam pedibus velle summitti. illam in subsellio ascondi. aliam expirature similem in pavimento palpitantem decumbere. Omnibus id erat remedii. si vel Cristine vestes possent contingere. Nec minus audax demon prorumpit ecclesiam. Quo monstro conspecto ancilla Christi quantulum perterrita.‡ sed concepto roborata spiritu. convertit se ad Dominum. fusisque precibus fantasticum illud monstrum eiecit. Illam tamen horror plus solito aliquod per tempus postea invasit. Unde mesta plurimum. illi in quo spem fixerat preces effundit cum gemitu. verens se derelictam a Domino. si monstruosas demonum effigies incipiat formidare. Cui super hiis in oracione sepius persistenti tale datur responsum. Pro huiusmodi supplicacionibus non indulseras. §pro quo autem supplicasti. ut vero scilicet. et eterno

---

* nulla *add. MS.*   † dominice *MS.*   ‡ preterita *MS.*   § *sic MS.*

Christina, incapable of being crushed by the cunning of the devil, having already overcome it many times by her faith, wondered what new offering she could make to God in order to enlighten the abbot and put an end to the shameless-ness of her detractors, whom she pitied. So the virgin, being endued with light which enlightened without consuming, proposed to offer a wax candle in the church as a gift every Sunday night. The proposal was endorsed by the sisters, who knew nothing of the reason for it. It was then Saturday. The devil, irritated by the virgin's constancy, which he could not inwardly disturb by any attempts of his own or of his followers, tried to frighten her outwardly by assuming a monstrous appearance. And so on the following night, that is, towards daybreak on Sunday, whilst Christina was in the monastery and whilst the others were getting ready for Matins, they saw a body without a head (for the devil had lost his head, God) sitting in the cloister near the entrance to the church. At this sight (for women are timid creatures) they were terrified and all of them fell on their faces at the feet of their mistress. You could see one trying to bury her-self in her bosom, another covering herself under her veil, another clinging to her knees, another wishing to hide at her feet, this one concealing herself under a bench, another lying on the ground and trembling as if at the hour of death. To all there was one way of escape; to touch, if possible, the garments of Christina. The devil, no less bold, burst into the church. At the sight of this monster the handmaid of Christ was somewhat afraid, but, taking her courage in her hands, she turned to the Lord and, uttering prayers, thrust out that monstrous phantom. But for some time afterwards a more than ordinary horror swept over her. Deeply grieved at this, she poured out prayers and laments to Him in whom she had placed her trust, fearing that if she began to be afraid of the monstrous appearances of the devil she was being abandoned by the Lord. As she continued to pray on this matter, this answer was given her: 'Your prayers on such things are unnecessary: but the prayers for your beloved friend, that

lumine tuus illustraretur dilectus pro certo te noveris impe-
trasse. Fantasticam tamen rabiem. et obtrectatorum invidi-
am. in proximo credas comprimendam. Sevi⟨a⟩t licet demon
interius. obtrectatorum accuat linguas exterius. nec a bono
desistendum. nec in adversis constancia est amittenda.

79. Hiis animata responsis simulque familiaris sui hilarata
salute in cordis sui secreta scrutinio frequencius studiosius-
que cepit discutere. utrumnam quis alium quam se. in hiis
dumtaxat que ad Dei pertinent amorem. plus diligat. Cumque in id studii versaretur. die quodam ipsa protela⟨n⟩cius in
monasterio suo orante. tanto tamque repentino suffusa est
gaudio. ut nec comprehendere. necdum illud cuiquam valeret
edicere. Quo diucius exhilarata (f. 166rᵇ) inter cetera que
cum Deo familiaria mente non verbis miscebat colloquia in
sacrario pectoris huiusmodi vocem percepit. Quem pro me
tantopere diligis. pro cuius salute me sollicitare non desinis.
velles ut pro me mortis subiret angustias? Clamore illa sed*
interiori affectu ingente non voce constanter respondit. Illud
quidem Domine gratanter sed et si vestra pateret voluntas
propriis manibus gratancius complerem. Nam si Abraham in
unici pignoris nece tibi devotus extitit.¹ cur et hunc non ego
pro te. si iuberes occiderem? Maxime cum illum in filio car-
nalis quoquo modo licet tuo non resistens amor afficeret. me
autem in isto tu solus nosti quis [amor] afficiat. Que mors
enim gloriosior quam pro sui conditoris amore suscepta?
Que vita iocundior. quam per graciam ex m[e]rito vivere?
Hiis alternis. sed secretis. sed dulcibus. sed indicibilibus
cum Domino colloquiis perstans: fortiter in dextro latere
non ledentis. sed admoventis modo se sensit impulsam. tanquam si quis diceret. Respice. Cumque respiceret ad altare
vidit benignum Ihesum cum habitu et vultu quo propiciatur

---

* sed+non *MS.*

¹ Gen. 22. 1–19.

he be enlightened with eternal light, have been granted. All the same, the frightful images and the envy of your detractors will, in a short time, be suppressed. For though the devil rages inwardly and sharpens the tongues of your detractors outwardly, you must not cease to do good nor lose constancy in time of difficulty.'

Encouraged by these replies and gladdened at the same time by the assurance of her friend's salvation, she began to examine more often and more closely in the depths of her heart whether anyone can love another more than himself, at least in matters that pertain to the love of God. And whilst she was engaged in this, as she prayed one day more protractedly in her monastery, she felt such overwhelming and sudden joy that she could not understand it, much less describe it. And cheered by this for some time, she heard as she was lovingly communing with God (not in words but in her mind) this voice in the sanctuary of her heart: 'He whom you love so much for My sake, for whose salvation you continue to implore, would you like him to suffer death for My sake?' With a cry, but inwardly, with a great surge of feeling, but in silence, she replied at once: 'That, indeed, O Lord, I gladly desire, and if Thy will was plain, I would even more gladly carry it out with my own hands. For if Abraham proved himself faithful to Thee in sacrificing his only begotten son,[1] why should not I, if Thou commandest me, sacrifice him for Thy sake? Especially as he (Abraham) was attached to his son by a love which, though not opposed to Thine, was carnal: whilst the kind of love that binds me to him, Thou alone understandest. For what death is more glorious than that which is accepted out of love for the Creator? What life is more pleasing than that which is honourably led under the influence of grace?' As she continued in these mutual, but inward and ineffably sweet communings with God, she felt herself nudged on the right side with a tap which struck but did not hurt her, as if someone said: 'Look!' And as she looked towards the altar, she saw Jesus standing at the altar in the loving attitude and mien of one who has compassion

peccatoribus altario assistere. Giransque oculos vidit illum
pro quo laborabat familiarem suum ad dexteram suam que
sinistra erat Domini consistere. Cumque ad orandum de-
cumberent. quoniam sinistra virginis ad dexteram erat
domini* utpote versis vultibus: timens ne ad sinistram esset
divinam. estuare cepit. quomodo ad dexteram transferri
valeret. intollerabile ferens [remotiorem] dilectum suum.
Dei dextere se esse coniunctiorem. Dexteram enim Dei di-
gniorem ipsius cernebat partem. Nec tamen dilecto suo in
oracione decumbenti . superferri volebat. sed quovis alio
modo transferri. Hoc ita permota desiderio. intellexit protinus illam (f. 166ᵛᵃ) se comprehendisse dexteram quam in
cunctis et pre cunctis sibi querebat clementem unde inter
cetera que sepius conferebant edificantia colloquia. illi suo
familiari replicare solebat. solam esse Dei dileccionem in
qua nullus alium sibimet preferre iuste liceat.

80. Contingit aliquando peregrinum quemdam. ignotum
quidem. sed reverendi admodum vultus venisse ad cellam
virginis Cristine. Quem illa sicut omnes dulce suscipiens.
nec percunctata est. nec illi tunc quis esset innotuit. Recessit
itaque habitus sui qualecumque memorie ipsius [in]signe
relinquens. Post tempus secundo revertitur. primum Domino
precum fundit libamina. Cristine de hinc grato fruitur colloquio. Interque loquendum fervorem illa senciens divinum
aut homines aut hominum commune meritum. ipsum sentit
excedere. unde plurimum delectata. humanitatis officio cibum
eciam illum cogit sumere. Discumbit ipse illa cum sorore
.M. dulce parat edulium. Cristina tamen attencius assidet
viro. Margareta laboriosius circa necessaria discurrit, ita ut
aliam Mariam. aliam videres et Martham. si Ihesum dis-
cumbentem daretur conspicere.¹ Itaque mensa parata. ori
panis apponitur et quasi cibum sumere videbatur. Sed si

† dominus *MS*.

¹ Luke 10. 39, 40.

on sinners. And turning her eyes she saw her close friend
for whom she was anxious standing at her right side, which
was the Lord's left side. And when they knelt to pray, as the
virgin's left was at the Lord's right (for they were facing
opposite ways), fearing lest he should be at the Lord's left,
she began to wonder how he could be transferred to the
right, feeling it intolerable that her beloved should be [at His
left] whilst she was nearer to His right. For she perceived
that the right side of God was the more dignified position.
Yet she did not wish to be placed above her beloved, who
was prostrate in prayer, but to be transferred in some other
way. Moved by this desire, she understood immediately that
the right hand, which in all things and above all things she
wanted to be merciful to her, was her possession: and so,
among the many edifying topics which they discussed together, she used to tell her friend that there was only one
thing in which a person should not place another before self,
God's love.

It happened once that a certain pilgrim, quite unknown
but of reverend mien, came to the virgin Christina's cell. She
welcomed him hospitably as she did everyone, not asking
him who he was nor being told by him at that time who he
was. So he went on his way, leaving on her memory a deep
impression. After a while he returned a second time: first he
offered prayers to the Lord and then he settled down to
enjoy Christina's conversation. Whilst they were talking,
she felt a divine fervour which made her recognize him as
being far beyond ordinary men or man's deserts. Greatly
delighted at this, she urged him with kindly hospitality to
take food. He sat down whilst she and her sister Margaret
prepared the repast. Christina paid more attention to the
man, whilst Margaret was busily moving about concerned
with the preparations of the meal, so that if it had been possible to see Jesus sitting down you would recognize another
Mary and another Martha.[1] And so, when the table was
prepared, he raised bread to his mouth and seemed to eat.
But if you had been present, you would have noticed that he

adesses plus gustantem eum adverteres quam edentem.
Cumque moneretur ut de apposito pisce vel modicum gu-
staret non esse opus respondit misero corpori. nisi de quo
tantum sustentetur. Inter que soror utraque vultus venustatem. decorem barbe. maturitatem habitus. nec sine pondere verba mirantes. tanto spirituali affecte sunt gaudio. ut
angelum non hominem se pre se sentirent ha(f. 166vb)bere.
commorandique si virginalis permisisset pudor expetivissent
assensum. Ille vero cum benediccione. suscepta licencia.
sororibus non nisi facie notus discessit. Tantam autem in
earum cordibus sui moris impressit memoriam. tantam in-
fudit dulcedinem. ut sepe in conferendo suspiriis affectum
monstrantibus dicerent: O si noster redibit peregrinus. O si
amplius eius dignabimur colloquio. O si maturitatis eius. et
venustatis exempla ipsum intuendo amodo percipiemus. Hiis
itaque ipsius viri desideriis sepius incitabant . . . -tatis . . . .
Hec Christina . . . ad suscipiendum natalis dominici festum
incerta tamen quid eius protenderet desiderium. Die vero
precedente ipsius festi vigiliam egritudine correpta gravi
decumbit lecto. tantus autem erat langoris vigor. ut nec
in die vigilie ecclesiam adire valeret. Quod audientes duo
monachi. qui et ipsi viri religiosi humanitatis ducti gracia
visitandam decernunt. Cumque decumbenti virgini horas
vigilie dominice psallerent: audit inter cetera totaque mente
concipit. versiculum hore none. speciale scilicet singularis
illius festi gaudium. *Hodie scietis quia veniet Dominus. et mane*
videbitis gloriam eius. Cuius versiculi percepto sensu tanto
spirituali gestivit gaudio. ut in residuo die vel in sub-
seque⟨n⟩ti nocte vix ab eius corde huiusmodi meditationes
exciderent. O qua hora veniet Dominus? O quomodo veniet?
Quis videbit venientem? Quis eius glorie visionem digna-
bitur? Qualis quantave illa erit gloria? Quale quantumve
gaudium erit intuentibus? In huiusmodi sacris persistens

tasted rather than ate. And when he was invited to taste a little of the fish that was set before him, he replied that there was no need to take more than would keep body and soul together. And whilst both sisters were admiring his well-shaped features, his handsome beard, his grave appearance, and his well-weighed words, they were filled with such spiritual joy that they felt they had before them an angel rather than a man, and, if their virginal modesty had allowed, they would have asked him to stay. But he, after imparting a blessing, and taking his leave of them, went on his way, still known to the sisters only by sight. On the other hand so deep an impression did his manner leave on their hearts, so much sweetness did he instil into them, that often when they were talking together they would say, with sighs that showed their feelings: 'If only our pilgrim would return. If only we could enjoy his company once more. If only we could gaze upon him and learn more from his grave and beautiful example.' With these yearnings for the man they often stimulated each other's desire. Christina, ⟨thinking over⟩ these things, prepared herself for the coming of the feast of Christmas, uncertain however where her yearnings would lead her. On the day preceding the vigil of the feast, she was confined to bed with an illness, and so strong was her weakness that she was unable to go to church on the vigil. Two monks, religiously inclined, hearing this decided to visit her out of courtesy. And whilst they were chanting the hours of the Christmas vigil to the sick virgin, she heard, and retained in her mind along with the rest the versicle of the hour of None, that special joy of that singular feast: *Today ye shall know that the Lord will come and tomorrow ye shall see His glory.* Realizing the significance of the verse, she was so moved with joy that for the rest of the day and the following night thoughts of this kind kept running through her mind: 'O at what hour will the Lord come? How will He come? Who shall see Him when He comes? Who will deserve to see His glory? What will that glory be like? and how great? What and how great will be the joy of those who see it?' Fixing

desideriis: quamquam lecto tunc nimis admodum egrotans decumberet. ad matutinalem sinaxim multo (f. 167ʳᵃ) [cum gaudio se prepa]ravit. Aud[iens preconia] festiva, [*Christus*] *natus est.* sic [   ] natum. ac si ad illius nativitatis gaudium comperit invitatam. Morbo enim omni sublato tanta spirituali iocunditate perfusa est ut non nisi divina mens eius ruminare valeret. Cumque cetere ymnum *Te Deum laudamus* psallerent. intendens in superna sensit se in ecclesia sancti Albani translatam. super gradus pulpiti. quo matutinarum leguntur lectiones consistere. Respiciensque in chorum. [vidi]t circa medium chori personam de[cent]iam psallencium applaudere. cuius [pulchram] formam describere. vires [et posse] transcendit humanum. Au[ream in] capite deferebat corona[m gemmi]s interlucentibus et eisdem [   ] ac insertis, quicquid homi[nis ingenio] confingitur precellere [videbat]ur. In summitate autem [fuit crux mi]rifici operis. et ipsa aurea. mi[nus manuf]acta quam divina. Depende[bant su]per faciem hinc inde due vitte [coro]ne adherentes exiles et perluc[ide: in gem]marum capitibus deorsum cerne[bantur] quasi roris guttule. Hac specie re-[fuls]erat persona illa cuius species [admira]bilis est enim speciosus pre filiis [hominum].¹ Cuius speciei decore conspe[cto se] quodammodo sensit in ali[um mundum rap]i. Ista tamen sive in corpo[re sive extr]a corpus viderit. deo teste se [fatetur] nescire.² In crastino scilicet na[tivitatis] die cum iam processionis [temp]us instaret. denunciatur sibi de[sider]atum illum suum adventasse peregrinum. Quo concepto gaudia gaudiis accumulans [et] accensi desiderii scintillas inflammans fructum percipere non modicum sperabat si illum in suo peregrino pasceret. de cuius pastu presencie se refocillata⟨m⟩ tam dulce senciebat. Iubet itaque fores (f. 167ʳᵇ) [claudi] . . . illo . . . omnes . . .

81. Igitur pro[ficis]centium [processi]onem sequitur peregrinus. [modestia] perpenditur in incessu. severitas [in aspec]tu. maturitas in habitu . . . cere videretur. virgineum

¹ Ps. 44. 3.   ² Cor. 12. 3.

her mind on holy desires of this kind, confined as she was to
bed with a severe illness, she prepared herself, with great joy
for the hours of Matins. And as she heard the ⟨anthem⟩ proper
to the feast, *Christ is born,* she understood that she had been
invited to the joy of His birth. Her illness disappeared and
she was filled with such spiritual happiness that her mind
could dwell on nothing but divine things. And when the
others sang the hymn *Te Deum laudamus,* she looked up and
felt as if she had been borne into the church of St. Albans
and stood on the steps of the lectern where the lessons of
Matins are read out. And looking down on the choir, she saw
a person in the middle of the choir looking approvingly at
the reverent behaviour of the monks singing. His beauty
exceeded the power and capacity of man to describe. On his
head he bore a golden crown thickly encrusted with precious
stones which seemed to excel any work of human skill. On
the top was a cross of gold of marvellous craftsmanship, not
so much man-made as divine. Hanging over his face, one on
either side, were two bands or fillets attached to the crown,
delicate and shining, and on the tops of the gems there were
seen as it were drops of dew. In this guise appeared the man
whose beauty had only to be seen to be loved, for He is
the fairest of the children of men.[1] And when she had
gazed on this beauty, she felt herself rapt in some way to
another world. But whether she saw these things in the body
or out of the body (God is her witness), she never knew.[2]
On the morrow of Christmas day, when the time for the
procession was near, a message was brought to her that her
beloved pilgrim had arrived. When she heard this, her joy
was unbounded, and added fire to the flames of her desire.
For she hoped to reap no little benefit by entertaining in the
person of this pilgrim Him whose presence had brought her
such sweet relief. She ordered the doors, therefore, [to be
closed.]

Therefore the pilgrim followed the procession of chanting
virgins: his modesty in gait, his grave expression, his mature
appearance, were closely observed, setting as it did the virgin's

chorum [simili] gravitatis studio. intendere d[ocebat]. In populo inquid gravi laudabo te.[1] Processione facta. misse cum reliquis interest peregrinus. Qua completa ceteros preveniens Christi virgo. neque peregrini sui ex[s]aturari poterat desiderio ecclesiam exit. ut egredientem prima suscipiat. Nullus enim erat locus exeundi pervius nisi per Christinam. Morante autem illo. dulci tedio afficitur virgo. Egredientibusque ceteris. ubi sit peregrinus inquirit. Ecce aiunt. orat in ecclesia. Illa more impaciens mittit que eum advocent. sed reverse quod eum nusquam repererint. denunciant prestolanti. Mirata virgo ubi sit clavis ianue quasi commota requirit. Ecce ait. cui talis erat cura tradita. Neque enim ex quo missa incepta est exitus ullus patuit. me ianuam sub clavis custodia soli⟨ci⟩cius observante. Sed nec erat aliquis qui vel de ecclesia eum exire vidisset. Quem illum nisi Dominum Ihesum aut eius dicemus angelum? Qui enim in nocte cum tanto scemate apparuit. qualis videndus est in gloria quoquo modo innotuit. Hec namque in presenti nobis est illa gloria. qui de illa non nisi per speculum videmus.[2] Unde caliginem Deus inhabitare dicitur.[3] non quod caliginem inhabitet. sed quia lux sua pre immensitate nos corporis graves pondere hebetare videtur. In die vero sub peregrini. sed maturioris viri specie videri voluit. quia qualiter (f. 167ᵛᵃ) *... perfudit.

82. [Porro timen]tibus Deum nichil deest[4] nec hiis qui eum diligunt in veritate. Ecce enim Domine ve[rit]atem dilexisti. incerta et occulta [sapien]cie tu manifestasti eis.[5] Inter quos enituit insignis ancilla tua Christina. que quanto veriore tibi appropinquavit amore. tanto manifestius mundo corde penetrare meruit occulta sapiencie tue. Hinc enim dedisti ei providere secretas cogitaciones hominum. et procul posita studioque occultata cognoscere tanquam presencia

---

* Four complete lines missing.

[1] Ps. 34. 18. [2] 1 Cor. 13. 12.
[3] 2 Paralip. 6. 1; Pseudo-Dionysius, *De Mystica Theologia*, c. 2, *PG* 3. 1025–6.
[4] Cf. Ps. 33. 10. [5] Ps. 50. 8.

choir an example of grave deportment, as it says in Scripture: 'I will give Thee thanks in the great congregation.'[1] In the procession and the Mass and the other parts of the service the pilgrim took part. And when they were over, the virgin of Christ, preceding the rest (for she could not have too much of her pilgrim), left the church so that she should be the first to greet him as he came out. For there was no other place of exit except where Christina was. As he stayed awhile, the virgin became impatient with waiting. And when they had all come out, she said: 'Where is the pilgrim?' 'He is praying in the church', they answered. Impatient of delay, she sent some of the nuns to call him. But they returned to say that he could not be found anywhere. The virgin, rather surprised and disturbed, said: 'Where is the key of the door?' 'Here it is', said the one who had charge of it. 'From the moment that Mass began no one could come out, since the door had been closed and I have guarded the key.' Nor was there anyone else who had even seen him come out of the Church. Who else could we say he was, except an angel or the Lord Jesus? For He who appeared that night in such a guise showed Himself in some sort of way as He will be seen in glory. For this is how that glory appears to us in this present life, since we see it only through a glass.[2] Hence God is said to dwell in darkness;[3] not that He dwells in darkness, but His light because of its brightness blinds us who are weighed down by the body. On that day He wished to appear under the guise of a pilgrim, of a grown-up man because, as . . . [*rest missing*].

However, nothing is lacking to those who fear God[4] nor to those who love Him in truth. Behold, O Lord, Thou desirest truth in the inward parts; and in the hidden parts Thou shalt make me to know wisdom.[5] Among these Thy handmaid Christina was pre-eminent, who the nearer she approached Thee in true love, the more clearly was she able to penetrate the hidden things of Thy wisdom with her pure heart. Hence Thou gavest her the power to know the secret thoughts of men, and to see those that were far off and deliberately concealed

sicut in subiectis constat manifestum. Cogitavit forte nescio quid una puellarum illius occulte facere. quod ancilla Dei sedens in alia domo mediis parietibus vidit. et prohibuit eam dicens: Ne facias. ne facias. Cui puella. Quid domina? Et illa. Hoc quod cogitasti nunc. Nichil inquid cogitavi quod prohibeatur fieri. Tunc vocavit eam ad se et dixit ei in aure quid hoc erat quod illam in corde gerere viderat. quo audito puella perfusa genas rubore verecundie. perhibuit testimonium veritati. obsecrans et obtestans illam. ut pro sui reverencia nequaquam id palam faceret. eo quod propalati pudore⟨m⟩ ferre nequiret.

83. Alio tempore sedentibus nobis ad mensam cum ancilla Christi apposuit prefata puella pulmentum ut manducaremus. Manducantibus itaque nobis inde: noluit Christina illud contingere. Rogantibus ut nobiscum una de pulmento comederet: minime consensit. vocata est godit (f. 167vb) hoc enim erat nom[en eius. Requirit] ab ea tacite Christina [an de vetitis] olus. Composuit illa timore v[isitan]cium. Iuraverat namque Christina se ni[chil] esuram usque ad tempus de vicino orto, cuius possessor possessio* avaricie [nu]per roganti sibi cerifolium negaverat. Interim accepta composicione siluit, pulmentum vero non gustavit, et post prandium mox convicit puellam te[sti]monio contuencium, et confessa est q[uod] in orto interdicto legerat quod gu[staverant].

84. Habuit hec virgo quemdam familiarem qui eam v[alde] diligebat. V . . . ecca . . . ori suo sub . . . retur per ministrum ei dirigebat. [ille] vero quedam ex commenda[tis sibi] furtim in via detrahebat et [in ali]quos usus nequiter expen[debat. Hoc] videns in spiritu virgo Dei . . . canti, et corripiens eum inter [se et] ipsum solum, extersit ab homine [crimen].

85. Soror erat Christine queda[m vivens in] seculo nomine Matildis. [Illam] et coniugem suum noct[e qua]dam

* possessio *sic MS.*

as if they were present. This was made manifest in what follows. One of her maidens was thinking of doing something or other secretly: and the handmaid of God, seated in another house, saw it through the walls and forbade her saying: 'Do it not, do it not.' The girl said: 'What, mistress?' She said: 'What you were thinking of then.' 'But I was not thinking of anything that is forbidden', said she. Then Christina called her to her and whispered in her ear what she had seen her thinking in her heart. On hearing it the girl blushed with shame, and proved that she spoke true. Then she besought and implored Christina for the sake of her good name not to tell anyone, because she would never be able to bear the shame of it if it were revealed.

On another occasion, as we were sitting at table with the maiden of Christ, the same girl placed food on the table for us to eat. And as we ate, Christina refused to touch it. And when we asked her to take a little food with us, she summoned Godit, for that was her name. Christina asked her, but quietly, out of respect for the guests, if she had made the salad from ingredients which had been forbidden, for Christina had been emphatic that for a time she would eat nothing from the garden next door because the owner, out of miserliness, had denied her a sprig of chervil when she had recently asked for it. In the meantime she accepted the salad, but refused to taste of the dish, and after the meal was over she proved the girl's guilt by the testimony of those who saw her. And the girl admitted that what they had eaten had been gathered in the forbidden garden.

This virgin had a certain friend who loved her very much. By her servant she sent to him ⟨certain things which might be of use to him⟩. But the servant abstracted some of them during the journey and turned them to his own evil purposes. When the maiden of God became aware of this in the spirit, she faced him with it and, chiding him without anyone else being present, cleansed him of his error.

Christina had a sister who was living in the world named Matilda. As she and her husband were lying one night in

in lecto suo iacentes h[untendo]ni, manebant namque illic,
[Christina] in cella sua consistens vi[dit et con]fabulantes
audivit, ita ut [postea con]venientibus ad se singul[is com-
me]moraret et locum et horam [et quid dixerint se]riatim.
Que omnia sic [facta fuisse] michi confessus est uter[que
sponsus].

86. Familiaris et amici [abbatis .G. quem] supradiximus,
Christina di[e ac noc]te memor erat, et circa e[um quod] illi
expediret probe satagebat ieiunando, vigilando, deum ex-
orando, [angelos et] alios sanctos in celo et in terra supplican-
do misericordiam Dei super illum precibus et obsequiis, que
minus recte videbatur gerere sapienter increpando: sa . . .

bed at Huntingdon, for that is where they lived, Christina, in her cell, saw them and heard them talking, so that later on when they came to visit her, she was able to tell each one exactly what they had said, at what time and where. Both husband and wife admitted to me that all this happened as she said.

Christina's thoughts were with her dear friend Abbot Geoffrey, whom we have mentioned earlier, night and day, and she busied herself with his interests by fasting, watching, calling upon God, the angels, and other holy folk in heaven and on earth, asking for the mercy of God with humble prayers, sensibly reproving him when his actions were not quite right . . .

ADDENDA ET CORRIGENDA

Page

1 n. 2, at end. *Add* (f. 123v).

2 n. 1, at end. *Read* ii.39–48.

   n. 2, l. 6. Read *apud Redborne*

3 ll. 28–9. Omit quotation marks and the words 'which is'.

5 n. 1 l. 2. Read *Analecta Monastica* iii.

7, 13, 14, 40 n. 4, 41. *For* Ralph (Flambard) *read* Ranulph

8 n. 1, 126 n. 1. On the foundation of St Clement (*c.*1130), see now D. Nicholl, *Thurstan, archbishop of York* (York, 1964), esp. pp. 199–200.

13 n. 1 For the date of Bishop Robert's death, see J. Le Neve, *Fasti Ecclesiae Anglicanae, 1066–1300*, iii, ed. D. E. Greenway (London, 1977), p. 1.

15 *For* 1147 *read* 1146 (death of Abbot Geoffrey: *Heads of Religious Houses, England and Wales, 940–1216*, ed. D. Knowles, C. N. L. Brooke, V.C.M. London (Cambridge, 1972), p. 67).

16 n. 2 l.1. *Read* Ligugé, 1928

      l.2. Read *Revue Bénédictine* xlv (1933)

   n. 4 l.4. *Read* fastidia

17 n. 5 l.2. *Omit* 'ibid. xxiii.425'; and for the text in Wilkins, i. 628, cf. *Councils and Synods* ii, ed. F. M. Powicke and C. R. Cheney (Oxford, 1964), 1, 262 n. 1.

17 n. 5 ll. 4ff. On this doubtful text see C. R. Cheney in *Councils and Synods*, ii, 1, 104 and *Eng.Hist.Rev.* l (1935), 393, 400–2.

19 n. 1, last 4 lines. Read *Gesta Abbatum Fontanellensium*. Milo was a benefactor to the monastery, Harduin to its library.

24 n. 1 l. 9. *Read* D. M. Parsons (later Lady Stenton)

26 n. 1 l. 5. *For* W. v. Wartburg *read* H. Skommodau

27 n. 2 Marcigny was probably founded *c.*1055: for its early history and these details see esp. J. Wollasch in *Cluniac Monasticism*, ed. N. Hunt (London, 1971), pp. 143–90; *Letters of Peter the Venerable*, ed. G. Constable (Cambridge, Mass., 1967), i, nos. 52–3, 56.

34 l. 28   *Read* gra. . .eri

36 l. 3   singula *may stand ('in every detail')*.

36 l. 20   *Read* eum (*so Grosjean, Analecta Bollandiana 78 (1960)*, 199)

36	l. 24	*For* [amoris eius captus] *read* . . . sit
42	l. 4	*Read* qua (*so Grosjean*)
42	l. 10	*Read* agnam (*so MS*)
44	l. 12	assensu *may stand.*
46	l. 6	*Read* impingentibus (*so MS*)
49	l. 31	*Delete asterisk.*
52	l. 14	*Transpose the words* corde suo (*so MS*).
56	l. 14	*Read* [ob]probria (*so MS?*)
58	n. 1	For the priors of Huntingdon, see now *Heads of Religious Houses*, p. 166.
66	l. 13	*Read* am[i-
66	n. 1	*For* pp. 135–6 *read* pp. 108–9
68	l. 6	*For* proles *read* probe (*so MS*)
68	l. 9	*Read* habere (*so MS*)
68	l. 18	*Replace* [sperabant fore] *by dots.*
76	l. 20	*Read* regine (*so MS*)
84	l. 3	*Read* sicuti (*so MS*)
84	n. 1	Ralph was postulated on 26 April, enthroned archbishop on 16 May 1114. *Fasti*, ed. Greenway, ii (1971), p. 3.
92	n. 3	*Read* Ps. 37.12–13
98	l. 5	*Read* [ten]-
98	l. 13	*Read* moder-
102	l. 2	eos *may stand.*
102	l. 17	*Read* coniun-
102	l. 18	*Read* pote-
104	n. 1	The quotation should read: 'fuge, tace, et quiesce.'
108	l. 21	*Read* Roberto
109	l. 25	*Omit* 3
110	n. 1	Thurstan was consecrated 19 Oct. 1119 and died *c.*6 Feb. 1140.
116	l. 18	[importunitate] *would be preferable* (*Talbot*).
122	l. 16	eo *may stand* ('*thither*').
126	n. 1	See under 8 n.1.
132	l. 6	*Read* experteque (*so MS*)
134	l. 20	*Add a full stop after* communicaverat
144	l. 24	*Read* loquendum (*so Grosjean*)
148	l. 28	*Read* eum (*so MS*)
154	l. 10	*For* inquid *read* quod (]uod *MS*)
156	n. *	*Read* columbam + aliam suam *MS, perhaps a corrupt dittograph of* alarum.

158   ll. 24–5 *Read* sollicitareris (*so Grosjean*)

160   l. 9   *For* fit *read* sic (*so Brooke and apparently the MS*)

165   l. 21   The double inverted commas should be transposed to follow the sentence ending 'intervention' in l. 19.

186   n. 2   *Read* 2 Cor. 12.3.

INDEX OF QUOTATIONS AND ALLUSIONS

A. BIBLICAL ALLUSIONS

Revelation
2.23   88–9

B. CITATIONS AND PARALLELS FROM CLASSICAL AND PATRISTIC SOURCES

GENERAL INDEX

MEDIEVAL ACADEMY REPRINTS FOR TEACHING